W9-DEM-764

GEORGE MÜLLER
OF BRISTOL

Mother

I've just read
pg 140 - 3rd para
Heb 8 'Jesus Christ
is the same yesterday,
today & forever'
Amen & so too
all that's in the word
can be prayed for us
also as we read the
scriptures - how amazing
x x

GEORGE MÜLLER
OF BRISTOL

ARTHUR T. PIERSON, D.D.
AUTHOR OF "THE CRISIS OF MISSIONS," "THE NEW ACTS
OF THE APOSTLES," ETC.

WITH AN INTRODUCTION BY

JAMES WRIGHT
SON-IN-LAW AND SUCCESSOR IN THE WORK OF
GEORGE MÜLLER

AMBASSADOR
Belfast Northern Ireland **Greenville** South Carolina

First published 1901
First Ambassador edition 1999
Reprinted 2001
Reprinted 2003

All rights reserved

ISBN 1 84030 058 2

Ambassador Publications
a division of
Ambassador Productions Ltd.
Providence House
Ardenlee Street
BELFAST
BT6 8QJ
Northern Ireland
www.ambassador-productions.com

Emerald House
427 Wade Hampton Blvd.
GREENVILLE
SC 29609, USA
www.emeraldhouse.com

Introduction

VERY soon after the decease of my beloved father-in-law I began to receive letters pressing upon me the desirableness of issuing as soon as possible a memoir of him and his work.

The well-known autobiography, entitled " Narrative of the Lord's Dealings with George Müller," had been, and was still being, so greatly used by God in the edification of believers and the conversion of unbelievers that I hesitated to countenance any attempt to supersede or even supplement it. But as, with prayer, I reflected upon the subject, several considerations impressed me:

1st. The last volume of the Narrative ends with the year 1885, so that there is no record of the last thirteen years of Mr. Müller's life excepting what is contained in the yearly reports of " The Scriptural Knowledge Institution."

2d. The last three volumes of the Narrative, being mainly a condensation of the yearly reports during the period embraced in them, contain much unavoidable repetition.

3d. A book of, say, four hundred and fifty pages, containing the substance of the four volumes of the Narrative, and carrying on the history to the date of the decease of the founder of the institution, would meet the desire of a large class of readers.

4th. Several brief sketches of Mr. Müller's career had issued from the press within a few days after the funeral;

and one (written by Mr. F. Warne and published by W. F. Mack & Co., Bristol), a very accurate and truly appreciative sketch, had had a large circulation; but I was convinced by the letters that reached me that a more comprehensive memoir was called for, and *would be* produced, so I was led especially to pray for *guidance* that such a book might be entrusted to the author fitted by God to undertake it.

While waiting for the answer to this definite petition, though greatly urged by publishers to proceed, I steadily declined to take any step until I had clearer light. Moreover, I was, personally, occupied during May and June in preparing the Annual Report of " The Scriptural Knowledge Institution," and could not give proper attention to the other matter.

Just then I learned from Dr. Arthur T. Pierson, of Brooklyn, N. Y., that he had been led to undertake the production of a memoir of Mr. Müller for *American* readers, and requesting my aid by furnishing him with some materials needed for the work.

Having complied with this request I was favoured by Dr. Pierson with a syllabus of the method and contents of his intended work.

The more I thought upon the subject the more satisfied I became that no one could be found more fitted to undertake the work which had been called for on this side of the Atlantic also than this my well-known and beloved friend.

He had had exceptional opportunities twenty years ago in the United States, and in later years when visiting Great Britain, for becoming intimately acquainted with Mr. Müller, with the principles on which the Orphanage and other branches of " The Scriptural Knowledge Institution " were carried on, and with many details of their working. I knew that Dr. Pierson most thoroughly sympathized with these principles as being according to the mind of God revealed in His word; and that he could, therefore, present not merely the history of the external facts and results of Mr. Müller's life and labours, but could and would, by God's help, unfold, with the ardour and force of *conviction*, the secret springs of that life and of those labours.

I therefore intimated to my dear friend that, provided he would allow me to read the manuscript and have thus the opportunity of making any suggestions that I felt necessary, I would, as my beloved father-in-law's executor and representative, gladly endorse his work as the authorized memoir for British as well as American readers.

To this Dr. Pierson readily assented; and now, after carefully going through the whole, I confidently recommend the book to esteemed readers on both sides of the Atlantic, with the earnest prayer that the result, in relation to the subject of this memoir, may be identical with that produced by the account of the Apostle Paul's " manner of life " upon the churches of Judea which were in Christ (Gal. i. 24), viz.,

" They glorified GOD " in him.

JAMES WRIGHT.

13 CHARLOTTE STREET, PARK STREET,
BRISTOL, ENG., March, 1899.

A Prefatory Word

Dr. Oliver W. Holmes wittily said that an autobiography is what every biography *ought to be*. The four volumes of "The Narrative of the Lord's Dealings with George Müller," already issued from the press and written by his own hand, with a fifth volume covering his missionary tours, and prepared by his wife, supplemented by the Annual Reports since published, constitute essentially an autobiography—Mr. Müller's own life-story, stamped with his own peculiar individuality, and singularly and minutely complete. To those who wish the simple journal of his life with the details of his history, these printed documents make any other sketch of him from other hands so far unnecessary.

There are, however, two considerations which have mainly prompted the preparation of this brief memoir: first, that the facts of this remarkable life might be set forth not so much with reference to the chronological order of their occurrence, as events, as for the sake of the lessons in living which they furnish, illustrating and enforcing grand spiritual principles and precepts; and secondly, because no man so humble as he would ever write of himself what, after his departure, another might properly write of him that others might glorify God in him.

No one could have undertaken this work of writing Mr. Müller's life-story without being deeply impressed with the opportunity thus afforded for impressing the most vital truths that concern holy living and holy serving; nor could any one have completed such a work without feeling over-awed by the argument which this narrative furnishes for a present, living, prayer-hearing God, and for a possible and practical daily walk with Him and work with Him. It has been a great help in the preparation of this book that the writer has had such frequent converse with Mr. James Wright, who was so long Mr. Müller's associate and knew him so intimately.

Table of Contents

HOUSE OF MR. MÜLLER, KINGSDOWN, BRISTOL.

IN LOVING MEMORY OF

GEORGE MÜLLER,
FOUNDER OF THE ASHLEY DOWN ORPHANAGE
BORN SEPTEMBER 27TH 1805,
FELL ASLEEP MARCH 10TH 1898.

HE TRUSTED IN GOD WITH WHOM
"NOTHING SHALL BE IMPOSSIBLE".
AND IN HIS BELOVED SON JESUS CHRIST OUR LORD
WHO SAID "I GO UNTO MY FATHER,
AND WHATSOEVER YE SHALL ASK IN MY NAME
THAT WILL I DO THAT THE FATHER,
MAY BE GLORIFIED IN THE SON".
AND IN HIS INSPIRED WORD WHICH DECLARES THAT
ALL THINGS ARE POSSIBLE TO HIM THAT BELIEVETH.
AND GOD FULFILLED THESE DECLARATIONS IN
THE EXPERIENCE OF HIS SERVANT BY ENABLING
HIM TO PROVIDE AND CARE FOR ABOUT
TEN THOUSAND ORPHANS.

THIS MEMORIAL WAS ERECTED BY THE
SPONTANEOUS AND LOVING GIFTS
OF MANY OF THESE ORPHANS.

MR. MÜLLER'S TOMBSTONE IN ARNO'S VALE CEMETERY.

George Müller of Bristol

CHAPTER I

FROM HIS BIRTH TO HIS NEW BIRTH

A HUMAN life, filled with the presence and power of God, is one of God's choicest gifts to His church and to the world.

Things which are unseen and eternal seem, to the carnal man, distant and indistinct, while what is seen and temporal is vivid and real. Practically, any object in nature that can be seen or felt is thus more real and actual to most men than the Living God. Every man who walks with God, and finds Him a present Help in every time of need ; who puts His promises to the practical proof and verifies them in actual experience ; every believer who with the key of faith unlocks God's mysteries, and with the key of prayer unlocks God's treasuries, thus furnishes to the race a demonstration and an illustration of the fact that " He is, and is a Rewarder of them that diligently seek Him."

George Müller was such an argument and example incarnated in human flesh. Here was a man of like passions as we are and tempted in all points like as we are, but who believed God and was established by believing; who prayed earnestly that he might live a life and do a work which should be a convincing proof that God hears prayer and that it is safe to trust Him at all times; and who has furnished just such a witness as he desired. Like Enoch, he truly walked with God, and had abundant testimony borne to him that he pleased God. And when, on the tenth day of March, 1898, it was told us of George Müller that "he was not," we knew that "God had taken him": it seemed more like a translation than like death.

To those who are familiar with his long life-story, and, most of all, to those who intimately knew him and felt the power of personal contact with him, he was one of God's ripest saints and himself a living proof that a life of faith is possible; that God may be known, communed with, found, and may become a conscious companion in the daily life. George Müller proved for himself and for all others who will receive his witness that, to those who are willing to take God at His word and to yield self to His will, He is "the same yesterday and to-day and forever": that the days of divine intervention and deliverance are past only to those with whom the days of faith and obedience are past—in a word, that believing prayer works still the wonders which our fathers told of in the days of old.

The life of this man may best be studied, perhaps, by dividing it into certain marked periods, into which it naturally falls, when we look at those leading events and experiences which are like punctuation-marks or paragraph divisions,—as, for example:

1. From his birth to his new birth or conversion: 1805–1825.

2. From his conversion to full entrance on his life-work: 1825–35.

3. From this point to the period of his mission tours : 1835–75.

4. From the beginning to the close of these tours : 1875–92.

5. From the close of his tours to his death : 1892–98.

Thus the first period would cover twenty years; the second, ten ; the third, forty ; the fourth, seventeen ; and the last, six.   However thus unequal in length, each forms a sort of epoch, marked by certain conspicuous and characteristic features which serve to distinguish it and make its lessons peculiarly important and memorable.   For example, the first period is that of the lost days of sin, in which the great lesson taught is the bitterness and worthlessness of a disobedient life.   In the second period may be traced the remarkable steps of preparation for the great work of his life.   The third period embraces the actual working out of the divine mission committed to him. Then for seventeen or eighteen years we find him bearing in all parts of the earth his world-wide witness to God; and the last six years were used of God in mellowing and maturing his Christian character.   During these years he was left in peculiar loneliness, yet this only made him lean more on the divine companionship, and it was noticeable with those who were brought into most intimate contact with him that he was more than ever before heavenly-minded, and the beauty of the Lord his God was upon him.

The first period may be passed rapidly by, for it covers only the wasted years of a sinful and profligate youth and early manhood.   It is of interest mainly as illustrating the sovereignty of that Grace which abounds even to the chief of sinners.   Who can read the story of that score of years and yet talk of piety as the product of evolution ?   In his case, instead of evolution, there was rather a *revolution*, as marked and complete as ever was found, perhaps, in the annals of salvation.   If Lord George Lyttelton could account

for the conversion of Saul of Tarsus only by supernatural
power, what would he have thought of George Müller's
transformation ! Saul had in his favor a conscience, however misguided, and a morality, however pharisaic. George
Müller was a flagrant sinner against common honesty and
decency, and his whole early career was a revolt, not
against God only, but against his own moral sense. If Saul
was a hardened transgressor, how callous must have been
George Müller !

He was a native of Prussia, born at Kroppenstaedt, near
Halberstadt, September 27, 1805. Less than five years later
his parents removed to Heimersleben, some four miles off,
where his father was made collector of the excise, again
removing about eleven years later to Schoenebeck, near
Magdeburg, where he had obtained another appointment.

George Müller had no proper parental training. His
father's favoritism toward him was harmful both to himself and to his brother, as in the family of Jacob, tending
to jealousy and estrangement. Money was put too freely into the hands of these boys, hoping that they might learn
how to use it and save it; but the result was, rather, careless
and vicious waste, for it became the source of many child-
ish sins of indulgence. Worse still, when called upon to
render any account of their stewardship, sins of lying and
deception were used to cloak wasteful spending. Young
George systematically deceived his father, either by false
entries of what he had received, or by false statements of
what he had spent or had on hand. When his tricks were
found out, the punishment which followed led to no
reformation, the only effect being more ingenious devices
of trickery and fraud. Like the Spartan lad, George
Müller reckoned it no fault to steal, but only to have his
theft found out.

His own brief account of his boyhood shows a very bad

boy and he attempts no disguise. Before he was ten years old he was a habitual thief and an expert at cheating; even government funds, entrusted to his father, were not safe from his hands. Suspicion led to the laying of a snare into which he fell: a sum of money was carefully counted and put where he would find it and have a chance to steal it. He took it and hid it under his foot in his shoe, but, he being searched and the money being found, it became clear to whom the various sums previously missing might be traced.

His father wished him educated for a clergyman, and before he was eleven he was sent to the cathedral classical school at Halberstadt to be fitted for the university. That such a lad should be deliberately set apart for such a sacred office and calling, by a father who knew his moral obliquities and offences, seems incredible; but, where a state church exists, the ministry of the Gospel is apt to be treated as a human profession rather than as a divine vocation, and so the standards of fitness often sink to the low secular level, and the main object in view becomes the so-called "living," which is, alas, too frequently independent of *holy* living.

From this time the lad's studies were mixed up with novel-reading and various vicious indulgences. Card-playing and even strong drink got hold of him. The night when his mother lay dying, her boy of fourteen was reeling through the streets, drunk; and even her death failed to arrest his wicked course or to arouse his sleeping conscience. And—as must always be the case when such solemn reminders make one no better—he only grew worse.

When he came to the age for confirmation he had to attend the class for preparatory religious teaching; but this being to him a mere form, and met in a careless spirit, another false step was taken : sacred things were treated as common, and so conscience became the more callous. On the very eve of confirmation and of his first approach to the Lord's Table he was guilty of gross sins; and on the day previous, when he met the clergyman for the customary " confession of sin," he planned and practised another shameless fraud, withholding from him eleven-twelfths of the confirmation fee entrusted to him by his father !

In such frames of mind and with such habits of life George Müller, in the Easter season of 1820, was confirmed and became a communicant. Confirmed, indeed ! but in sin, not only immoral and unregenerate, but so ignorant of the very rudiments of the Gospel of Christ that he could not have stated to an inquiring soul the simple terms of the plan of salvation. There was, it is true about such serious and sacred transactions, a vague solemnity which left a transient impression and led to shallow resolves to live a better life ; but there was no real sense of sin or of repentance toward God, nor was there any dependence upon a higher strength: and, without these, efforts at self-amendment never prove of value or work lasting results.

The story of this wicked boyhood presents but little variety, except that of sin and crime. It is one long tale of evil-doing and of the sorrow which it brings. Once, when his money was all recklessly wasted, hunger drove him to steal a bit of coarse bread from a soldier who was a fellow lodger; and looking back, long afterward, to that hour of extremity, he exclaimed, " What a bitter thing is the service of Satan, even in this world ! "

On his father's removal to Schoenebeck in 1821 he asked to be sent to the cathedral school at Magdeburg, inwardly hoping thus to break away from his sinful snares and vicious companions, and, amid new scenes, find help in self-reform. He was not, therefore, without at least occasional aspirations after moral improvement ; but again he made the common and fatal mistake of overlooking the Source of all true betterment. "God was not in all his thoughts." He found that to leave one place for another was not to leave his sin behind, for he took himself along.

His father, with a strange fatuity, left him to superintend sundry alterations in his house at Heimersleben, arranging for him meanwhile to read classics with the resident clergyman, Rev. Dr. Nagel. Being thus for a time his own master, temptation opened wide doors before him. He was allowed to collect dues from his father's debtors, and again he resorted to fraud, spending large sums of this money and concealing the fact that it had been paid.

In November, 1821, he went to Magdeburg and to Brunswick, to which latter place he was drawn by his passion for a young Roman Catholic girl whom he had met there soon after confirmation. In this absence from home he took one step after another in the path of wicked indulgence. First of all, by lying to his tutor he got his consent to his going; then came a week of sin at Magdeburg and a wasting of his father's means at a costly hotel in Brunswick. His money being gone, he went to the house of an uncle until he was sent away; then, at another expensive hotel, he ran up bills until, payment being demanded, he had to leave his best clothes as a security, barely escaping arrest. Then, at Wolfenbüttel, he tried the same bold scheme again, until, having nothing for deposit, he ran off, but this time was caught and sent to jail. This boy of sixteen was already a liar and thief, swindler and drunkard, accomplished only in crime, a companion of convicted felons and himself in a felon's cell. This cell, a few days later, a thief shared: and these two held con-

verse as fellow thieves, relating their adventures to one
another, and young Müller, that he might not be outdone,
invented lying tales of villainy to make himself out the
more famous fellow of the two !

Ten or twelve days passed in this wretched fellowship,
until disagreement led to a sullen silence between them.
And so passed away twenty-four dark days, from December
18, 1821, until the 12th of January ensuing, during all of
which George Müller was shut up in prison and during
part of which he sought as a favour the company of a thief.

His father learned of his disgrace and sent money to
meet his hotel dues and other " costs " and pay for his return home. Yet such was his persistent wickedness that,
going from a convict's cell to confront his outraged but in-
dulgent parent, he chose as his companion in travel an
avowedly wicked man.

He was severely chastised by his father and felt that he
must make some effort to reinstate himself in his favour.
He therefore studied hard and took pupils in arithmetic
and German, French and Latin. This outward reform so
pleased his father that he shortly forgot as well as forgave
his evil-doing ; but again it was only the outside of the
cup and platter that was made clean: the secret heart was
still desperately wicked and the whole life, as God saw it,
was an abomination.

George Müller now began to forge what he afterward
called " a whole chain of lies." When his father would
no longer consent to his staying at home, he left, ostensibly
for Halle, the university town, to be examined, but really
for Nordhausen to seek entrance into the gymnasium. He
avoided Halle because he dreaded its severe discipline, and
foresaw that restraint would be doubly irksome when constantly meeting young fellows of his acquaintance who,
as students in the university, would have much more free-

dom than himself. On returning home he tried to conceal this fraud from his father; but just before he was to leave again for Nordhausen the truth became known, which made needful new links in that chain of lies to account for his systematic disobedience and deception. His father, though angry, permitted him to go to Nordhausen, where he remained from October, 1822, till Easter, 1825.

During these two and a half years he studied classics, French, history, etc., living with the director of the gymnasium. His conduct so improved that he rose in favour and was pointed to as an example for the other lads, and permitted to accompany the master in his walks, to converse with him in Latin. At this time he was a hard student, rising at four A.M. the year through, and applying himself to his books till ten at night.

Nevertheless, by his own confession, behind all this formal propriety there lay secret sin and utter alienation from God. His vices induced an illness which for thirteen weeks kept him in his room. He was not without a religious bent, which led to the reading of such books as Klopstock's works, but he neither cared for God's word, nor had he any compunction for trampling upon God's law. In his library, now numbering about three hundred books, no Bible was found. Cicero and Horace, Molière and Voltaire, he knew and valued, but of the Holy Scriptures he was grossly ignorant, and as indifferent to them as he was ignorant of them. Twice a year, according to prevailing custom, he went to the Lord's Supper, like others who had passed the age of confirmation, and he could not at such seasons quite avoid religious impressions. When the consecrated bread and wine touched his lips he would sometimes take an oath to reform, and for a few days refrain from some open sins; but there was no spiritual life to act as a force within, and his vows were forgotten almost as soon as made. The old Satan was too strong for the young Müller, and, when the mighty passions of his evil nature were roused, his resolves and endeavours were as powerless to 'hold him as were the new cords which bound Samson, to restrain him, when he awoke from his slumber.

It is hard to believe that this young man of twenty could lie without a blush and with the air of perfect candor. When dissipation dragged him into the mire of debt, and his allowance would not help him out, he resorted again to the most ingenious devices of falsehood. He pretended that the money wasted in riotous living had been stolen by violence, and, to carry out the deception he studied the part of an actor. Forcing the locks of his trunk and guitar-case, he ran into the director's room half dressed and feigning fright, declaring that he was the victim of a robbery, and excited such pity that friends made up a purse to cover his supposed losses. Suspicion was, however, awakened that he had been playing a false part, and he never regained the master's confidence ; and though he had even then no sense of sin, shame at being detected in such meanness and hypocrisy made him shrink from ever again facing the director's wife, who, in his long sickness, had nursed him like a mother.

Such was the man who was not only admitted to honourable standing as a university student, but accepted as a candidate for holy orders, with permission to preach in the Lutheran establishment. This student of divinity knew nothing of God or salvation, and was ignorant even of the gospel plan of saving grace. He felt the need for a better life, but no godly motives swayed him. Reformation was a matter purely of expediency : to continue in profligacy would bring final exposure, and no parish would have him as a pastor. To get a valuable " cure " and a good "living" he must make attainments in divinity, pass a good examination, and have at least a decent reputation. Worldly policy urged him to apply himself on the one hand to his studies and on the other to self-reform.

Again he met defeat, for he had never yet found the one source and secret of all strength. Scarce had he entered Halle before his resolves proved frail as a spider's web, unable to restrain him from vicious indulgences. He refrained indeed from street brawls and duelling, because they would curtail his liberty, but he knew as yet no moral restraints. His money was soon spent, and he borrowed till he could find no one to lend, and then pawned his watch and clothes.

He could not but be wretched, for it was plain to what a goal of poverty and misery, dishonour and disgrace, such paths lead. Policy loudly urged him to abandon his evil-doing, but piety had as yet no voice in his life. He went so far, however, as to choose for a friend a young man and former schoolmate, named Beta, whose quiet seriousness might, as he hoped, steady his own course. But he was leaning on a broken reed, for Beta was himself a back-slider. Again he was taken ill. God made him to "possess the iniquities of his youth." After some weeks he was better, and once more his conduct took on the semblance of improvement.

The true mainspring of all well-regulated lives was still lacking, and sin soon broke out in unholy indulgence. George Müller was an adept at the ingenuity of vice. What he had left he pawned to get money, and with Beta and two others went on a four days' pleasure-drive, and then planned a longer tour in the Alps. Barriers were in the way, for both money and passports were lacking ; but fertility of invention swept all such barriers away. Forged letters, purporting to be from their parents, brought passports for the party, and books, put in pawn, secured money. Forty-three days were spent in travel, mostly afoot; and during this tour George Müller, holding, like Judas, the common purse, proved, like him, a thief, for he managed to make his companions pay one third of his own expenses.

The party were back in Halle before the end of September, and George Müller went home to spend the rest of his vacation. To account plausibly to his father for the use of his allowance a new chain of lies was readily devised. So soon and so sadly were all his good resolves again broken.

When once more in Halle, he little knew that the time had come when he was to become a new man in Christ Jesus. He was to find God, and that discovery was to turn into a new channel the whole current of his life. The sin and misery of these twenty years would not have been reluctantly chronicled but to make the more clear that his conversion was a supernatural work, inexplicable without God. There was certainly nothing in himself to 'evolve' such a result, nor was there anything in his 'environment.' In that university town there were no natural forces that could bring about a revolution in character and conduct such as he experienced. Twelve hundred and sixty students were there gathered, and nine hundred of them were divinity students, yet even of the latter number, though all were permitted to preach, not one hundredth part, he says, actually " feared the Lord." Formalism displaced pure and undefiled religion, and with many of them immorality and infidelity were cloaked behind a profession of piety. Surely such a man, with such surroundings, could undergo no radical change of character and life without the intervention of some mighty power from without and from above ! What this force was, and how it wrought upon him and in him, we are now to see.

CHAPTER II

THE NEW BIRTH AND THE NEW LIFE

THE lost days of sin, now forever past, the days of heaven upon earth began to dawn, to grow brighter till the perfect day.

We enter the second period of this life we are reviewing. After a score of years of evil-doing George Müller was converted to God, and the radical nature of the change strikingly proves and displays the sovereignty of Almighty Grace. He had been kept amid scenes of outrageous and flagrant sin, and brought through many perils, as well as two serious illnesses, because divine purposes of mercy were to be fulfilled in him. No other explanation can adequately account for the facts.

Let those who would explain such a conversion without taking God into account remember that it was at a time when this young sinner was as careless as ever; when he had not for years read the Bible or had a copy of it in his possession ; when he had seldom gone to a service of worship, and had never yet even heard one gospel sermon; when he had never been told by any believer what it is to believe on the Lord Jesus Christ and to live by God's help and according to His Word ; when, in fact, he had no conception of the first principles of the doctrine of Christ, and knew not the real nature of a holy life, but thought all others to be as himself, except in the degree of depravity and iniquity. This young man had thus grown to manhood without having learned that rudimental truth that sinners and saints differ not in degree but in kind; that if any man be in Christ, he is a new creation; yet the hard heart of such a man, at such a time and in such conditions, was so wrought upon by the Holy Spirit that he suddenly found entrance into a new sphere of life, with new adaptations to its new atmosphere.

The divine Hand in this history is doubly plain when, as we now look back, we see that this was also the period of preparation for his life-work—a preparation the more mysterious because he had as yet no conception or forecast of that work. During the next ten years we shall watch the divine Potter, to Whom George Müller was a chosen vessel for service, moulding and fitting the vessel for His use. Every step is one of preparation, but can be understood only in the light which that future casts backward over the unique ministry to the church and the world, to which this new convert was all unconsciously separated by God and was to become so peculiarly consecrated.

One Saturday afternoon about the middle of November, 1825, Beta said to Müller, as they were returning from a walk, that he was going that evening to a meeting at a believer's house, where he was wont to go on Saturdays, and where a few friends met to sing, to pray, and to read the word of God and a printed sermon. Such a programme held out nothing fitted to draw a man of the world who sought his daily gratifications at the card-table and in the wine-cup, the dance and the drama, and whose companionships were found in dissipated young fellows : and yet George Müller felt at once a wish to go to this meeting, though he could not have told why. There was no doubt a conscious void within him never yet filled, and some instinctive inner voice whispered that he might there find food for his soul-hunger—a satisfying something after which he had all his life been unconsciously and blindly groping. He expressed the desire to go, which his friend hesitated to encourage lest such a gay and reckless devotee of vicious pleasures might feel ill at ease in such an assembly. However, he called for young Müller and took him to the meeting.

During his wanderings as a backslider, Beta had both joined and aided George Müller in his evil courses, but, on coming back from the Swiss tour, his sense of sin had so revived as to constrain him to make a full confession to his father ; and, through a Christian friend, one Dr. Richter, a former student at Halle, he had been made acquainted with the Mr. Wagner at whose dwelling the meetings were held. The two young men therefore went together, and the former backslider was used of God to " convert a sinner from the error of his way and save a soul from death and hide a multitude of sins."

That Saturday evening was the turning-point in George Müller's history and destiny. He found himself in strange company, amid novel surroundings, and breathing a new atmosphere. His awkwardness made him feel so uncertain of his welcome that he made some apology for being there. But he never forgot brother Wagner's gracious answer : " Come as often as you please ! house and heart are open to you." He little knew then what he afterward learned from blessed experience, what joy fills and thrills the hearts of praying saints when an evil-doer turns his feet, however timidly, toward a place of prayer !

All present sat down and sang a hymn. Then a brother —who afterward went to Africa under the London Missionary Society—fell on his knees and prayed for God's blessing on the meeting. That *kneeling before God in prayer* made upon Müller an impression never lost. He was in his twenty-first year, and yet he had *never before seen any one on his knees praying,* and of course had never himself knelt before God,—the Prussian habit being to stand in public prayer.

A chapter was read from the word of God, and—all meetings where the Scriptures were expounded, unless by an ordained clergyman, being under the ban as irregular—a printed sermon was read. When, after another hymn, the master of the house prayed, George Müller was inwardly saying: "I am much more learned than this illiterate man, but I could not pray as well as he." Strange to say, a new joy was already springing up in his soul for which he could have given as little explanation as for his unaccountable desire to go to that meeting. But so it was; and on the way home he could not forbear saying to Beta: "All we saw on our journey to Switzerland, and all our former pleasures, are as nothing compared to this evening."

Whether or not, on reaching his own room, he himself knelt to pray he could not recall, but he never forgot that a new and strange peace and rest somehow found him as he lay in bed that night. Was it God's wings that folded over him, after all his vain flight away from the true nest where the divine Eagle flutters over His young?

How sovereign are God's ways of working! In such a sinner as Müller, theologians would have demanded a great 'law work' as the necessary doorway to a new life. Yet there was at this time as little deep conviction of guilt and condemnation as there was deep knowledge of God and of divine things, and perhaps it was because there was so little of the latter that there was so little of the former.

Our rigid theories of conversion all fail in view of such facts. We have heard of a little child who so simply trusted Christ for salvation that she could give no account of any 'law work.' And as one of the old examiners, who thought there could be no genuine conversion without a period of deep conviction, asked her, " But, my dear, how about the Slough of Despond ? " she dropped a courtesy and said, *" Please, sir, I didn't come that way! "*

George Müller's eyes were but half opened, as though he saw men as trees walking ; but Christ had touched those eyes. He knew little of the great Healer, but somehow he had touched the hem of His garment of grace, and virtue came out of Him who wears that seamless robe, and who responds even to the faintest contact of the soul that is groping after salvation. And so we meet here another proof of the infinite variety of God's working which, like the fact of that working, is so wonderful. That Saturday evening in November, 1825, was to this young student of Halle *the parting of the ways.* He had tasted that the Lord is gracious, though he himself could not account for the new relish for divine things which made it seem too long to wait a week for another meal ; so that thrice before the Saturday following he sought the house of brother Wagner, there, with the help of brethren, to search the Scriptures.

We should lose one of the main lessons of this life-story by passing too hastily over such an event as this conversion and the exact manner of it, for here is to be found the first great step in God's preparation of the workman for his work.

Nothing is more wonderful in history than the unmistakable signs and proofs of *preadaptation.* Our life-occurrences are not *disjecta membra*—scattered, disconnected, and accidental fragments. In God's book all these events were written beforehand, when as yet there was nothing in existence but the plan in God's mind—to be fashioned in continuance in actual history—as is perhaps suggested in Psalm cxxxix. 16 (margin).

We see stones and timbers brought to a building site—the stones from different quarries and the timbers from various shops—and different workmen have been busy upon them at times and places which forbade all conscious contact or cooperation. The conditions oppose all preconcerted action, and yet, without chipping or cutting, stone fits stone, and timber fits timber—tenons and mortises, and proportions and dimensions, all corresponding so that when the building is complete it is as perfectly proportioned and as accurately fitted as though it had been all prepared in one workshop and put together in advance as a test. In such circumstances no sane man would doubt that *one presiding mind*—one architect and master builder—had planned that structure, however many were the quarries and workshops and labourers.

And so it is with this life-story we are writing. The materials to be built into one structure of service were from a thousand sources and moulded into form by many hands, but there was a mutual fitness and a common adaptation to the end in view which prove that He whose mind and plan span the ages had a supreme purpose to which all human agents were unconsciously tributary. The awe of this vision of God's workmanship will grow upon us as we look beneath and behind the mere human occurrences to see the divine Hand shaping and building together all these seemingly disconnected events and experiences into one life-work.

For example, what have we found to be the initial step and stage in George Müller's spiritual history ? In a little gathering of believers, where for the first time he saw a child of God pray on his knees, he found his first approach to a pardoning God. Let us observe : this man was henceforth to be singularly and peculiarly identified with simple scriptural assemblies of believers after the most primitive and apostolic pattern—meetings for prayer and praise, reading and expounding of the Word, such as doubtless were held at the house of Mary the mother of John Mark—assemblies mainly and primarily for believers, held wherever a place could be found, with no stress laid on consecrated buildings and with absolutely no secular or æsthetic attractions. Such assemblies were to be so linked with the whole life, work, and witness of George Müller as to be inseparable from his name, and it was in such an assembly that the night before he died he gave out his last hymn and offered his last prayer.

Not only so, but *prayer, on the knees, both in secret and in such companionship of believers,* was henceforth to be the one great central secret of his holy living and holy serving. Upon this corner-stone of prayer all his life-work was to be built. Of Sir Henry Lawrence the native soldiers during the Lucknow mutiny were wont to say that, " when he looked twice up to heaven, once down to earth, and then stroked his beard, he knew what to do." And of George Müller it may well be said that he was to be, for more than seventy years, the man who conspicuously looked up to heaven to learn what he was to do. Prayer for direct divine guidance in every crisis, great or small, was to be the secret of his whole career. Is there any accident in the exact way in which he was first led to God, and in the precise character of the scenes which were thus stamped with such lasting interest and importance ?

The thought of a divine plan which is thus emphasized at this point we are to see singularly illustrated as we mark how stone after stone and timber after timber are brought to the building site, and all so mutually fitted that no sound of any human tool is to be heard while the life-work is in building.

Of course a man that had been so profligate and prodigal

must at least begin at conversion to live a changed life. Not that all at once the old sins were abandoned, for such total transformation demands deeper knowledge of the word and will of God than George Müller yet had. But within him a new separating and sanctifying Power was at work. There was a distaste for wicked joys and former companions ; the frequenting of taverns entirely ceased, and a lying tongue felt new and strange bands about it. A watch was set at the door of the lips, and every word that went forth was liable to a challenge, so that old habits of untamed speech were arrested and corrected.

At this time he was translating into German for the press a French novel, hoping to use the proceeds of his work for a visit to Paris, etc. At first the plan for the pleasure-trip was abandoned, then the question arose whether the work itself should not be. Whether his convictions were not clear or his moral courage not sufficient, he went on with the novel. It was finished, but never published. Providential hindrances prevented or delayed the sale and publication of the manuscript until clearer spiritual vision showed him that the whole matter was not of faith and was therefore sin, so that he would neither sell nor print the novel, but burned it—another significant step, for it was his *first courageous act of self-denial in surrender to the voice of the Spirit*—and another stone or timber was thus ready for the coming building.

He now began in different directions a good fight against evil. Though as yet weak and often vanquished before temptation, he did not habitually ' continue in sin,' nor offend against God without godly sorrow. Open sins became less frequent and secret sins less ensnaring. He read the word of God, prayed often, loved fellow disciples, sought church assemblies from right motives, and boldly took his stand on the side of his new Master, at the cost of reproach and ridicule from his fellow students.

George Müller's next marked step in his new path was *the discovery of the preciousness of the word of God.*

At first he had a mere hint of the deep mines of wealth which he afterward explored. But his whole life-history so circles about certain great texts that whenever they come into this narrative they should appear in capitals to mark their prominence. And, of them all, that 'little gospel' in John iii. 16 is the first, for by it he found a full salvation:

" GOD SO LOVED THE WORLD THAT HE GAVE HIS ONLY-BEGOTTEN SON, THAT WHOSOEVER BELIEVETH IN HIM SHOULD NOT PERISH, BUT HAVE EVERLASTING LIFE."

From these words he got his first glimpse of the philosophy of the plan of salvation—why and how the Lord Jesus Christ bore our sins in His own body on the tree as our vicarious Substitute and suffering Surety, and how His sufferings in Gethsemane and Golgotha made it forever needless that the penitent believing sinner should bear his own iniquity and die for it.

Truly to grasp this fact is the beginning of a true and saving faith—what the Spirit calls " laying hold." He who believes and knows that God so loved him first, finds himself loving God in return, and faith works by love to purify the heart, transform the life, and overcome the world.

It was so with George Müller. He found in the word of God *one great fact:* the love of God in Christ. Upon that fact faith, not feeling, laid hold ; and then the feeling came naturally without being waited for or sought after. The love of God in Christ constrained him to a love—infinitely unworthy, indeed, of that to which it responded, yet supplying a new impulse unknown before. What all his father's injunctions, chastisements, entreaties, with all the urgent dictates of his own conscience, motives of expediency, and repeated resolves of amendment, utterly failed to effect, the love of God both impelled and enabled him to do—renounce a life of sinful self-indulgence. Thus early he learned that double truth, which he afterwards passionately loved to teach others, that in the blood of God's atoning Lamb is the Fountain of both forgiveness and cleansing. Whether we seek pardon for sin or power over sin, the sole source and secret are in Christ's work for us.

The new year 1826 was indeed a *new year* to this new-born soul. He now began to read *missionary* journals, which kindled a new flame in his heart. He felt a yearning—not very intelligent as yet—to be himself a messenger to the nations, and frequent praying deepened and confirmed the impression. As his knowledge of the world-field enlarged, new facts as to the destitution and the desolation of heathen peoples became as fuel to feed this flame of the mission spirit.

A carnal attachment, however, for a time almost quenched this fire of God within. He was drawn to a young woman of like age, a professed believer, whom he had met at the Saturday-evening meetings; but he had reason to think that her parents would not give her up to a missionary life, and he began, half-unconsciously, to weigh in the balance his yearning for service over against his passion for a fellow creature. Inclination, alas, outweighed duty. Prayer lost its power and for the time was almost discontinued, with corresponding decline in joy. His heart was turned from the foreign field, and in fact from all self-denying service. Six weeks passed in this state of spiritual declension, when God took a strange way to reclaim the backslider.

A young brother, Hermann Ball, wealthy, cultured, and

with every promising prospect for this world to attract
him, made a great self-sacrifice. He chose Poland as a
field, and work among the Jews as his mission, refusing to
stay at home to rest in the soft nest of self-indulgent and
luxurious ease. This choice made on young Müller a deep
impression. He was compelled to contrast with it his own
course. For the sake of a passionate love for a young
woman he had given up the work to which he felt drawn
of God, and had become both joyless and prayerless : another young man, with far more to draw him worldward,
had, for the sake of a self-denying service among despised
Polish Jews, resigned all the pleasures and treasures of the
world. Hermann Ball was acting and choosing as Moses
did in the crisis of his history, while he, George Müller,
was acting and choosing more like that profane person
Esau, when for one morsel of meat he bartered his birth-
right. The result was a new renunciation—he gave up
the girl he loved, and forsook a connection which had been
formed without faith and prayer and had proved a source
of alienation from God.

Here we mark another new and significant step in
preparation for his life-work—a decided step forward,
which became a pattern for his after-life. For the second
time a *decision for God had cost him marked self-denial.*
Before, he had burned his novel; now, on the same altar,
he gave up to the consuming fire a human passion which
had over him an unhallowed influence. According to the
measure of his light thus far, George Müller was *fully,
unreservedly given up to God,* and therefore walking in the
light. He did not have to wait long for the recompense
of the reward, for the smile of God repaid him for the loss
of a human love, and the peace of God was his because the
God of peace was with him.

Every new spring of inward joy demands a channel for

outflow, and so he felt impelled to bear witness. He wrote to his father and brother of his own happy experience, begging. them to seek and find a like rest in God, thinking that they had but to know the path that leads to such joy to be equally eager to enter it. But an angry response was all the reply that his letter evoked.

About the same time the famous Dr. Tholuck took the chair of professor of divinity at Halle, and the advent of such a godly man to the faculty drew pious students from other schools of learning, and so enlarged George Müller's circle of fellow believers, who helped him much through grace. Of course the missionary spirit revived, and with such increased fervor, that he sought his father's permission to connect himself with some missionary institution in Germany. His father was not only much displeased, but greatly disappointed, and dealt in reproaches very hard to bear. He reminded George of all the money he had spent on his education in the expectation that he would re-pay him by getting such a ' living ' as would insure to the parent a comfortable home and support for his old age; and in a fit of rage he exclaimed that he would no longer look on him as a son.

Then, seeing that son unmoved in his quiet steadfast-ness, he changed tone, and from threats turned to tears of entreaty that were much harder to resist than reproaches. The result of the interview was a *third* significant step in preparation for his son's life's mission. His resolve was un-broken to follow the Lord's leading at any cost, but he now clearly saw that he could be *independent of man only by being more entirely dependent on God, and that henceforth he should take no more money from his father.* To receive such support implied obedience to his wishes, for it seemed plainly wrong to look to him for the cost of his training when he had no prospect nor intention of meeting his known expectations. If he was to live on his father's money, he was under a tacit obligation to carry out his plans and seek a good living as a clergyman at home. Thus early in life George Müller learned the valuable lesson that one must preserve his independence if he would not endanger his integrity.

God was leading His servant in his youth to *cast himself upon Him for temporal supplies.* This step was not taken without cost, for the two years yet to be spent at the university would require more outlay than during any time previous. But thus early also did he find God a faithful Provider and Friend in need. Shortly after, certain American gentlemen, three of whom were college professors,* being in Halle and wishing instruction in German, were by Dr. Tholuck recommended to employ George Müller as tutor; and the pay was so ample for the lessons taught them and the lectures written out for them, that all wants were more than met. Thus also in his early life was written large in the chambers of his memory another golden text from the word of God :

" O FEAR THE LORD, YE HIS SAINTS !
FOR THERE IS NO WANT TO THEM THAT FEAR HIM."
(Psalm xxxiv. 9.)

* One of them, the Rev. Charles Hodge, afterward so well known as professor at Princeton Theological Seminary, etc.

CHAPTER III

MAKING READY THE CHOSEN VESSEL

THE workman of God needs to wait on Him to know the work he is to do and the sphere where he is to serve Him.

Mature disciples at Halle advised George Müller for the time thus quietly to wait for divine guidance, and meanwhile to take no further steps toward the mission field. He felt unable, however, to dismiss the question, and was so impatient to settle it that he made the common blunder of attempting to come to a decision in a carnal way. *He resorted to the lot,* and not only so, but to the lot as cast in the lap of the *lottery!* In other words, he first drew a lot in private, and then bought a ticket in a royal lottery, expecting his steps to be guided in a matter so solemn as the choice of a field for the service of God, by the turn of the 'wheel of fortune'! Should his ticket draw a prize he would *go;* if not, *stay* at home. Having drawn a small sum, he accordingly accepted this as a 'sign,' and at once applied to the Berlin Missionary Society, but was not accepted because his application was not accompanied with his father's consent.

Thus a higher Hand had disposed while man proposed. God kept out of the mission field, at this juncture, one so utterly unfit for His work that he had not even learned that primary lesson that he who would work with God must first wait on Him and wait for Him, and that all undue haste in such a matter is worse than waste.   He who kept Moses waiting forty years before He sent him to lead out captive Israel, who withdrew Saul of Tarsus three years into Arabia before he sent him as an apostle to the nations, and who left even His own Son thirty years in obscurity before His manifestation as Messiah—this God is in no hurry to put other servants at work.   He says to all impatient souls : " My time is not yet full come, but your time is always ready."

Only twice after this did George Müller ever resort to the lot : once at a literal parting of the ways when he was led by it to take the wrong fork of the road, and afterward in a far more important matter, but with a like result : in both cases he found he had been misled, and henceforth abandoned all such chance methods of determining the mind of God.

He learned two lessons, which new dealings of God more and more deeply impressed :

First, that the safe guide in every crisis is believing prayer in connection with the word of God ;

Secondly, that continued uncertainty as to one's course is a reason for continued waiting.

These lessons should not be lightly passed over, for they are too valuable.   The flesh is impatient of all delay, both in decision and action; hence all carnal choices are immature and premature, and all carnal courses are mistaken and unspiritual.   God is often moved to delay that we may be led to pray, and even the answers to prayer are deferred that the natural and carnal spirit may be kept in check and self-will may bow before the will of God.

In a calm review of his course many years later George Müller saw that he " ran hastily to the lot " as a shorter way of settling a doubtful matter, and that, especially in the question of God's call to the mission field, this was shockingly improper. He saw also how unfit he had been at that time for the work he sought : he should rather have asked himself how one so ignorant and so needing to be taught could think of teaching others ! Though a child of God, he could not as yet have given a clear statement or explanation of the most elementary gospel truths. The one thing needful was therefore to have sought through much prayer and Bible study to get first of all a deeper knowledge and a deeper experience of divine things. Impatience to settle a matter so important was itself seen to be a positive disqualification for true service, revealing unfitness to endure hardship as a good soldier of Jesus Christ. There is a constant strain and drain on patient waiting which is a necessary feature of missionary trial and particularly the trial of deferred harvests. One who, at the outset, could not brook delay in making his first decision, and wait for God to make known His will in His own way and time, would not on the field have had long patience as a husbandman, waiting for the precious fruit of his toil, or 'have met with quietness of spirit the thousand perplexing problems of work among the heathen !

Moreover the conviction grew that, could he have followed the lot, his choice would have been a life-mistake. His mind, at that time, was bent upon the East Indies as a field. Yet all subsequent events clearly showed that God's choice for him was totally different. His repeated offers met as repeated refusals, and though on subsequent occasions he acted most deliberately and solemnly, no open door was found, but he was in every case kept from following out his honest purpose. Nor could the lot be justified as an indication of his *ultimate* call to the mission field, for the purpose of it was definite, namely, to ascertain, not whether *at some period of his life* he was to go forth, but whether *at that time* he was to go or stay. The

whole after-life of George Müller proved that God had
for him an entirely different plan, which He was not ready
yet to reveal, and which His servant was not yet prepared
to see or follow. If any man's life ever was a plan of God,
surely this life was; and the Lord's distinct, emphatic leading, when made known, was *not* in this direction. He
had purposed for George Müller a larger field than the
Indies, and a wider witness than even the gospel message
to heathen peoples. He was 'not suffered' to go into
'Bithynia' because 'Macedonia' was waiting for his ministry.

With increasing frequency, earnestness, and minuteness,
was George Müller led to put before God, in prayer, all
matters that lay upon his mind. This man was to be
peculiarly an example to believers as an *intercessor;* and so
God gave him from the outset a very *simple, childlike disposition* toward Himself. In many things he was in
knowledge and in strength to outgrow childhood and become a man, for it marks immaturity when we err through
ignorance and are overcome through weakness. But in faith
and in the filial spirit, he always continued to be a little
child. Mr. J. Hudson Taylor well reminds us that while
in *nature* the normal order of growth is from childhood
to manhood and so to maturity, in *grace* the true development is perpetually backward toward the cradle : we
must become and continue as little children, not losing,
but rather gaining, childlikeness of spirit. The disciple's
maturest manhood is only the perfection of his childhood.
George Müller was never so really, truly, fully a little
child in all his relations to his Father, as when in the
ninety-third year of his age.

Being thus providentially kept from the Indies, he
began definite work at home, though yet having little real
knowledge of the divine art of coworking with God. He

spoke to others of their soul's welfare, and wrote to former
companions in sin, and circulated tracts and missionary
papers. Nor were his labours without encouragement,
though sometimes his methods were awkward or even gro-
tesque, as when, speaking to a beggar in the fields about his
need of salvation, he tried to overcome apathetic indifference by speaking louder and louder, as though mere
bawling in his ears would subdue the hardness of his
heart !

In 1826 he first attempted to *preach*. An unconverted
schoolmaster some six miles from Halle he was the means
of turning to the Lord; and this schoolmaster asked him to
come and help an aged, infirm clergyman in the parish.
Being a student of divinity he was at liberty to preach, but
conscious ignorance had hitherto restrained him. He
thought, however, that by committing some other man's
sermon to memory he might profit the hearers, and so he
undertook it. It was slavish work to prepare, for it took most
of a week to memorize the sermon, and it was joyless work
to deliver it, for there was none of the living power that
attends a man's God-given message and witness. His conscience was not yet enlightened enough to see that he was
acting a false part in preaching another's sermon as his
own ; nor had he the spiritual insight to perceive that it
is not God's way to set up a man to preach who knows not
enough of either His word or the life of the Spirit within
him, to prepare his own discourse. How few even among
preachers feel preaching to be *a divine vocation and not a
mere human profession;* that a ministry of the truth implies the witness of experience, and that to preach another
man's sermon is, at the best, unnatural walking on stilts !

George Müller ' got through ' his painful effort of August 27, 1826, reciting this memoriter sermon at eight A.M.
in the chapel of ease, and three hours later in the parish

church. Being asked to preach again in the afternoon, but having no second sermon committed to memory, he had to keep silent, or *depend on the Lord for help*. He thought he could at least read the fifth chapter of Matthew, and simply expound it. But he had no sooner begun the first beatitude than he felt himself greatly assisted. Not only were his lips opened, but the Scriptures were opened too, his own soul expanded, and a peace and power, wholly unknown to his tame, mechanical repetitions of the morning, accompanied the simpler expositions of the afternoon, with this added advantage, that he talked on a level with the people and not over their heads, his colloquial, earnest speech riveting their attention.

Going back to Halle, he said to himself, 'This is the *true way to preach*,' albeit he felt misgivings lest such a simple style of exposition might not suit so well a cultured refined city congregation. He had yet to learn how the enticing words of man's wisdom make the cross of Christ of none effect, and how the very simplicity that makes preaching intelligible to the illiterate makes sure that the most cultivated will also understand it, whereas the reverse is not true.

Here was another very important *step in his preparation* for subsequent service. He was to rank throughout life among the simplest and most scriptural of preachers. This first trial of pulpit-work led to frequent sermons, and in proportion as his speech was in the simplicity that is in Christ did he find joy in his work and a harvest from it. The committed sermon of some great preacher might draw forth human praise, but it was the simple witness of the Word, and of the believer to the Word, that had praise of God. His preaching was not then much owned of God in fruit. Doubtless the Lord saw that he was not ready for reaping, and scarcely for sowing: there was yet too little prayer in preparation and too little unction in delivery, and so his labours were comparatively barren of results.

About this same time he took another step—perhaps the most significant thus far in its bearing on the precise form of work so closely linked with his name. For some two months he availed himself of the free lodgings furnished for poor divinity students in the famous *Orphan Houses built by A. H. Francke.* This saintly man, a professor of divinity at Halle, who had died a hundred years before (1727), had been led to found an orphanage in entire dependence upon God. Half unconsciously George Müller's whole life-work at Bristol found both its suggestion and pattern in Francke's orphanage at Halle. The very building where this young student lodged was to him an object lesson—a visible, veritable, tangible proof that the Living God hears prayer, and can, in answer to prayer alone, build a house for orphan children. That lesson was never lost, and George Müller fell into the apostolic succession of such holy labour! He often records how much his own faith-work was indebted to that example of simple trust in prayer exhibited by Francke. Seven years later he read his life, and was thereby still more prompted to follow him as he followed Christ.

George Müller's spiritual life in these early days was strangely chequered. For instance, he who, as a Lutheran divinity student, was essaying to preach, hung up in his room a framed crucifix, hoping thereby to keep in mind the sufferings of Christ and so less frequently fall into sin. Such helps, however, availed him little, for while he rested upon such artificial props, it seemed as though he sinned the oftener.

He was at this time overworking, writing sometimes fourteen hours a day, and this induced nervous depression, which exposed him to various temptations. He ventured into a confectioner's shop where wine and beer were sold, and then suffered reproaches of conscience for conduct so unbecoming a believer ; and he found himself indulging ungracious and ungrateful thoughts of God, who, instead of visiting him with deserved chastisement, multiplied His tender mercies.

He wrote to a rich, liberal and titled lady, asking a loan, and received the exact sum asked for, with a letter, not from her, but from another into whose hands his letter had fallen by "a peculiar providence," and who signed it as "An adoring worshipper of the Saviour Jesus Christ." While led to send the money asked for, the writer added wise words of caution and counsel—words so fitted to George Müller's exact need that he saw plainly the higher Hand that had guided the anonymous writer. In that letter he was urged to "seek by watching and prayer to be delivered from all vanity and self-complacency," to make it his "chief aim to be more and more humble, faithful, and quiet," and not to be of those who "say 'Lord, Lord,' but have Him not deeply in their hearts." He was also reminded that "Christianity consists not in words but in power, and that there must be life in us."

He was deeply moved by this message from God through an unknown party, and the more as it had come, with its enclosure, at the time when he was not only guilty of conduct unbecoming a disciple, but indulging hard thoughts of his heavenly Father. He went out to walk alone, and was so deeply wrought on by God's goodness and his own ingratitude that he knelt behind a hedge, and, though in snow a foot deep, he forgot himself for a half-hour in praise, prayer, and self-surrender.

Yet so deceitful is the human heart that a few weeks later he was in such a backslidden state that, for a time, he was again both careless and prayerless, and one day sought to drown the voice of conscience in the wine-cup. The merciful Father gave not up his child to folly and sin. He who once could have gone to great lengths in dissipation now found a few glasses of wine more than enough ; his relish for such pleasures was gone, and so was the power to silence the still small voice of conscience and of the Spirit of God.

Such vacillations in Christian experience were due in part to the lack of holy associations and devout companionships. Every disciple needs help in holy living, and this young believer yearned for that spiritual uplift afforded by sympathetic fellow believers. In vacation times he had found at Gnadau, the Moravian settlement some three miles from his father's residence, such soul refreshment, but Halle itself supplied little help. He went often to church, but seldom heard the Gospel, and in that town of over 30,000, with all its ministers, he found not one enlightened clergyman. When, therefore, he could hear such a preacher as Dr. Tholuck, he would walk ten or fifteen miles to enjoy such a privilege. The meetings continued at Mr. Wagner's house; and on the Lord's day evenings some six or more believing students were wont to gather, and both these assemblies were means of grace. From Easter, 1827, so long as he remained in Halle, this latter meeting was held in his own room, and must rank alongside those little gatherings of the " Holy Club " in Lincoln College, Oxford, which a hundred years before had shaped the Wesleys and Whitefield for their great careers. Before George Müller left Halle the attendance at this weekly meeting in his room had grown to twenty.

These assemblies were throughout very simple and primitive. In addition to prayer, singing, and reading of God's word, one or more brethren exhorted or read extracts from devout books. Here young Müller freely opened his heart to others, and through their counsels and prayers was delivered from many snares.

One lesson, yet to be learned, was that the one fountain of all wisdom and strength is the Holy Scriptures. Many disciples practically prefer religious books to the Book of God. He had indeed found much of the reading with which too many professed believers occupy their minds to be but worthless chaff—such as French and German novels; but as yet he had not formed the habit of reading the word of God daily and systematically as in later life, almost to the exclusion of other books. In his ninety-second year, he said to the writer, that for every page of any other reading he was sure he read ten of the Bible. But, up to that November day in 1825 when he first met a praying band of disciples, he had never to his recollection read one chapter in the Book of books ; and for the first four years of his new life he gave to the works of uninspired men practical preference over the Living Oracles.

After a true relish for the Scriptures had been created, he could not understand how he could ever have treated God's Book with such neglect. It seemed obvious that *God having condescended to become an Author,* inspiring holy men to write the Scriptures, He would in them impart the most vital truths; His message would cover all matters which concern man's welfare, and therefore, under the double impulse of duty and delight, we should instinctively and habitually turn to the Bible. Moreover, as he read and studied this Book of God, he felt himself admitted to more and more *intimate acquaintance with the Author.* During the last twenty years of his life he read it carefully through, four or five times annually, with a growing sense of his own rapid increase in the knowledge of God thereby.

Such motives for Bible study it is strange that any true believer should overlook. Ruskin, in writing "Of the King's Treasuries," refers to the universal ambition for 'advancement in life,' which means 'getting into good society.' How many obstacles one finds in securing an introduction to the great and good of this world, and even then in getting access to them, in securing an audience with the kings and queens of human society! Yet there is open to us a society of people of the very first rank who will meet us and converse with us so long as we like, whatever our ignorance, poverty, or low estate—namely, the society of authors; and the key that unlocks their private audience-chamber is their books.

So writes Ruskin, and all this is beautifully true; but how few, even among believers, appreciate the privilege of access to the great Author of the universe through His word! Poor and rich, high and low, ignorant and learned, young and old, all alike are welcomed to the audience-chamber of the King of kings. The most intimate knowledge of God is possible on one condition—that we search His Holy Scriptures, prayerfully and habitually, and translate what we there find, into obedience. Of him who thus meditates on God's law day and night, who looks and continues looking into this perfect law of liberty, the promise is unique, and found in both Testaments: "Whatsoever he doeth shall prosper"; "that man shall be blessed in his deed." (Comp. Psalm i. 3; Joshua i. 8; James i. 25.)

So soon as George Müller found this well-spring of delight and success, he drank habitually at this fountain of living waters. In later life he lamented that, owing to his early neglect of this source of divine wisdom and strength, he remained so long in spiritual infancy, with its ignorance and impotence. So long and so far as his growth in knowledge of God was thus arrested his growth in grace was likewise hindered. His close walk with God began at the point where he learned that such walk is always in the light of that inspired word which is divinely declared to be to the obedient soul " a lamp unto the feet and a light unto the path." He who would keep up intimate converse with the Lord must habitually find in the Scriptures the highway of such companionship. God's aristocracy, His nobility, the princes of His realm, are not the wise, mighty, and high-born of earth, but often the poor, weak, despised of men, who abide in His presence and devoutly commune with Him through His inspired word.

Blessed are they who have thus learned to use the key which gives free access, not only to the King's Treasuries, but to the King Himself !

CHAPTER IV

NEW STEPS AND STAGES OF PREPARATION

PASSION for souls is a divine fire, and in the heart of George Müller that fire now began to burn more brightly, and demanded vent.

In August, 1827, his mind was more definitely than before turned toward mission work. Hearing that the Continental Society of Britain sought a minister for Bucharest, he offered himself through Dr. Tholuck, who, in behalf of the Society, was on the lookout for a suitable candidate. To his great surprise his father gave consent, though Bucharest was more than a thousand miles distant and as truly missionary ground as any other field. After a short visit home he came back to Halle, his face steadfastly set toward his far-off field, and his heart seeking prayerful preparation for expected self-sacrifice and hardship. But God had other plans for His servant, and he never went to Bucharest.

In October following, Hermann Ball, passing through Halle, and being at the little weekly meeting in Müller's room, told him how failing health forbade his continuing his work among Polish Jews; and at once there sprang up in George Müller's mind a strong desire to take his place. Such work doubly attracted him, because it would bring him into close contact with God's chosen but erring people, Israel; and because it would afford opportunity to utilize those Hebrew studies which so engrossed him.

At this very time, calling upon Dr. Tholuck, he was asked, to his surprise, whether he had ever felt a desire to *labour among the Jews*—Dr. Tholuck then acting as agent for the London Missionary Society for promoting missions among them. This question naturally fanned the flame of his already kindled desire; but, shortly after, Bucharest being the seat of the war then raging between the Russians and Turks, the project of sending a minister there was for the time abandoned. But a door seemed to open before him just as another shut behind him.

The committee in London, learning that he was available as a missionary to the Jews, proposed his coming to that city for six months as a missionary student to prepare for the work. To enter thus on a sort of probation was trying to the flesh, but, as it seemed right that there should be opportunity for mutual acquaintance between committee and candidate, to insure harmonious cooperation, his mind was disposed to accede to the proposal.

There was, however, a formidable obstacle. Prussian male subjects must commonly serve three years in the army, and classical students who have passed the university examinations, at least one year. George Müller, who had not served out even this shorter term, could not, without royal exemption, even get a passport out of the country. Application was made for such exemption, but it failed. Meanwhile he was taken ill, and after ten weeks suffered a relapse. While at Leipsic with an American professor with whom he went to the opera, he unwisely partook of some refreshments between the acts, which again brought on illness. He had broken a blood-vessel in the stomach, and he returned to Halle, never again to enter a theatre. Subsequently being asked to go to Berlin for a

few weeks to teach German, he went, hoping at the Prussian capital to find access to the court through persons of
rank and secure the desired exemption. But here again he
failed. There now seemed no way of escaping a soldier's
term, and he submitted himself for examination, but was
pronounced physically unfit for military duty. In God's
providence he fell into kind hands, and, being a second
time examined and found unfit, he was thenceforth *completely exempted for life from all service in the army.*

God's lines of purpose mysteriously converged. The
time had come ; the Master spake and it was done : all
things moved in one direction—to set His servant free
from the service of his country, that, under the Cap-
tain of his salvation, he might endure hardness as a good
soldier of Jesus Christ, without entanglement in the affairs
of this life. Aside from this, his stay at the capital had
not been unprofitable, for he had preached five times a
week in the poorhouse and conversed on the Lord's days
with the convicts in the prison.

In February, 1829, he left for London, on the way visiting his father at Heimersleben, where he had returned
after retirement from office ; and he reached the English
metropolis March 19th. His liberty was much curtailed as
a student in this new seminary, but, as no rule conflicted
with his conscience, he submitted. He studied about
twelve hours daily, giving attention mainly to Hebrew
and cognate branches closely connected with his expected
field. Sensible of the risk of that deadness of soul which
often results from undue absorption in mental studies,
he committed to memory much of the Hebrew Old Testament and pursued his tasks in a prayerful spirit, seeking
God's help in matters, however minute, connected with
daily duty.

Tempted to the continual use of his native tongue by

living with his German countrymen, he made little progress in English, which he afterward regretted; and he was wont, therefore, to counsel those who propose to work among a foreign people; not only to live among them in order to learn their language, but to keep aloof as far as may be from their own countrymen, so as to be compelled to use the tongue which is to give them access to those among whom they labour.

In connection with this removal to Britain a seemingly trivial occurrence left upon him a lasting impress—another proof that there are no little things in life. Upon a very small hinge a huge door may swing and turn. It is, in fact, often the apparently trifling events that mould our history, work, and destiny.

A student incidentally mentioned a dentist in Exeter—a Mr. Groves—who for the Lord's sake had resigned his calling with fifteen hundred pounds a year, and with wife and children offered himself as a misionary to Persia, *simply trusting the Lord for all temporal supplies.* This act of self-denying trust had a strange charm for Mr. Müller, and he could not dismiss it from his mind ; indeed, he distinctly entered it in his journal and wrote about it to friends at home. It was *another lesson in faith,* and in the very line of that trust of which for more than sixty years he was to be so conspicuous an example and illustration.

In the middle of May, 1829, he was taken ill and felt himself to be past recovery. Sickness is often attended with strange *self-disclosure.* His conviction of sin and guilt at his conversion was too superficial and shallow to leave any after-remembrance. But, as is often true in the history of God's saints, the sense of guilt, which at first seemed to have no roots in conscience and scarce an existence, struck deeper into his being and grew stronger as he knew more of God and grew more like Him. This common experience of saved souls is susceptible of easy explanation. Our conceptions of things depend mainly upon two conditions : first, the clearness of our vision of truth and duty; and secondly, the standard of measurement and comparison. The more we live in God and unto God, the more do our eyes become enlightened to see the enormity and deformity of sin, so that we recognize the hatefulness of evil more distinctly: and the more clearly do we recognize the perfection of God's holiness and make it the pattern and model of our own holy living.

The amateur musician or artist has a false complacency in his own very imperfect work only so far as his ear or eye or taste is not yet trained to accurate discrimination ; but, as he becomes more accomplished in a fine art, and more appreciative of it, he recognizes every defect or blemish of his previous work, until the musical performance seems a wretched failure and the painting a mere daub. The change, however, is wholly in the *workman* and not in the *work:* both the music and the painting are in themselves just what they were, but the man is capable of something so much better, that his standard of comparison is raised to a higher level, and his capacity for a true judgment is correspondingly enlarged.

Even so a child of God who, like Elijah, stands before Him as a waiting, willing, obedient servant, and has both likeness to God and power with God, may get under the juniper-tree of despondency, cast down with the sense of unworthiness and ill desert. As godliness increases the sense of ungodliness becomes more acute, and so feelings never accurately gauge real assimilation to God. We shall seem worst in our own eyes when in His we are best, and conversely.

A Mohammedan servant ventured publicly to challenge

a preacher who, in an Indian bazaar, was asserting the universal depravity of the race, by affirming that he knew at least one woman who was immaculate, absolutely without fault, and that woman, his own Christian mistress. The preacher bethought himself to ask in reply whether he had any means of knowing whether that was her opinion of herself, which caused the Mohammedan to confess that there lay the mystery : she had been often overheard in prayer confessing herself the most unworthy of sinners.

To return from this digression, Mr. Müller, not only during this illness, but down to life's sudden close, had a growing sense of sin and guilt which would at times have been overwhelming, had he not known upon the testimony of the Word that "whoso covereth his sins shall not prosper, but he that confesseth and forsaketh them shall find mercy." From his own guilt he turned his eyes to the cross where it was atoned for, and to the mercy-seat where forgiveness meets the penitent sinner ; and so sorrow for sin was turned into the joy of the justified.

This confidence of acceptance in the Beloved so stripped death of its terrors that during this illness he longed rather to depart and to be with Christ; but after a fortnight he was pronounced better, and, though still longing for the heavenly rest, he submitted to the will of God for a longer sojourn in the land of his pilgrimage, little foreseeing what joy he was to find in living for God, or how much he was to know of the days of heaven upon earth.

During this illness, also, he showed the growing tendency to bring before the Lord in prayer even the minutest matters which his later life so signally exhibited. He constantly besought God to guide his physician, and every new dose of medicine was accompanied by a new petition that God would use it for his good and enable him with patience to await His will. As he advanced toward recovery he sought rest at Teignmouth, where, shortly after his arrival, " Ebenezer " chapel was reopened. It was here also that Mr. Müller became acquainted with Mr. Henry Craik, who was for so many years not only his friend, but fellow labourer.

It was also about this time that, as he records, certain great truths began to be made clear to him and to stand out in much prominence. This period of personal preparation is so important in its bearing on his whole after-career that the reader should have access to his own witness.

On returning to London, prospered in soul-health as also in bodily vigor, he proposed to fellow students a daily morning meeting, from 6 to 8, for prayer and Bible study, when each should give to the others such views of any passage read as the Lord might give him. These spiritual exercises proved so helpful and so nourished the appetite for divine things that, after continuing in prayer late into the evening hours, he sometimes at midnight sought the fellowship of some like-minded brother, and thus prolonged the prayer season until one or two o'clock in the morning; and even then sleep was often further postponed by his overflowing joy in God. Thus, under his great Teacher, did this pupil, early in his spiritual history, learn that supreme lesson that to every child of God the word of God is the bread of life, and the prayer of faith the breath of life.

Mr. Müller had been back in London scarcely ten days before health again declined, and the conviction took strong hold upon him that he should not spend his little strength in confining study, but at once get about his work; and this conviction was confirmed by the remem-

brance of the added light which God had given him and
the deeper passion he now felt to serve Him more freely
and fully. Under the pressure of this persuasion that
both his physical and spiritual welfare would be promoted
by actual labours for souls, he sought of the Society a
prompt appointment to his field of service; and that they
might with the more confidence commission him, he asked
that some experienced man might be sent out with him
as a fellow counsellor and labourer.

After waiting in vain for six weeks for an answer to
this application, he felt another strong conviction : that
*to wait on his fellow men to be sent out to his field and work
was unscriptural and therefore wrong.* Barnabas and Saul
were called by name and sent forth by the Holy Spirit,
before the church at Antioch had taken any action ; and
he felt himself so called of the Spirit to his work that he
was prompted to begin at once, without waiting for human
authority,—and why not among the Jews in London ?
Accustomed to act promptly upon conviction, he undertook to distribute among them tracts bearing his name
and address, so that any who wished personal guidance
could find him. He sought them at their gathering-places,
read the Scriptures at stated times with some fifty Jewish
lads, and taught in a Sunday-school. Thus, instead of
lying like a vessel in dry-dock for repairs, he was launched
into Christian work, though, like other labourers among
the despised Jews, he found himself exposed to petty trials
and persecutions, called to suffer reproach for the name
of Christ.

Before the autumn of 1829 had passed, a further misgiving laid hold of him as to whether he could in good
conscience remain longer connected in the usual way with
this London Society, and on December 12th he concluded
to dissolve all such ties except upon certain conditions. To

do full justice both to Mr. Müller and the Society, his own words will again be found in the Appendix.

Early in the following year it was made clear that he could labour in connection with such a society only as they would consent to his *serving without salary and labouring when and where the Lord might seem to direct.* He so wrote, eliciting a firm but kind response to the effect that they felt it "inexpedient to employ those who were unwilling to submit to their guidance with respect to missionary operations," etc.

Thus this link with the Society was broken. He felt that he was acting up to the light God gave, and, while imputing to the Society no blame, he never afterward repented this step nor reversed this judgment. To those who review this long life, so full of the fruits of unusual service to God and man, it will be quite apparent that the Lord was gently but persistently thrusting George Müller out of the common path into one where he was to walk very closely with Himself; and the decisions which, even in lesser matters furthered God's purpose were wiser and weightier than could at the time be seen.

One is constantly reminded in reading Mr. Müller's journal that he was a man of like frailties as others. On Christmas morning of this year, after a season of peculiar joy, he awoke to find himself in the Slough of Despond, without any sense of enjoyment, prayer seeming as fruitless as the vain struggles of a man in the mire. At the usual morning meeting he was urged by a brother to continue in prayer, notwithstanding, until he was again melted before the Lord—a wise counsel for all disciples when the Lord's presence seems strangely withdrawn. Steadfast continuance in prayer must never be hindered by the want of sensible enjoyment ; in fact, it is a safe maxim that the less joy, the more need Cessation of communion with God, for whatever cause, only makes the more difficult its resumption and the recovery of the prayer habit and prayer spirit; whereas the persistent outpouring of supplication, together with continued activity in the service of God, soon brings back the lost joy. Whenever, therefore, one yields to spiritual depression so as to abandon, or even to suspend, closet communion or Christian work, the devil triumphs.

So rapid was Mr. Müller's recovery out of this Satanic snare, through continuance in prayer, that, on the evening of that same Christmas day whose dawn had been so overcast, he expounded the Word at family worship in the house where he dined by invitation, and with such help from God that two servants who were present were deeply convicted of sin and sought his counsel.

Here we reach another mile-stone in this life-journey. George Müller 'had now come to the end of the year 1829, and he had been led of the Lord in a truly remarkable path. It was but about four years since he first found the narrow way and began to walk in it, and he was as yet a young man, in his twenty-fifth year. Yet already he had been taught some of the grand secrets of a holy, happy, and useful life, which became the basis of the whole structure of his after-service.

Indeed, as we look back over these four years, they seem crowded with significant and eventful experiences, all of which forecast his future work, though he as yet saw not in them the Lord's sign. His conversion in a primitive assembly of believers where worship and the word of God were the only attractions, was the starting-point in a career every step of which seems a stride forward. Think of a young convert, with such an ensnaring past to reproach and retard him, within these few years learning such advanced lessons in *renunciation:* burning his manuscript novel, giving up the girl he loved, turning his back on the seductive prospect of ease and wealth, to accept self-denial for God, cutting loose from dependence on his father and then refusing all stated salary lest his liberty of witness be curtailed, and choosing a simple expository mode of preaching, instead of catering to popular taste ! Then mark how he fed on the word of God; how he cultivated the habits of searching the Scriptures and praying in secret ; how he threw himself on God, not only for temporal supplies, but for support in bearing all burdens, however great or small ; and how thus early he offered himself for the mission field and was impatiently eager to enter it. Then look at the sovereign love of God, imparting to him in so eminent a degree the childlike spirit, teaching him to trust not his own variable moods of feeling, but the changeless word of His promise ; teaching him to wait patiently on Him for orders, and not to look to human authority or direction ; and so singularly releasing him from military service for life, and mysteriously withholding him from the far-off mission field, that He might train him for his unique mission to the race and the ages to come !

These are a few of the salient points of this narrative, thus far, which must, to any candid mind, demonstrate that a higher Hand was moulding this chosen vessel on His potter's wheel, and shaping it unmistakably for the singular service to which it was destined !

CHAPTER V

THE PULPIT AND THE PASTORATE

No work for God surpasses in dignity and responsibility the Christian ministry. It is at once the consummate flower of the divine planting, the priceless dower of His church, and through it works the power of God for salvation.

Though George Müller had begun his 'candidacy for holy orders' as an unconverted man, seeking simply a human calling with a hope of a lucrative living, he had heard God's summons to a divine vocation, and he was from time to time preaching the Gospel, but not in any settled field.

While at Teignmouth, early in 1830, preaching by invitation, he was asked to take the place of the minister who was about to leave, but he replied that he felt at that time called of God, not to a stationary charge, but rather to a sort of itinerant evangelism. During this time he preached at Shaldon for Henry Craik, thus coming into closer contact with this brother, to whom his heart became knit in bonds of love and sympathy which grew stronger as the acquaintance became more intimate.

Certain hearers at Teignmouth, and among them some preachers, disliked his sermons, albeit they were owned of God; and this caused him to reflect upon the probable causes of this opposition, and whether it was any indication of his duty. He felt that they doubtless looked for outward graces of oratory in a preacher, and hence were not attracted to a foreigner whose speech had no rhetorical charms and who could not even use English with fluency. But he felt sure of a deeper cause for their dislike, especially as he was compelled to notice that, the summer previous, when he himself was less spiritually minded and had less insight into the truth, the same parties who now opposed him were pleased with him. His final conclusion was that the Lord meant to work through him at Teignmouth, but that Satan was acting, as usual, the part of a hinderer, and stirring up brethren themselves to oppose the truth. And as, notwithstanding the opposers, the wish that he should minister at the chapel was expressed so often and by so many, he determined to remain for a time until he was openly rejected as God's witness, or had some clear divine leading to another field of labour.

He announced this purpose, at the same time plainly stating that, should they withhold salary, it would not affect his decision, inasmuch as he did not preach as a hireling of man, but as the servant of God, and would willingly commit to Him the provision for his temporal needs. At the same time, however, he reminded them that it was alike their duty and privilege to minister in carnal things to those who served them in things spiritual, and that while he did not desire a gift, he did desire fruit that might abound to their account.

These experiences at Teignmouth were typical: "Some believed the things which were spoken, and some believed not;" some left the chapel, while others stayed; and some were led and fed, while others maintained a cold indifference, if they did not exhibit an open hostility. But the Lord stood by him and strengthened him, setting His seal upon his testimony; and Jehovah Jireh also moved two brethren, unasked, to supply all the daily wants of His servant. After a while the little church of eighteen members unanimously called the young preacher to the pastorate, and he consented to abide with them for a season, without abandoning his original intention of going from place to place as the Lord might lead. A stipend, of fifty-five pounds annually, was offered him, which somewhat increased as the church membership grew ; and so the university student of Halle was settled in his first pulpit and pastorate.

While at Sidmouth, preaching, in April, 1830, three believing sisters held in his presence a conversation about 'believers' baptism,' which proved the suggestion of another important step in his life, which has a wider bearing than at first is apparent.

They naturally asked his opinion on the subject about which they were talking, and he replied that, having been baptized as a child, he saw no need of being baptized again. Being further asked if he had ever yet prayerfully searched the word of God as to its testimony in this matter, he frankly confessed that he had not.

At once, with unmistakable plainness of speech and with rare fidelity, one of these sisters in Christ promptly said : *" I entreat you, then, never again to speak any more about it till you have done so."*

Such a reply George Müller was not the man either to resent or to resist. He was too honest and conscientious to dismiss without due reflection any challenge to search the oracles of God for their witness upon any given question. Moreover, if, at that very time, his preaching was emphatic in any direction, it was in the boldness with which he insisted that *all pulpit teaching and Christian practice must be subjected to one great test,* namely, *the touchstone of the word of God.* Already an Elijah in spirit, his great aim was to repair the broken-down altar of the Lord, to expose and rebuke all that hindered a thoroughly scriptural worship and service, and, if possible, to restore apostolic simplicity of doctrine and life.

As he thought and prayed about this matter, he was forced to admit to himself that he had never yet earnestly examined the Scriptures for their teaching as to the position and relation of baptism in the believer's life, nor had he even prayed for light upon it. He had nevertheless repeatedly spoken against believers' baptism, and so he saw it to be possible that he might himself have been opposing the teaching of the Word. He therefore determined to study the subject until he should reach a final, satisfactory, and scriptural conclusion ; and thenceforth, whether led to defend infant baptism or believers' baptism, to do it only on scriptural grounds.

The mode of study which he followed was characteristically simple, thorough, and business-like, and was always pursued afterward. He first sought from God the Spirit's teaching that his eyes might be opened to the Word's witness, and his mind illumined ; then he set about a systematic examination of the New Testament from beginning to end. So far as possible he sought absolutely to rid himself of all bias of previous opinion or practice, prepossession or prejudice; he prayed and endeavoured to be free from the influence of human tradition, popular custom, and churchly sanction, or that more subtle hindrance, *personal pride in his own consistency.* He was humble enough to be willing to retract any erroneous teaching and renounce any false position, and to espouse that wise maxim : " Don't be *consistent,* but simply be *true.*" Whatever may have been the case with others who claim to have examined the same question for themselves, the result in his case was that he came to the conclu-

sion, and, as he believed, from the word of God and the
Spirit of God, that none but believers are the proper subjects of baptism, and that only immersion is its proper
mode. Two passages of Scripture were very marked in the
prominence which they had in compelling him to these
conclusions, namely: Acts viii. 36–38, and Romans vi. 3–5.
The case of the Ethiopian eunuch strongly convinced
him that baptism is proper, only as the act of a believer
confessing Christ ; and the passage in the Epistle to the
Romans equally satisfied him that only immersion in water
can express the typical burial with Christ and resurrection
with Him, there and elsewhere made so prominent. He
intended no assault upon brethren who hold other views,
when he thus plainly stated in his journal the honest and
unavoidable convictions to which he came ; but he was
too loyal both to the word of God and to his own conscience to withhold his views when so carefully and prayerfully arrived at through the searching of the Scriptures.
Conviction compelled action, for in him there was no
spirit of compromise ; and he was accordingly promptly
baptized. Years after, in reviewing his course, he records
the solemn conviction that " of all revealed truths, not
one is more clearly revealed in the Scriptures—not even
the doctrine of justification by faith—and that the subject has only become obscured by men not having been
willing to take *the Scriptures alone* to decide the point."
He also bears witness incidentally that not one true
friend in the Lord had ever turned his back upon him in
consequence of his baptism, as he supposed some would
have done ; and that almost all such friends had, since
then, been themselves baptized. It is true that in one way
he suffered some pecuniary loss through this step taken in
obedience to conviction, but the Lord did not suffer him
to be ultimately the loser even in this respect, for He

bountifully made up to him any such sacrifice, even in things that pertain to this life. He concludes this review of his course by adding that through his example many others were led both to examine the question of baptism anew and to submit themselves to the ordinance.

Such experiences as these suggest the honest question whether there is not imperative need of subjecting all current religious customs and practices to the one test of conformity to the scripture pattern. Our Lord sharply rebuked the Pharisees of His day for making "the commandment of God of none effect by their tradition," and, after giving one instance, He added, "and many other such like things do ye."* It is very easy for doctrines and practices to gain acceptance, which are the outgrowth of ecclesiasticism, and neither have sanction in the word of God, nor will bear the searching light of its testimony. Cyprian has forewarned us that even *antiquity* is not *authority*, but may be only *vetustas erroris*—the old age of error. What radical reforms would be made in modern worship, teaching and practice,—in the whole conduct of disciples and the administration of the church of God,— if the one final criterion of all judgment were : 'What do the Scriptures teach ?' And what revolutions in our own lives as believers might take place, if we should first put every notion of truth and custom of life to this one test of scripture authority, and then with the courage of conviction dare to do according to that word—counting no cost, but studying to show ourselves approved of God ! Is it possible that there are any modern disciples who "reject the commandment of God that they may keep their own tradition " ?

This step, taken by Mr. Müller as to baptism, was only

---

* Matthew xv. 6.   + Mark vii 9–13.

a precursor of many others, all of which, as he believed, were according to that Word which, as the lamp to the believer's feet, is to throw light upon his path.

During this same summer of 1830 the further study of the Word satisfied him that, though there is no direct *command* so to do, the scriptural and apostolic *practice* was to *break bread every Lord's day*. (Acts xx 7, etc.) Also, that the Spirit of God should have unhindered liberty to work through any believer according to the gifts He had bestowed, seemed to him plainly taught in Romans xii. ; 1 Cor. xii. ; Ephes. iv., etc. These conclusions likewise this servant of God sought to translate at once into conduct, and such conformity brought increasing spiritual prosperity.

Conscientious misgivings, about the same time, ripened into settled convictions that he could no longer, upon the same principle of obedience to the word of God, consent to *receive any stated salary* as a minister of Christ. For this latter position, which so influenced his life, he assigns the following grounds, which are here stated as showing the basis of his life-long attitude :

1. A stated salary implies a fixed sum, which cannot well be paid without a fixed income through pew-rentals or some like source of revenue. This seemed plainly at war with the teaching of the Spirit of God in James ii. 1–6, since the poor brother cannot afford as good sittings as the rich, thus introducing into church assemblies invidious distinctions and respect of persons, and so encouraging the caste spirit.

2. A fixed pew-rental may at times become, even to the willing disciple, a burden. He who would gladly contribute to a pastor's support, if allowed to do so according to his ability and at his own convenience, might be oppressed by the demand to pay a stated sum at a stated

time.   Circumstances so change that one who has the same cheerful mind as before may be unable to give as formerly, and thus be subjected to painful embarrassment and humiliation if constrained to give a fixed sum.

3. The whole system tends to the bondage of the servant of Christ.   One must be unusually faithful and intrepid if he feels no temptation to keep back or in some degree modify his message in order to please men, when he remembers that the very parties, most open to rebuke and most liable to offence, are perhaps the main contributors toward his salary.

Whatever others may think of such reasons as these, they were so satisfactory to his mind that he frankly and promptly announced them to his brethren ; and thus, as early as the autumn of 1830, when just completing his twenty-fifth year, he took a position from which he never retreated, that he would thenceforth *receive no fixed salary for any service rendered to God's people.*   While calmly assigning scriptural grounds for such a position he, on the same grounds, urged *voluntary offerings*, whether of money or other means of support, as the proper acknowledgment of service rendered by God's minister, and as a sacrifice acceptable, well-pleasing to God.   A little later, seeing that, when such voluntary gifts came direct from the givers personally, there was a danger that some might feel self-complacent over the largeness of the amount given by them, and others equally humbled by the smallness of their offerings, with consequent damage to both classes of givers, he took a step further : he had a *box put up in the chapel,* over which was written, that whoever had a desire to do something for his support might put such an offering therein as ability and disposition might direct.   His intention was, that thus the act might be wholly as in God's sight, without the risk of a sinful pride or false humility.

He further felt that, to be entirely consistent, he should *ask no help from man*, even in bearing necessary costs of travel in the Lord's service, nor even state his needs beforehand in such a way as indirectly to appeal for aid. All of these methods he conceived to be forms of trusting in an arm of ·flesh, going to man for help instead of going at once, always and only, to the Lord. And he adds: "*To come to this conclusion before God required more grace than to give up my salary.*"

These successive steps are here recorded explicitly and in their exact order because they lead up directly to the ultimate goal of his life-work and witness. Such decisions were vital links connecting this remarkable man and his "Father's business," upon which he was soon more fully to enter; and they were all necessary to the fulness of the world-wide witness which he was to bear to a prayer-hearing God and the absolute safety of trusting in Him and in Him alone.

On October 7, 1830, George Müller, in finding a wife, found a good thing and obtained new favour from the Lord. Miss Mary Groves, sister of the self-denying dentist whose surrender of all things for the mission field had so impressed him years before, was married to this man of God, and for forty blessed years proved an help meet for him. It was almost, if not quite, an ideal union, for which he continually thanked God; and, although her kingdom was one which came not 'with observation,' the sceptre of her influence was far wider in its sway than will ever be appreciated by those who were strangers to her personal and domestic life. She was a rare woman and her price was above rubies. The heart of her husband safely trusted in her, and the great family of orphans who were to her as children rise up even to this day to call her blessed.

Married life has often its period of estrangement, even

when temporary alienation yields to a deeper love, as the parties become more truly wedded by the assimilation of their inmost being to one another. But to Mr. and Mrs. Müller there never came any such experience of even temporary alienation. From the first, love grew, and with it, mutual confidence and trust. One of the earliest ties which bound these two in one was the bond of a *common self-denial*. Yielding literal obedience to Luke xii. 33, they sold what little they had and gave alms, henceforth laying up no treasures on earth (Matthew vi. 19–34; xix. 21.) The step then taken—accepting, for Christ's sake, voluntary poverty—was never regretted, but rather increasingly rejoiced in ; how faithfully it was followed in the same path of continued self-sacrifice will sufficiently appear when it is remembered that, nearly sixty-eight years afterward, George Müller passed suddenly into the life beyond, a poor man; his will, when admitted to probate, showing his entire personal property, under oath, to be but one hundred and sixty pounds ! And even that would not have been in his possession had there been no daily need of requisite comforts for the body and of tools for his work. Part of this amount was in money, shortly before received and not yet laid out for his Master, but held at His disposal. Nothing, even to the clothes he wore, did he treat as his own. He was a consistent steward.

This final farewell to all earthly posssessions, in 1830, left this newly married husband and wife to look only to the Lord. Thenceforth they were to put to ample daily test both their faith in the Great Provider and the faithfulness of the Great Promiser. It may not be improper here to anticipate, what is yet to be more fully recorded, that, from day to day and hour to hour, during more than threescore years, George Müller was enabled to set to his seal that God is true. If few men have ever been permitted so to trace in the smallest matters God's care over His children, it is partly because few have so completely abandoned themselves to that care. He dared to trust Him, with whom the hairs of our head are all numbered, and who touchingly reminds us that He cares for what has been quaintly called "*the odd sparrow.*" Matthew records (x. 29) how two sparrows are sold for a farthing, and Luke (xii. 6) how five are sold for two farthings ; and so it would appear that, when two farthings were offered, an odd sparrow was thrown in, as of so little value that it could be given away with the other four. And yet even for that one sparrow, not worth taking into account in the bargain, *God cares.* Not one of them is forgotten before God, or falls to the ground without Him. With what force then comes the assurance : " Fear ye not therefore ; ye are of more value than many sparrows " !

So George Müller found it to be. He was permitted henceforth to know as never before, and as few others have ever learned, how truly God may be approached as " Thou that hearest prayer." God can keep His trusting children not only from falling but from stumbling ; for, during all those after-years that spanned the lifetime of two generations, there was no drawing back. Those precious promises, which in faith and hope were " laid hold " of in 1830, were " held fast " until the end. (Heb. vi. 18, x. 23.) And the divine faithfulness proved a safe anchorage-ground in the most prolonged and violent tempests. The anchor of hope, sure and steadfast, and entering into that within the veil, was never dragged from its secure hold on God. In fifty thousand cases, Mr. Müller calculated that he could trace distinct answers to definite prayers; and in multitudes of instances in which God's care was not definitely traced, it was day by day like an encombut invisible presence or atmosphere of life and ~~~gon.

On August 9, 1831, Mrs. Müller gave birth to a still-born babe, and for six weeks remained seriously ill. Her husband meanwhile laments that his heart was so cold and carnal, and his prayers often so hesitating and formal; and he detects, even behind his zeal for God, most unspiritual frames. He especially chides himself for not having more seriously thought of the peril of child-bearing, so as to pray more earnestly for his wife; and he saw clearly that the prospect of parenthood had not been rejoiced in as a blessing, but rather as implying a new burden and hindrance in the Lord's work.

While this man of God lays bare his heart in his journal, the reader must feel that "as in water face answereth to face, so the heart of man to man." How many a servant of God has no more exalted idea of the divine privilege of a sanctified parenthood! A wife and a child are most precious gifts of God when received, in answer to prayer, from His hand. Not only are they not hindrances, but they are helps, most useful in fitting a servant of Christ for certain parts of his work for which no other preparation is so adequate. They serve to teach him many most valuable lessons, and to round out his character into a far more symmetrical beauty and serviceableness. And when it is remembered how a godly *association* in holiness and usefulness may thus be supplied, and above all a godly *succession* through many generations, it will be seen how wicked is the spirit that treats holy wedlock and its fruits in offspring, with lightness and contempt. Nor let us forget that promise: "If two of you agree on earth as touching any thing that they shall ask, it shall be done for them of My Father which is in heaven." (Matt. xviii. 19.) The Greek word for "agree" is *symphonize*, and suggests a

musical harmony where chords are tuned to the same
key and struck by a master hand. Consider what a blessed
preparation for such habitual symphony in prayer is to be
found in the union of a husband and wife in the Lord!
May it not be that to this the Spirit refers when He bids
husband and wife dwell in unity, as " heirs together of
the grace of life," and adds, " *that your prayers be not
hindered* " ? (1 Peter iii. 7.)

God used this severe lesson for permanent blessing to
George Müller. He showed him how open was his heart
to the subtle power of selfishness and carnality, and how
needful was this chastisement to teach him the sacredness
of marital life and parental responsibility. Henceforth
he judged himself, that he might not be judged of the
Lord." (1 Cor. xi. 31.)

A crisis like his wife's critical illness created a demand
for much extra expense, for which no provision had been
made, not through carelessness and improvidence, but
upon principle. Mr. Müller held that to lay by in store
is inconsistent with full trust in God, who in such case
would send us to our hoardings before answering prayer
for more supplies. Experience in this emergency justified
his faith; for not only were all unforeseen wants supplied,
but even the delicacies and refreshments needful for the
sick and weak ; and the two medical attendants graciously
declined all remuneration for services which extended
through six weeks. Thus was there given of the Lord
more than could have been laid up against this season of
trial, even had the attempt been made.

The principle of committing future wants to the Lord's
care, thus acted upon at this time, he and his wife consistently followed so long as they lived and worked together. Experience confirmed them in the conviction
that a life of trust forbids laying up treasures against un-

foreseen needs, since with God *no emergency is unforeseen and no want unprovided for;* and He may be as implicitly trusted for extraordinary needs as for our common daily bread.

Yet another law, kindred to this and thoroughly inwrought into Mr. Müller's habit of life, was *never to contract debt,* whether for personal purposes or the Lord's work. This matter was settled on scriptural grounds once for all (Romans xiii. 8), and he and his wife determined if need be to suffer starvation rather than to buy anything without paying for it when bought. Thus they always knew how much they had to buy with, and what they had left to give to others or use for others' wants.

There was yet another law of life early framed into Mr. Müller's personal decalogue. He regarded any money which was in his hands *already designated for, or appropriated to, a specific use,* as *not his to use, even temporarily, for any other ends.* Thus, though he was often reduced to the lowest point of temporal supplies, he took no account of any such funds set apart for other outlays or due for other purposes. Thousands of times he was in straits where such diversion of funds for a time seemed the only and the easy way out, but where this would only have led him into new embarrassments. This principle, intelligently adopted, was firmly adhered to, that what properly belongs to a particular branch of work, or has been already put aside for a certain use, even though yet in hand, is not to be reckoned on as available for any other need, however pressing. Trust in God implies such knowledge on His part of the exact circumstances that He will not constrain us to any such misappropriation. Mistakes, most serious and fatal, have come from lack of conscience as well as of faith in such exigencies—drawing on one fund to meet the overdraught upon another, hoping afterward to replace what is thus withdrawn. A well-known college president had nearly involved the institution of which he was the head, in bankruptcy, and himself in worse moral ruin, all the result of one error—money given for endowing certain chairs had been used for current expenses until public confidence had been almost hopelessly impaired.

Thus a life of *faith* must be no less a life of *conscience*. Faith and trust in God, and truth and faithfulness toward man, walked side by side in this life-journey in unbroken agreement.

CHAPTER VI

"THE NARRATIVE OF THE LORD'S DEALINGS"

THINGS which are sacred forbid even a careless touch.

The record written by George Müller of the Lord's dealings reads, especially in parts, almost like an inspired writing, because it is simply the tracing of divine guidance in a human life—not this man's own working or planning, suffering or serving, but *the Lord's dealings* with him and workings through him.

It reminds us of that conspicuous passage in the Acts of the Apostles where, within the compass of twenty verses, God is fifteen times put boldly forward as the one Actor in all events. Paul and Barnabas rehearsed, in the ears of the church at Antioch, and afterward at Jerusalem, not what *they had done* for the Lord, but all that *He had done with them*, and how *He had opened* the door of faith unto the Gentiles ; what miracles and wonders *God had wrought* among the Gentiles *by them*. And, in the same spirit, Peter before the council emphasizes how God had made choice of his mouth, as that whereby the Gentiles should hear the word of the Gospel and believe; how He had given them the Holy Ghost and put no difference between Jew and Gentile, purifying their hearts by faith ; and how He who knew all hearts had thus borne them witness. Then James, in the same strain, refers to the way in which *God had visited* the Gentiles to *take out* of them a people for His name; and concludes by two quotations or adaptations

from the Old Testament, which fitly sum up the whole
matter :

" The Lord *who doeth all* these things."

" Known unto God are *all His works* from the beginning
of the world."   (Acts xiv. 27 to xv. 18.)

The meaning of such repeated phraseology cannot be
mistaken. God is here presented as the one agent or actor,
and even the most conspicuous apostles, like Paul and
Peter, as only His instruments. No twenty verses in the
word of God contain more emphatic and repeated lessons
on man's insufficiency and nothingness, and God's all-suffi-
ciency and almightiness. It was God that wrought upon
man through man. It was He who chose Peter to be His
mouthpiece, He whose key unlocked shut doors, He who
visited the nations, who turned sinners into saints, who
was even then taking out a people for His name, purifying
hearts and bearing them witness ; it was He and He alone
who did all these wondrous things, and according to His
knowledge and plan of what He would do, from the beginning. We are not reading so much the Acts of the
Apostles as the acts of God through the apostles. Was it
not this very passage in this inspired book that suggested,
perhaps, the name of this journal : " *The Lord's dealings
with George Müller* " ?

At this narrative or journal, as a whole, we can only
rapidly glance. In this shorter account, purposely condensed to secure a wider reading even from busy people,
that narrative could not be more fully treated, for in its
original form it covers about three thousand printed pages,
and contains close to one million words. To such as can
and will read that more minute account it is accessible at a
low rate,* and is strongly recommended for careful and

---

* Five volumes at 16s. Published by Jas. Nisbet & Co., London.
With subsequent Annual Reports at 3d. each.

leisurely perusal. But for the present purpose the life-story, as found in these pages, takes both a briefer and a different form.

The journal is largely composed of, condensed from, and then supplemented by, annual reports of the work, and naturally and necessarily includes, not only thousands of little details, but much inevitable repetition year by year, because each new report was likely to fall into the hands of some who had never read reports of the previous years. The desire and design of this briefer memoir is to present the salient points of the narrative, to review the whole life-story as from the great summits or outlooks found in this remarkable journal ; so that, like the observer who from some high mountain-peak looks toward the different points of the compass, and thus gets a rapid, impressive, comparative, and comprehensive view of the whole landscape, the reader may, as at a glance, take in those marked features of this godly man's character and career which incite to new and advance steps in faith and holy living. Some few characteristic entries in the journal will find here a place; others, only in substance; while of the bulk of them it will be sufficient to give a general survey, classifying the leading facts, and under each class giving a few representative examples and illustrations.

Looking at this narrative as a whole, certain prominent peculiarities must be carefully noted. We have here a record and revelation of seven conspicuous experiences:

1. An experience of frequent and at times prolonged *financial straits.*

The money in hand for personal needs, and for the needs of hundreds and thousands of orphans, and for the various branches of the work of the Scriptural Knowledge Institution, was often reduced to a single *pound*, or even *penny*, and sometimes to *nothing.* There was therefore a necessity for constant waiting on God, looking to Him directly for all supplies. For months, if not years, together, and at several periods in the work, supplies were furnished only from month to month, week to week, day to day, *hour to hour!* Faith was thus kept in lively exercise and under perpetual training.

2. An experience of the *unchanging faithfulness of the Father-God.*

The straits were long and trying, but never was there one case of failure to receive help; never a meal-time without at least a frugal meal, never a want or a crisis unmet by divine supply and support. Mr. Müller said to the writer : " Not once, or five times, or five hundred times, but thousands of times in these threescore years, have we had in hand not enough *for one more meal,* either in food or in funds ; but not once has God failed us ; not once have we or the orphans gone hungry or lacked any good thing." From 1838 to 1844 was a period of peculiar and prolonged straits, yet when the time of need actually came the supply was always given, though often at the last moment.

3. An experience of the working of God upon the minds, hearts, and consciences of *contributors to the work.*

It will amply repay one to plod, step by step, over these thousands of pages, if only to trace the hand of God touching the springs of human action all over the world in ways of His own, and at times of great need, and adjusting the amount and the exact day and hour of the supply, to the existing want. Literally from the earth's ends, men, women, and children who had never seen Mr. Müller and could have known nothing of the pressure at the time, have been led at the exact crisis of affairs to send aid in the very sum or form most needful. In countless cases, while he was on his knees asking, the answer has come in such close correspondence with the request as to shut out *chance* as an explanation, and compel belief in a prayer-hearing God.

4. An experience of habitual *hanging upon the unseen God* and nothing else.

The reports, issued annually to acquaint the public with the history and progress of the work, and give an account of stewardship to the many donors who had a right to a report—these made *no direct appeal for aid.* At one time, and that of great need, Mr. Müller felt led to *withhold* the usual annual statement, lest some might construe the account of work already done as an appeal for aid in work yet to be done, and thus detract from the glory of the Great Provider.* The Living God alone was and is the Patron of these institutions; and not even the wisest and wealthiest, the noblest and the most influential of human beings, has ever been looked to as their dependence.

5. An experience of conscientious *care in accepting and using gifts.*

Here is a pattern for all who act as stewards for God. Whenever there was any ground of misgiving as to the propriety or expediency of receiving what was offered, it was declined, however pressing the need, unless or until all such objectionable features no more existed. If the party contributing was known to dishonour lawful debts, so that the money was righteously due to others ; if the gift was encumbered and embarrassed by restrictions that

---

* For example, Vol. II, 102, records that the report given is for 1846-1848, no report having been issued for 1847; and on page 113, under date of May 25th, occur these words: "not being nearly enough to meet the housekeeping expenses," etc.; and, May 28th and 30th, such other words as these: "now our poverty," "in this our great need," "in these days of straitness." Mr. Wright thinks that *on that very account* Mr. Müller did not publish the report for 1847.

hindered its free use for God ; if it was designated for endowment purposes or as a provision for Mr. Müller's old age, or for the future of the institutions ; or if there was any evidence or suspicion that the donation was given grudgingly, reluctantly, or for self-glory, it was promptly declined and returned. In some cases, even where large amounts were involved, parties were urged to wait until more prayer and deliberation made clear that they were acting under divine leading.

6. An experience of extreme caution lest there should be even a careless *betrayal of the fact of pressing need,* to the outside public.

The helpers in the institutions were allowed to come into such close fellowship and to have such knowledge of the exact state of the work as aids not only in common labours, but in common prayers and self-denials. Without such acquaintance they could not serve, pray, nor sacrifice intelligently. But these associates were most solemnly and repeatedly charged never to reveal to those without, not even in the most serious crises, any want whatsoever of the work. The one and only resort was ever to be the God who hears the cry of the needy ; and the greater the exigency, the greater the caution lest there should even seem to be a looking away from divine to human help.

7. An experience of growing boldness of faith in *asking and trusting for great things.*

As faith was exercised it was energized, so that it became as easy and natural to ask confidently for a hundred, a thousand, or ten thousand pounds, as once it had been for a pound or a penny. After confidence in God had been strengthened through discipline, and God had been proven faithful, it required no more *venture* to cast himself on God for provision for two thousand children and an annual outlay of at least twenty-five thousand pounds for them than in the earlier periods of the work to look to Him to care for twenty homeless orphans at a cost of two hundred and fifty pounds a year. Only by *using* faith are we kept from practically *losing* it, and, on the contrary, to use faith is to lose the unbelief that hinders God's mighty acts.

This brief résumé of the contents of thousands of entries is the result of a repeated and careful examination of page after page where have been patiently recorded with scrupulous and punctilious exactness the innumerable details of Mr. Müller's long experience as a co-worker with God. He felt himself not only the steward of a celestial Master, but the trustee of human gifts, and hence he sought to " provide things honest in the sight of all men." He might never have published a report or spread these minute matters before the public eye, and yet have been an equally faithful steward toward *God;* but he would not in such case have been an equally faithful trustee toward *man.*

Frequently, in these days, men receive considerable sums of money from various sources for benevolent work, and yet give no account of such trusteeship. However honest such parties may be, they not only act unwisely, but, by their course, lend sanction to others with whom such irresponsible action is a cloak for systematic fraud. Mr. Müller's whole career is the more without fault because in this respect his administration of his great trust challenges the closest investigation.

The brief review of the lessons taught in his journal may well startle the incredulous and unbelieving spirit of our skeptical day. Those who doubt the power of prayer to bring down actual blessing, or who confound faith in God with credulity and superstition, may well wonder and perhaps stumble at such an array of facts. But, if any reader is still doubtful as to the facts, or thinks they are here arrayed in a deceptive garb or invested with an imaginative halo, he is hereby invited to examine for himself the singularly minute records which George Müller has been led of God to put before the world in a printed form which thus admits no change, and to accompany with a bold and repeated challenge to any one so inclined, to subject every statement to the severest scrutiny, and prove, if possible, one item to be in any respect false, exaggerated, or misleading. The absence of all enthusiasm in the calm and mathematical precision of the narrative compels the reader to feel that the writer was almost mechanically exact in the record, and inspires confidence that it contains the absolute, naked truth.

One caution should, like Habakkuk's gospel message— " The just shall live by his faith "—be written large and plain so that even a cursory glance may take it in. Let no one ascribe to George Müller such a *miraculous gift of faith* as lifted him above common believers and out of the reach of the temptations and infirmities to which all fallible souls are exposed. He was constantly liable to satanic assaults, and we find him making frequent confession of the same sins as others, and even of unbelief, and at times overwhelmed with genuine sorrow for his departures from God. In fact he felt himself rather more than usually wicked by nature, and utterly helpless even as a believer : was it not this poverty of spirit and mourning over sin, this consciousness of entire unworthiness and dependence, that so drove him to the throne of grace and the all-merciful and all-powerful Father ? Because he was so weak, he leaned hard on the strong arm of Him whose strength is not only manifested, but can only be made perfect, in weakness.*

* 1 Cor. xii. 1–10.

To those who think that no man can wield such power in prayer or live such a life of faith who is not an exception to common mortal frailties, it will be helpful to find in this very journal that is so lighted up with the records of God's goodness, the dark shadows of conscious sin and guilt. Even in the midst of abounding mercies and interpositions he suffered from temptations to distrust and disobedience, and sometimes had to mourn their power over him, as when once he found himself inwardly complaining of the cold leg of mutton which formed the staple of his Sunday dinner! We discover as we read that we are communing with a man who was not only of like passions with ourselves, but who felt himself rather more than most others subject to the sway of evil, and needing therefore a special keeping power. Scarce had he started upon his new path of entire dependence on God, when he confessed himself " so sinful " as for some time to entertain the thought that " it would be of no use to trust in the Lord in this way," and fearing that he had perhaps gone already too far in this direction in having committed himself to such a course.* True, this temptation was speedily overcome and Satan confounded ; but from time to time similar fiery darts were hurled at him which had to be quenched by the same shield of faith. Never, to the last hour of life, could he trust himself, or for one moment relax his hold on God, and neglect the word of God and prayer, without falling into sin. The ' old man ' of sin always continued too strong for George Müller alone, and the longer he lived a ' life of trust ' the less was his trust placed upon himself.

Another fact that grows more conspicuous with the perusal of every new page in his journal is that in things

* Vol. I. 73.

common and small, as well as uncommon and great, he took no step without first asking counsel of the oracles of God and seeking guidance from Him in believing prayer. It was his life-motto to learn the will of God before undertaking anything, and to wait till it is clear, because only so can one either be blessed in his own soul or prospered in the work of his hands.* Many disciples who are comparatively bold to seek God's help in great crises, fail to come to Him with like boldness in matters that seem too trivial to occupy the thought of God or invite the interposition of Him who numbers the very hairs of our heads and suffers not one hair to perish. The writer of this journal escaped this great snare and carried even the smallest matter to the Lord.

Again, in his journal he constantly seeks to save from reproach the good name of Him whom he serves : he cannot have such a God accounted a hard Master. So early as July, 1831, a false rumour found circulation that he and his wife were half-starving and that certain bodily ailments were the result of a lack of the necessities of life ; and he is constrained to put on record that, though often brought so low as not to have one penny left and to have the last bread on the table, they had never yet sat down to a meal unprovided with some nourishing food. This witness was repeated from time to time, and until just before his departure for the Father's house on high; and it may therefore be accepted as covering that whole life of faith which reached over nearly threescore years and ten.

A kindred word of testimony, first given at this same time and in like manner reiterated from point to point in his pilgrimage, concerns the Lord's faithfulness in ac-

* Vol. I. 74.

companying His word with power, in accordance with
that positive and unequivocal promise in Isaiah lv. 11 :
" My word shall not return unto Me void ; but it shall
accomplish that which I please, and it shall prosper in
the thing whereto I sent it." It is very noticeable that
this is not said of *man's* word, however wise, important,
or sincere, but of *God's* word. We are therefore justified
in both expecting and claiming that, just so far as our
message is not of human invention or authority, but is
God's message through us, it shall never fail to accomplish His pleasure and its divine errand, whatever be its
apparent failure at the time. Mr. Müller, referring to his
own preaching, bears witness that in almost if not quite
every place where he spoke God's word, whether in larger
chapels or smaller rooms, the Lord gave the seal of His
own testimony. He observed, however, that blessing did
not so obviously or abundantly follow his open-air services: only in one instance had it come to his knowledge
that there were marked results, and that was in the case
of an army officer who came to make sport. Mr. Müller
thought that it might please the Lord not to let him see
the real fruit of his work in open-air meetings, or that
there had not been concerning them enough believing
prayer ; but he concluded that such manner of preaching
was not his present work, since God had not so conspicuously sealed it with blessing.

His journal makes very frequent reference to the
physical weakness and disability from which he suffered.
The struggle against bodily infirmity was almost life-long,
and adds a new lesson to his life-story. The strength of
faith had to triumph over the weakness of the flesh. We
often find him suffering from bodily ills, and sometimes
so seriously as to be incapacitated for labour.

For example, early in 1832 he broke a blood-vessel in

the stomach and lost much blood by the hemo
The very day following was the Lord's day, and fo
side preaching stations needed to be provided for, from
which his disablement would withdraw one labourer to
take his place at home. After an hour of prayer he felt
that faith was given him to rise, dress, and go to the
chapel; and, though very weak, so that the short walk
wearied him, he was helped to preach as usual. After the
service a medical friend remonstrated against his course
as tending to permanent injury ; but he replied that he
should himself have regarded it presumptuous had not
the Lord given him the faith. He preached both afternoon and evening, growing stronger rather than weaker
with each effort, and suffering from no reaction afterward.

In reading Mr. Müller's biography and the record of
such experiences, it is not probable that all will agree as to
the wisdom of his course in every case. Some will com-
mend, while others will, perhaps, condemn. He himself
qualifies this entry in his journal with a wholesome caution
that no reader should in such a matter follow his example,
who *has not faith given him;* but assuring him that if God
does give faith so to undertake for Him, such trust will
prove like good coin and be honoured when presented. He
himself did not always pursue a like course, because he
had not always a like faith, and this leads him in his
journal to draw a valuable distinction between the *gift
of faith* and the *grace of faith,* which deserves careful consideration.

He observed that repeatedly he prayed with the sick
till they were restored, he *asking unconditionally for the
blessing of bodily health,* a thing which, he says, later on, he
could not have done. Almost always in such cases the
petition was granted, yet in some instances not. Once,
in his own case, as early as 1829, he had been healed

of a bodily infirmity of long standing, and which never returned. Yet this same man of God subsequently suffered from disease which was not in like manner healed, and in more than one case submitted to a costly operation at the hands of a skilful surgeon.

Some will doubtless say that even this man of faith lacked the faith necessary for the healing of his own body; but we must let him speak for himself, and especially as he gives his own view of the gift and the grace of faith. He says that the *gift* of faith is exercised, whenever we " do or believe a thing where the not doing or not believing would *not* be sin "; but the *grace* of faith, " where we do or believe what not to do or believe *would* be sin "; in one case we have no unequivocal command or promise to guide us, and in the other we have. The gift of faith is not always in exercise, but the grace must be, since it has the definite word of God to rest on, and the absence or even weakness of faith in such circumstances implies sin. There were instances, he adds, in which it pleased the Lord at times to bestow upon him something like the gift of faith so that he could ask unconditionally and expect confidently.

This journal we may now dismiss as a whole, having thus looked at the general features which characterize its many pages. But let it be repeated that to any reader who will for himself carefully examine its contents its perusal will prove a means of grace. To read a little at a time, and follow it with reflection and self-examination, will be found most stimulating to faith, though often most humiliating by reason of the conscious contrast suggested by the reader's unbelief and unfaithfulness. This man lived peculiarly with God and in God, and his senses were exercised to discern good and evil. His conscience became increasingly sensitive and his judgment singularly discriminating, so that he detected fallacies where they escape the common eye, and foresaw dangers which, like hidden rocks ahead, risk damage and, perhaps, destruction to service if not to character. And, therefore, so far is the writer of this memoir from desiring to displace that journal, that he rather seeks to incite many who have not read it to examine it for themselves. It will to such be found to mark a path of close daily walk with God, where, step by step, with circumspect vigilance, conduct and even motive are watched and weighed in God's own balances.

To sum up very briefly the impression made by the close perusal of this whole narrative with the supplementary annual reports, it is simply this : CONFIDENCE IN GOD.

In a little sketch of Beaté Paulus, the Frau Pastorin pleads with God in a great crisis not to forsake her, quaintly adding that she was " willing to be the *second* whom He might forsake," but she was " determined not to be the *first*." * George Müller believed that, in all ages, there had never yet been one true and trusting believer to whom God had proven false or faithless, and he was perfectly sure that He could be safely trusted who, " if we believe not, yet abideth faithful : He cannot deny Himself." † God has not only *spoken*, but *sworn;* His word is confirmed by His oath : because He could swear by no greater He sware by Himself. And all this that we might have a strong consolation ; that we might have boldness in venturing upon Him, laying hold and holding fast His promise. Unbelief makes God a *liar* and, worse still,

* Faith's Miracles, p. 43.   † 2 Timothy ii. 13.

a *perjurer,* for it accounts Him as not only false to His word, but to His oath. George Müller believed, and because he believed, prayed ; and praying. expected ; and expecting, received. Blessed is he that believes, for there shall be a performance of those things which are spoken of the Lord.

CHAPTER VII

LED OF GOD INTO A NEW SPHERE

If much hangs and turns upon the choice of the *work* we are to do and the *field* where we are to do it, it must not be forgotten how much also depends on the *time* when it is undertaken, the *way* in which it is performed, and the *associates* in the labour. In all these matters the true workman will wait for the Master's beck, glance, or signal, before a step is taken.

We have come now to a new fork in the road where the path ahead begins to be more plain. The future and permanent centre of his life-work is at this point clearly indicated to God's servant by divine leading.

In March, 1832, his friend Mr. Henry Craik left Shaldon for four weeks of labour *in Bristol,* where Mr. Müller's strong impression was that the Lord had for Mr. Craik some more lasting sphere of work, though as yet it had not dawned upon his mind that he himself was to be a co-worker in that sphere, and to find in that very city the place of his permanent abode and the centre of his life's activities. God again led the blind by a way he knew not. The conviction, however, had grown upon him that the Lord was loosing him from Teignmouth, and, without having in view any other definite field, he felt that his ministry there was drawing to a close; and he inclined to go about again from place to place, seeking especially to bring believers to a fuller trust in God and a deeper sense of His faithfulness, and to a more thorough search into His word. His inclination to such itinerant work was strengthened by the fact that outside of Teignmouth his preaching both gave him much more enjoyment and sense of power, and drew more hearers.

On April 13th a letter from Mr. Craik, inviting Mr. Müller to join in his work at Bristol, made such an impression on his mind that he began prayerfully to consider whether it was not God's call, and whether a field more suited to his gifts was not opening to him. The following Lord's day, preaching on the Lord's coming, he referred to the effect of this blessed hope in impelling God's messenger to bear witness more widely and from place to place, and reminded the brethren that he had refused to bind himself to abide with them that he might at any moment be free to follow the divine leading elsewhere.

On April 20th Mr. Müller left for Bristol. On the journey he was dumb, having no liberty in speaking for Christ or even in giving away tracts, and this led him to reflect. He saw that the so-called ' work of the Lord ' had tempted him to substitute *action for meditation and communion.* He had neglected that ' still hour ' with God which supplies to spiritual life alike its breath and its bread. No lesson is more important for us to learn, yet how slow are we to learn it : that for the lack of habitual seasons set apart for devout meditation upon the word of God and for prayer, nothing else will compensate.

We are prone to think, for example, that converse with Christian brethren, and the general round of Christian activity, especially when we are much busied with preaching the Word and visits to inquiring or needy souls, make

up for the loss of aloneness with God in the secret place.
We hurry to a public service with but a few minutes of private prayer, allowing precious time to be absorbed in social
pleasures, restrained from withdrawing from others by a
false delicacy, when to excuse ourselves for needful communion with God and his word would have been perhaps
the best witness possible to those whose company was
holding us unduly ! How often we rush from one public
engagement to another without any proper interval for
renewing our strength in waiting on the Lord, as though
God cared more for the quantity than the quality of our
service !

Here Mr. Müller had the grace to detect one of the foremost perils of a busy man in this day of insane hurry. He
saw that if we are to feed others we must be fed ; and
that even public and united exercises of praise and prayer
can never supply that food which is dealt out to the believer only in the closet—the shut-in place with its closed
door and open window, where he meets God alone. In a
previous chapter reference has been made to the fact that
three times in the word of God we find a divine prescrip-
tion for a true prosperity. God says to Joshua, " This
book of the law shall not depart out of thy mouth; but
thou shalt meditate therein day and night, that thou
mayest observe to do according to all that is written
therein : *for then thou shalt make thy way prosperous, and
then thou shalt have good success.*" (Joshua i. 8.) Five
hundred years later the inspired author of the first Psalm
repeats the promise in unmistakable terms. The Spirit
there says of him whose delight is in the law of the Lord
and who in His law doth meditate day and night, that " he
shall be like a tree planted by the rivers of water, that
bringeth forth his fruit in his season ; his leaf also shall
not wither ; and *whatsoever he doeth shall prosper.*" Here

the devout meditative student of the blessed book of God is likened to an evergreen tree planted beside unfailing supplies of moisture; his fruit is perennial, and so is his verdure—and *whatsoever he doeth* prospers ! More than a thousand years pass away, and, before the New Testament is sealed up as complete, once more the Spirit bears essentially the same blessed witness. " Whoso looketh into the perfect law of liberty and *continueth* " (i.e. continueth *looking*—meditating on what he there beholds, lest he forget the impression received through the mirror of the Word), " *this man shall be blessed in his deed.*" (James i. 25.)

Here then we have a threefold witness to the secret of true prosperity and unmingled blessing : devout meditation and reflection upon the Scriptures, which are at once a book of law, a river of life, and a mirror of self—fitted to convey the will of God, the life of God, and the transforming power of God. That believer makes a fatal mistake who *for any cause* neglects the prayerful study of the word of God. To read God's holy book, by it search one's self, and turn it into prayer and so into holy living, is the one great secret of growth in grace and godliness. The worker *for* God must first be a worker *with* God : he must have power with God and must prevail with Him in prayer, if he is to have power with men and prevail with men in preaching or in any form of witnessing and serving. At all costs let us make sure of that highest preparation for our work—the preparation of our own souls; and for this we must *take time* to be alone with His word and His Spirit, that we may truly meet God, and understand His will and the revelation of Himself.

If we seek the secrets of the life George Müller lived and the work he did, this is the very key to the whole mystery, and with that key any believer can unlock the doors to a prosperous growth in grace and power in service.

God's word is HIS WORD—the expression of His thought,
the revealing of His mind and heart. The supreme end
of life is to know God and make Him known ; and how is
this possible so long as we neglect the very means He has
chosen for conveying to us that knowledge ! Even Christ,
the Living Word, is to be found enshrined in the written
word. Our knowledge of Christ is dependent upon our
acquaintance with the Holy Scriptures, which are the reflection of His character and glory—the firmament across
the expanse of which He moves as the Sun of righteous-
ness.

On April 22, 1832, George Müller first stood in the pulpit of Gideon Chapel. The fact and the date are to be
carefully marked as the new turning-point in a career of
great usefulness. Henceforth, for almost exactly sixty-six
years, Bristol is to be inseparably associated with his name.
Could he have foreseen, on that Lord's day, what a work
the Lord would do through him in that city; how from
it as a centre his influence would radiate to the earth's
ends, and how, even after his departure, he should continue to bear witness by the works which should follow
him, how his heart would have swelled and burst with
holy gratitude and praise,—while in humility he shrank
back in awe and wonder from a responsibility and an opportunity so vast and overwhelming !

In the afternoon of this first Sabbath he preached at
Pithay Chapel a sermon conspicuously owned of God.
Among others converted by it was a young man, a notori-
ous drunkard. And, before the sun had set, Mr. Müller,
who in the evening heard Mr. Craik preach, was fully
persuaded that the Lord had brought him to Bristol for
a purpose, and that for a while, at least, there he was to
labour. Both he and his brother Craik felt, however, that
Bristol was not the place to reach a clear decision, for the

judgment was liable to be unduly biassed when subject to the pressure of personal urgency, and so they determined to return to their respective fields of previous labour, there to wait quietly upon the Lord for the promised wisdom from above. They left for Devonshire on the first of May; but already a brother had been led to assume the responsibility for the rent of Bethesda Chapel as a place for their joint labours, thus securing a second commodious building for public worship.

Such blessing had rested on these nine days of united testimony in Bristol that they both gathered that the Lord had assuredly called them thither. The seal of His sanction had been on all they had undertaken, and the last service at Gideon Chapel on April 29th had been so thronged that many went away for lack of room.

Mr. Müller found opportunity for the exercise of humility, for he saw that by many his brother's gifts were much preferred to his own; yet, as Mr. Craik would come to Bristol only with him as a yokefellow, God's grace enabled him to accept the humiliation of being the less popular, and comforted him with the thought that two are better than one, and that each might possibly fill up some lack in the other, and thus both together prove a greater benefit and blessing alike to sinners and to saints—as the result showed. That same grace of God helped Mr. Müller to rise higher—nay, let us rather say, to sink lower and, "in honor preferring one another," to rejoice rather than to be envious; and, like John the Baptist, to say within himself: "A man can receive nothing except it be given him from above." Such a humble spirit has even in this life oftentimes its recompense of reward. Marked as was the impress of Mr. Craik upon Bristol, Mr. Müller's influence was even deeper and wider. As Henry Craik died in 1866, his own work reached through a much longer period; and as he was permitted to make such extensive mission tours throughout the world, his witness was far more outreaching. The lowly-minded man who bowed down to take the lower place, consenting to be the more obscure, was by God exalted to the higher seat and greater throne of influence.

Within a few weeks the Lord's will, as to their new sphere, became so plain to both these brethren that on May 23d Mr. Müller left Teignmouth for Bristol, to be followed next day by Mr. Craik. At the believers' meeting at Gideon Chapel they stated their terms, which were acceded to : that they were to be regarded as accepting no fixed relationship to the congregation, preaching in such manner and for such a season as should seem to them according to the Lord's will ; that they should not be under bondage to any rules among them; that *pew-rents should be done away with;* and that they should, as in Devonshire, *look to the Lord to supply all temporal wants through the voluntary offerings of those to whom they ministered.*

Within a month Bethesda Chapel had been so engaged for a year as to risk no debt, and on July 6th services began there as at Gideon. From the very first, the Spirit set His seal on the joint work of these two brethren. Ten days after the opening service at Bethesda, an evening being set for inquirers, the throng of those seeking counsel was so great that more than four hours were consumed in ministering to individual souls, and so from time to time similar meetings were held with like encouragement.

August 13, 1832, was a memorable day. On that evening at Bethesda Chapel Mr. Müller, Mr. Craik, one other brother, and four sisters—*only seven in all*—sat down together, uniting in church fellowship " *without any rules,— desiring to act only as the Lord should be pleased to give light through His word.*"

This is a very short and simple entry in Mr. Müller's journal, but it has most solemn significance. It records what was to him separation to the hallowed work of building up a simple apostolic church, with no manual of guidance but the New Testament; and in fact it introduces us to the THIRD PERIOD of his life, when he entered fully upon the work to which God had set him apart. The further steps now followed in rapid succession. God having prepared the workman and gathered the material, the structure went on quietly and rapidly until the life-work was complete.

Cholera was at this time raging in Bristol. This terrible ' scourge of God' first appeared about the middle of July and continued for three months, prayer-meetings being held often, and for a time daily, to plead for the removal of this visitation. Death stalked abroad, the knell of funeral-bells almost constantly sounding, and much solemnity hanging like a dark pall over the community. Of course many visits to the sick, dying, and afflicted became necessary, but it is remarkable that, among all the children of God among whom Mr. Müller and Mr. Craik laboured, but one died of this disease.

In the midst of all this gloom and sorrow of a fatal epidemic, a little daughter was born to Mr. and Mrs. Müller September 17, 1832. About her name, Lydia, sweet fragrance lingers, for she became one of God's purest saints and the beloved wife of James Wright. How little do we forecast at the time the future of a new-born babe who, like Samuel, may in God's decree be established to be a prophet of the Lord, or be set apart to some peculiar sphere of service, as in the case of another Lydia, whose heart the Lord opened and whom He called to be the nucleus of the first Christian church in Europe.

Mr. Müller's unfeigned humility, and the docility that

always accompanies that unconscious grace, found new exercise when the meetings with inquirers revealed the fact that his colleague's preaching was much more used of God than his own, in conviction and conversion. This discovery led to much self-searching, and he concluded that three reasons lay back of this fact : first, Mr. Craik was more spiritually minded than himself; second, he was more earnest in prayer for converting power; and third, he oftener spoke directly to the unsaved, in his public ministrations. Such disclosures of his own comparative lack did not exhaust themselves in vain self-reproaches, but led at once to more importunate prayer, more diligent preparation for addressing the unconverted, and more frequent appeals to this class. From this time on, Mr. Müller's preaching had the seal of God upon it equally with his brother's. What a wholesome lesson to learn, that for every defect in our service there is a cause, and that the one all-sufficient remedy is the throne of grace, where in every time of need we may boldly come to find grace and help !

It has been already noted that Mr. Müller did not satisfy himself with more prayer, but gave new diligence and study to the preparation of discourses adapted to awaken careless souls. In the supernatural as well as the natural sphere, there is a law of *cause and effect*. Even the Spirit of God works not without order and method; He has His chosen channels through which He pours blessing. There is no accident in the spiritual world. " The Spirit bloweth where He listeth." but even the wind has its circuits. There is a kind of preaching, fitted to bring conviction and conversion, and there is another kind which is not so fitted. Even in the faithful use of truth there is room for discrimination and selection. In the armory of the word of God are many weapons, and all have their various uses and adaptations. Blessed is the workman or warrior who seeks to know what particular implement or instrument God appoints for each particular work or conflict. We are to study to keep in such communion with His word and Spirit as that we shall be true workmen that need "not to be ashamed, rightly dividing the word of truth." (2 Tim. ii. 15.)

This expression, found in Paul's second letter to Timothy, is a very peculiar one (ορθοτομοῦντα τον λόγον τῆς αληθειας). It seems to be nearly equivalent to the Latin phrase *recte viam secare—to cut a straight road* —and to hint that the true workman of God is like the civil engineer to whom it is given to construct a direct road to a certain point. The hearer's heart and conscience is the objective point, and the aim of the preacher should be, so to use God's truth as to reach most directly and effectively the needs of the hearer. He is to avoid all circuitous routes, all evasions, all deceptive apologies and by-ways of argument, and seek by God's help to find the shortest, straightest, quickest road to the convictions and resolutions of those to whom he speaks. And if the road-builder, before he takes any other step, first carefully *surveys his territory and lays out his route,* how much more should the preacher first study the needs of his hearers and the best ways of successfully dealing with them, and then with even more carefulness and prayerfulness study the adaptation of the word of God and the gospel message to meet those wants.

Early in the year 1833, letters from missionaries in Bagdad urged Messrs. Müller and Craik to join them in labours in that distant field, accompanying the invitation with drafts for two hundred pounds for costs of travel. Two weeks of prayerful inquiry as to the mind of the Lord, however, led them to a clear decision *not* to go—a choice never regretted, and which is here recorded only as part of a complete biography, and as illustrating the manner in which each new call for service was weighed and decided.

We now reach another stage of Mr. Müller's entrance upon his complete life-work. In February, 1832, he had begun to read the biography of A. H. Francké, the founder of the Orphan Houses of Halle. As that life and work were undoubtedly used of God to make him a like instrument in a kindred service, and to mould even the methods of his philanthropy, a brief sketch of Francké's career may be helpful.

August H. Francké was Müller's fellow countryman. About 1696, at Halle in Prussia, he had commenced the largest enterprise for poor children then existing in the world. He trusted in God, and He whom he trusted did not fail him, but helped him throughout abundantly.

The institutions, which resembled rather a large street than a building, were erected, and in them about two thousand orphan children were housed, fed, clad, and taught. For about thirty years all went on under Francké's own eyes, until 1727, when it pleased the Master to call the servant up higher ; and after his departure his like minded son-in-law became the director. Two hundred years have passed, and these Orphan Houses are still in existence, serving their noble purpose.

It is needful only to look at these facts and compare with Francké's work in Halle George Müller's monuments to a prayer-hearing God on Ashley Down, to see that in the main the latter work so far resembles the former as to be in not a few respects its counterpart. Mr. Müller began his orphan work a little more than one hundred years after Francké's death ; ultimately housed, fed, clothed, and taught over two thousand orphans year by year ; personally supervised the work for over sixty years—twice as long a period as that of Francké's personal manage-

ment,—and at his decease likewise left his like minded
son-in-law to be his successor as the sole director of the
work. It need not be added that, beginning his enterprise like Francké in dependence on God alone, the
founder of the Bristol Orphan Houses trusted from first to
last only in Him.

It is very noticeable how, when God is preparing a workman for a certain definite service, He often leads him out
of the beaten track into a path peculiarly His own by
means of some striking biography, or by contact with some
other living servant who is doing some such work, and
exhibiting the spirit which must guide if there is to be a
true success. Meditation on Francké's life and work naturally led this man who was hungering for a wider usefulness to think more of the poor homeless waifs about him,
and to ask whether he also could not plan under God some
way to provide for them ; and as he was musing the fire
burned.

As early as June 12, 1833, when not yet twenty-eight
years old, the inward flame began to find vent in a scheme
which proved the first forward step toward his orphan
work. It occurred to him to gather out of the streets,
at about eight o'clock each morning, the poor children,
give them a bit of bread for breakfast, and then, for about
an hour and a half, teach them to read or read to them
the Holy Scriptures ; and later on to do a like service to
the adult and aged poor. He began at once to feed from
thirty to forty such persons, confident that, as the number
increased, the Lord's provision would increase also. Un-
burdening his heart to Mr. Craik, he was guided to a place
which could hold one hundred and fifty children and
which could be rented for ten shillings yearly ; as also to
an aged brother who would gladly undertake the teaching.

Unexpected obstacles, however, prevented the carrying

out of this plan. The work already pressing upon Mr. Müller and Mr. Craik, the rapid increase of applicants for food, and the annoyance to neighbours of having crowds of idlers congregating in the streets and lying about in troops—these were some of the reasons why this method was abandoned. But the *central thought and aim* were never lost sight of : God had planted a seed in the soil of Mr. Müller's heart, presently to spring up in the orphan work, and in the Scriptural Knowledge Institution with its many branches and far-reaching fruits.

From time to time a backward glance over the Lord's dealings encouraged his heart, as he looked forward to unknown paths and untried scenes. He records at this time—the close of the year 1833—that during the four years since he first began to trust in the Lord alone for temporal supplies he had suffered no want. He had received during the first year one hundred and thirty pounds, during the second one hundred and fifty-one, during the third one hundred and ninety-five, and during the last two hundred and sixty-seven—all in free-will offerings and without ever asking any human being for a penny. He had looked alone to the Lord, yet he had not only received a supply, but an increasing supply, year by year. Yet he also noticed that at each year's close he had very little, if anything, left, and that much had come through strange channels, from distances very remote, and from parties whom he had never seen. He observed also that in every case, according as the need was greater or less, the supply corresponded. He carefully records for the benefit of others that, when the calls for help were many, the Great Provider showed Himself able and willing to send help accordingly.* The ways of divine dealing

* Vol. I. 105.

which he had thus found true of the early years of his life of trust were marked and magnified in all his after-experience, and the lessons learned in these first four years prepared him for others taught in the same school of God and under the same Teacher.

Thus God had brought His servant by a way which he knew not to the very place and sphere of his life's widest and most enduring work. He had moulded and shaped His chosen vessel, and we are now to see to what purposes of world-wide usefulness that earthen vessel was to be put, and how conspicuously the excellency of the power was to be of God and not of man.

CHAPTER VIII

A TREE OF GOD'S OWN PLANTING

THE time was now fully come when the divine Husbandman was to glorify Himself by a product of His own husbandry in the soil of Bristol.

On February 20, 1834, George Müller was led of God to sow the seed of what ultimately developed into a great means of good, known as " The Scriptural Knowledge Institution, for Home and Abroad." As in all other steps of his life, this was the result of much prayer, meditation on the Word, searching of his own heart, and patient waiting to know the mind of God.

A brief statement of the reasons for founding such an institution, and the principles on which it was based, will be helpful at this point. Motives of conscience controlled Mr. Müller and Mr. Craik in starting a new work rather than in uniting with existing societies already established for missionary purposes, Bible and tract distribution, and for the promotion of Christian schools. As they had sought to conform personal life and church conduct wholly to the scriptural pattern, they felt that all work for God should be carefully carried on in exact accordance with His known will, in order to have His fullest blessing. Many features of the existing societies seemed to them *extra*-scriptural, if not decidedly anti-scriptural, and these they felt constrained to avoid.

For example, they felt that the *end proposed* by such

organizations, namely, *the conversion of the world* in this dispensation, was not justified by the Word, which everywhere represents this as the age of the *outgathering of the church* from the world, and not the *ingathering of the world* into the church. To set such an end before themselves as the world's conversion would therefore not only be unwarranted by Scripture, but delusive and disappointing, disheartening God's servants by the failure to realize the result, and dishonoring to God Himself by making Him to appear unfaithful.

Again, these existing societies seemed to Mr. Müller and Mr. Craik to sustain a *wrong relation to the world*—mixed up with it, instead of separate from it. Any one by paying a certain fixed sum of money might become a member or even a director, having a voice or vote in the conduct of affairs and becoming eligible to office. Unscriptural means were commonly used to *raise money*, such as appealing for aid to unconverted persons, asking for donations simply for money's sake and without regard to the character of the donors or the manner in which the money was obtained. The custom of *seeking patronage* from men of the world and asking such to preside at public meetings, and the habit of *contracting debts*,—these and some other methods of management seemed so unscriptural and unspiritual that the founders of this new institution could not with a good conscience give them sanction. Hence they hoped that by basing their work upon thoroughly biblical principles they might secure many blessed results.

First of all, they confidently believed that the work of the Lord could be best and most successfully carried on within the landmarks and limits set up in His word; that the fact of thus carrying it on would give boldness in prayer and confidence in labour. But they also desired the work itself to be a witness to the living God, and a testimony to believers, by calling attention to the objectionable methods already in use and encouraging all God's true servants in adhering to the principles and practices which He has sanctioned.

On March 5th at a public meeting a formal announcement of the intention to found such an institution was accompanied by a full statement of its purposes and principles,* in substance as follows :

1. Every believer's duty and privilege is to help on the cause and work of Christ.

2. The patronage of the world is not to be sought after, depended upon, or countenanced.

3. Pecuniary aid, or help in managing or carrying on its affairs, is not to be asked for or sought from those who are not believers.

4. Debts are not to be contracted or allowed for any cause in the work of the Lord.

5. The standard of success is not to be a numerical or financial standard.

6. All compromise of the truth or any measures that impair testimony to God are to be avoided.

Thus the word of God was accepted as counsellor, and all dependence was on God's blessing in answer to prayer.

The *objects* of the institution were likewise announced as follows :

I. To establish or aid day-schools, Sunday-schools, and adult-schools, taught and conducted only by believers and on thoroughly scriptural principles.

2. To circulate the Holy Scriptures, wholly or in portions, over the widest possible territory.

3. To aid missionary efforts and assist labourers, in the Lord's vineyard anywhere, who are working upon a biblical basis and looking only to the Lord for support.

To project such a work, on such a scale, and at such a time, was doubly an act of faith ; for not only was the work already in hand enough to tax all available time and strength, but at this very time this record appears in Mr. Müller's journal : *"We have only one shilling left."* Surely no advance step would have been taken, had not the eyes been turned, not on the empty purse, but on the full and exhaustless treasury of a rich and bountiful Lord !

It was plainly God's purpose that, out of such abundance of poverty, the riches of His liberality should be manifested. It pleased Him, from whom and by whom are all things, that the work should be begun when His servants were poorest and weakest, that its growth to such giant proportions might the more prove it to be a plant of His own right hand's planting, and that His word might be fulfilled in its whole history :

"I the Lord do keep it :
I will water it every moment :
Lest any hurt it, I will keep it night and day :"

(Isa. xxvii. 3.)

Whatever may be thought as to the need of such a new organization, or as to such scruples as moved its founders to insist even in minor matters upon the closest adherence to scripture teaching, this at least is plain, that for more than half a century it has stood upon its original foundation, and its increase and usefulness have surpassed the most enthusiastic dreams of its founders ; nor have the principles first avowed ever been abandoned. With the Living God as its sole patron, and prayer as its only appeal, it has attained vast proportions, and its world-wide work has been signally owned and blessed.

On March 19th Mrs. Müller gave birth to a son, to the great joy of his parents ; and, after much prayer, they gave him the name Elijah—" My God is Jah "—the name itself being one of George Müller's life-mottoes. Up to this time the families of Mr. Müller and Mr. Craik had dwelt under one roof, but henceforth it was thought wise that they should have separate lodgings.

When, at the close of 1834, the usual backward glance was cast over the Lord's leadings and dealings, Mr. Müller gratefully recognized the divine goodness which had thus helped him to start upon its career the work with its several departments. Looking to the Lord alone for light and help, he had laid the corner-stone of this "little institution"; and in October, after only seven months' existence, it had already begun to be established. In the Sunday-school there were one hundred and twenty children; in the adult classes, forty; in the four day-schools, two hundred and nine boys and girls; four hundred and eighty-two Bibles and five hundred and twenty Testaments had been put into circulation, and fifty-seven pounds had been spent in aid of missionary operations. During these seven months the Lord had sent, in answer to prayer, over one hundred and sixty-seven pounds in money, and much blessing upon the work itself. The brothers and sisters who were in charge had likewise been given by the same prayer-hearing God, in direct response to the cry of need and the supplication of faith.

Meanwhile *another object* was coming into greater prominence before the mind and heart of Mr. Müller: it was the thought of *making some permanent provision for fatherless and motherless children.*

An orphan boy who had been in the school had been taken to the poorhouse, no longer able to attend on account of extreme poverty; and this little incident set Mr. Müller thinking and praying about orphans. Could not something be done to meet the temporal and spiritual wants of this class of very poor children? Unconsciously to himself, God had set a seed in his soul, and was watching and watering it. The idea of a definite orphan work had taken root within him, and, like any other living germ, it was springing up and growing, he knew not how. As yet it was only in the blade, but in time there would come the ear and the full-grown corn in the ear, the new seed of a larger harvest.

Meanwhile the church was growing. In these two and a half years over two hundred had been added, making the total membership two hundred and fifty-seven; but the enlargement of the work generally neither caused the church life to be neglected nor any one department of duty to suffer declension—a very noticeable fact in this history.

The point to which we have now come is one of double interest and importance, as at once a point of arrival and of departure. The work of God's chosen servant may be considered as fairly if not fully inaugurated *in all its main forms of service.* He himself is in his thirtieth year, the age when his divine Master began to be fully manifest to the world and to go about doing good. Through the preparatory steps and stages leading up to his complete mission and ministry to the church and the world, Christ's humble disciple has likewise been brought, and his fuller career of usefulness now begins, with the various agencies in operation whereby for more than threescore years he was to show both proof and example of what God can do through one man who is willing to be simply the instrument for Him to work with. Nothing is more marked in George Müller, to the very day of his death, than this, that he so looked to God and leaned on God that he felt himself to be nothing, and God everything. He sought to be always and in all things surrendered as a passive tool to the will and hand of the Master Workman.

This point of arrival and of departure is also a point of *prospect*. Here, halting and looking backward, we may take in at a glance the various successive steps and stages of preparation whereby the Lord had made His servant ready for the sphere of service to which He called, and for which He fitted him. One has only, from this height, to look over the ten years that were past, to see beyond dispute or doubt the divine design that lay back of George Müller's life, and to feel an awe of the God who thus chooses and shapes, and then uses, His vessels of service.

It will be well, even if it involves some repetition, to pass in review the more important steps in the process by which the divine Potter had shaped His vessel for His purpose, educating and preparing George Müller for His work.

1. First of all, his *conversion*. In the most unforeseen manner and at the most unexpected time God led him to turn from the error of his way, and brought him to a saving knowledge of Jesus Christ.

2. Next, his *missionary spirit*. That consuming flame was kindled within him which, when it is fanned by the Spirit and fed by the fuel of facts, inclines to unselfish service and makes one willing to go wherever, and to do whatever, the Lord will.

3. Next, his *renunciation of self*. In more than one instance he was enabled to give up for Christ's sake an earthly attachment that was idolatrous, because it was a hindrance to his full obedience and single-eyed loyalty to his heavenly Master.

4. Then his *taking counsel of God*. Early in his Christian life he formed the habit, in things great and small, of ascertaining the will of the Lord before taking action, asking guidance in every matter, through the Word and the Spirit.

5. His humble and *childlike temper.* The Father drew His child to Himself, imparting to him the simple mind that asks believingly and trusts confidently, and the filial spirit that submits to fatherly counsel and guidance.

6. His *method of preaching.* Under this same divine tuition he early learned how to preach the Word, in simple dependence on the Spirit of God, studying the Scriptures in the original and expounding them without wisdom of words.

7. His *cutting loose from man.* Step by step, all dependence on man or appeals to man for pecuniary support were abandoned, together with all borrowing, running into debt, stated salary, etc. His eyes were turned to God alone as the Provider.

8. His *satisfaction in the Word.* As knowledge of the Scriptures grew, love for the divine oracles increased, until all other books, even of a religious sort, lost their charms in comparison with God's own text-book, as explained and illumined by the divine Interpreter.

9. His *thorough Bible study.* Few young men have ever been led to such a systematic search into the treasures of God's truth. He read the Book of God through and through, fixing its teachings on his mind by meditation and translating them into practice.

10. His *freedom from human control.* He felt the need of independence of man in order to complete dependence on God, and boldly broke all fetters that hindered his liberty in preaching, in teaching, or in following the heavenly Guide and serving the heavenly Master.

11. His *use of opportunity.* He felt the value of souls, and he formed habits of approaching others as to matters of salvation, even in public conveyances. By a word of witness, a tract, a humble example, he sought constantly to lead some one to Christ.

12. His *release from civil obligations.* This was purely providential. In a strange way God set him free from all liability to military service, and left him free to pursue his heavenly calling as His soldier, without entanglement in the affairs of this life.

13. His *companions in service.* Two most efficient co-workers were divinely provided : first his brother Craik so like-minded with himself, and secondly, his wife, so peculiarly God's gift, both of them proving great aids in working and in bearing burdens of responsibility.

14. His *view of the Lord's coming.* He thanked God for unveiling to him that great truth, considered by him as second to no other in its influence upon his piety and usefulness ; and in the light of it he saw clearly the purpose of this gospel age, to be not to convert the world but to call out from it a believing church as Christ's bride.

15. His *waiting on God for a message.* For every new occasion he asked of Him a word in season ; then a mode of treatment, and unction in delivery ; and, in godly simplicity and sincerity, with the demonstration of the Spirit, he aimed to reach the hearers.

16. His submission to the *authority of the Word.* In the light of the holy oracles he reviewed all customs, however ancient, and all traditions of men, however popular, submitted all opinions and practices to the test of Scripture, and then, regardless of consequences, walked according to any new light God gave him.

17. His *pattern of church life.* From his first entrance upon pastoral work, he sought to lead others only by himself following the Shepherd and Bishop of Souls. He urged the assembly of believers to conform in all things to New Testament models so far as they could be clearly found in the Word, and thus reform all existing abuses.

18. His stress upon *voluntary offerings*. While he courageously gave up all fixed salary for himself, he taught
that all the work of God should be maintained by the free-
will gifts of believers, and that pew-rents promote invidious distinctions among saints.

19. His *surrender of all earthly possessions*. Both himself and his wife literally sold all they had and gave alms,
henceforth to live by the day, hoarding no money even
against a time of future need, sickness, old age, or any
other possible crisis of want.

20. His habit of *secret prayer*. He learned so to prize
closet communion with God that he came to regard it as
his highest duty and privilege. To him nothing could
compensate for the lack or loss of that fellowship with God
and meditation on His word which are the support of all
spiritual life.

21. His *jealousy of his testimony*. In taking oversight of
a congregation he took care to guard himself from all
possible interference with fulness and freedom of utterance and of service. He could not brook any restraints
upon his speech or action that might compromise his al-
legiance to the Lord or his fidelity to man.

22. His *organizing of work*. God led him to project a
plan embracing several departments of holy activity, such
as the spreading of the knowledge of the word of God
everywhere, and the encouraging of world-wide evangelization and the Christian education of the young ; and to
guard the new Institution from all dependence on worldly
patronage, methods, or appeals.

23. His *sympathy with orphans*. His loving heart had
been drawn out toward poverty and misery everywhere,
but especially in the case of destitute children bereft of
both parents ; and familiarity with Francké's work at
Halle suggested similar work at Bristol.

24. Beside all these steps of preparation, he had been guided by the Lord from his birthplace in Prussia to London, Teignmouth, and Bristol in Britain, and thus the chosen vessel, shaped for its great use, had by the same divine Hand been borne to the very place where it was to be of such signal service in testimony to the Living God.

Surely no candid observer can survey this course of divine discipline and preparation, and remember how brief was the period of time it covers, being less than ten years, and mark the many distinct steps by which this education for a life of service was made singularly complete, without a feeling of wonder and awe. Every prominent feature, afterward to appear conspicuous in the career of this servant of God, was anticipated in the training whereby he was fitted for his work and introduced to it. We have had a vivid vision of the divine Potter sitting at His wheel, taking the clay in His hands, softening its hardness, subduing it to His own will ; then gradually and skilfully shaping from it the earthen vessel ; then baking it in His oven of discipline till it attained the requisite solidity and firmness, then filling it with the rich treasures of His word and Spirit, and finally setting it down where He would have it serve His special uses in conveying to others the excellency of His power !

To lose sight of this sovereign shaping Hand is to miss one of the main lessons God means to teach us by George Müller's whole career. He himself saw and felt that he was only an earthen vessel ; that God had both chosen and filled him for the work he was to do ; and, while this conviction made him happy in his work, it made him humble, and the older he grew the humbler he became. He felt more and more his own utter insufficiency. It grieved him that human eyes should ever turn away from the

Master to the servant, and he perpetually sought to avert their gaze from himself to God alone. " For of Him, and through Him, and to Him are all things—to Whom be glory for ever and ever. Amen."

There are several important episodes in Mr. Müller's history which may be lightly passed by, because not so characteristic of him as that they might not have been common to many others, and therefore not constituting features so distinguishing this life from others as to make it a special lesson to believers.

For example, early in 1835 he made a visit to Germany upon a particular errand. He went to aid Mr. Groves, who had come from the East Indies to get missionary recruits, and who asked help of him, as of one knowing the language of the country, in setting the claims of India before German brethren, and pleading for its unsaved millions.

When Mr. Müller went to the alien office in London to get a passport, he found that, through ignorance, he had broken the law which required every alien semi-annually to renew his certificate of residence, under penalty of fifty pounds fine or imprisonment. He confessed to the officer his non-compliance, excusing himself only on the ground of ignorance, and trusted all consequences with God, who graciously inclined the officer to pass over his non-compliance with the law. Another hindrance which still interfered with obtaining his passport, was also removed in answer to prayer; so that at the outset he was much impressed with the Lord's sanction of his undertaking.

His sojourn abroad continued for nearly two months, during which time he was at Paris, Strasburg, Basle, Tubingen, Würtemberg, Schaffhausen, Stuttgart, Halle, Sandersleben, Aschersleben, Heimersleben, Halberstadt, and Hamburg. At Halle, calling on Dr. Tholuck after seven years of separation, he was warmly welcomed and constrained to lodge at his house. From Dr. Tholuck he heard many delightful incidents as to former fellow students who had been turned to the Lord from impious paths, or had been strengthened in their Christian faith and devotion. He also visited Francké's orphan houses, spending an evening in the very room where God's work of grace had begun in his heart, and meeting again several of the same little company of believers that in those days had prayed together.

He likewise gave everywhere faithful witness to the Lord. While at his father's house the way was opened for him to bear testimony indirectly to his father and brother. He had found that a direct approach to his father upon the subject of his soul's salvation only aroused his anger, and he therefore judged that it was wiser to refrain from a course which would only repel one whom he desired to win. An unconverted friend of his father was visiting him at this time, before whom he put the truth very frankly and fully, in the presence of both his father and brother, and thus quite as effectively gave witness to them also. But he was especially moved to pray that he might by his *whole life* bear witness at his home, manifesting his love for his kindred and his own joy in God, his satisfaction in Christ, and his utter indifference to all former fascinations of a worldly and sinful life, through the supreme attraction he found in Him ; for this, he felt sure, would have far more influence than any mere words : our *walk* counts for more than our *talk*, always.

The effect was most happy. God so helped the son to live before the father that, just before his leaving for England, he said to him : " My son, may God help me to follow your example, and to act according to what you have said to me ! "

On June 22, 1835, Mr. Müller's father-in-law, Mr. Groves, died ; and both of his own children were very ill, and four days later little Elijah was taken. Both parents had been singularly prepared for these bereavements, and were divinely upheld. They had felt no liberty in prayer for the child's recovery, dear as he was ; and grandfather and grandson were laid in one grave. Henceforth Mr. and Mrs. Müller were to have no son, and Lydia was to remain their one and only child.

About the middle of the following month, Mr. Müller was quite disabled from work by weakness of the chest, which made necessary rest and change. The Lord tenderly provided for his need through those whose hearts He touched, leading them to offer him and his wife hospitalities in the Isle of Wight, while at the same time money was sent him which was designated for "a change of air.' On his thirtieth birthday, in connection with specially refreshing communion with God, and for the first time since his illness, there was given him a spirit of believing prayer for his own recovery ; and his strength so rapidly grew that by the middle of October he was back in Bristol.

It was just before this, on the ninth of the same month, that *the reading of John Newton's Life stirred him up to bear a similar witness to the Lord's dealings with himself.* Truly there are no little things in our life, since what seems to be trivial may be the means of bringing about results of great consequence. This is the second time that a chance reading of a book had proved a turning-point with George Müller. Franké's life stirred his heart to begin an orphan work, and Newton's life suggested the narrative of the Lord's dealings. To what is called an accident are owing, under God, those pages of his life-journal which read like new chapters in the Acts of the Apostles, and will yet be so widely read, and so largely used of God.

CHAPTER IX

THE GROWTH OF GOD'S OWN PLANT

THE last great step of full entrance upon Mr. Müller's life-service was the *founding of the orphan work*, a step so important and so prominent that even the lesser particulars leading to it have a strange significance and fascination.

In the year 1835, on November 20th, in taking tea at the house of a Christian sister, he again saw a copy of Francké's life. For no little time he had thought of like labours, though on no such scale, nor in mere imitation of Francké, but under a sense of similar divine leading. This impression had grown into a conviction, and the conviction had blossomed into a resolution which now rapidly ripened into corresponding action. He was emboldened to take this forward step in sole reliance on God, by the fact that at that very time, in answer to prayer, ten pounds more had been sent him than he had asked for other existing work, as though God gave him a token of both willingness and readiness to supply all needs.

Nothing is more worthy of imitation, perhaps, than the uniformly deliberate, self-searching, and prayerful way in which he set about any work which he felt led to undertake. It was preeminently so in attempting this new form of service, the future growth of which was not then even in his thought. In daily prayer he sought as in his

Master's presence to sift from the pure grain of a godly purpose to glorify Him, all the chaff of selfish and carnal motives, to get rid of every taint of worldly self-seeking or lust of applause, and to bring every thought into captivity to the Lord. He constantly probed his own heart to discover the secret and subtle impulses which are unworthy of a true servant of God; and, believing that a spiritually minded brother often helps one to an insight into his own heart, he spoke often to his brother Craik about his plans, praying God to use him as a means of exposing any unworthy motive, or of suggesting any scriptural objections to his project. His honest aim being to please God, he yearned to know his own heart, and welcomed any light which revealed his real self and prevented a mistake.

Mr. Craik so decidedly encouraged him, and further prayer so confirmed previous impressions of God's guidance, that on December 2, 1835, the *first formal step was taken* in ordering printed bills announcing a public meeting for the week following, when the proposal to open an orphan house was to be laid before brethren, and further light to be sought unitedly as to the mind of the Lord.

Three days later, in reading the Psalms, he was struck with these nine words :

"OPEN THY MOUTH WIDE,

AND I WILL FILL IT." (Psalm lxxxi. 10.)

From that moment this text formed one of his great life-mottoes, and this promise became a power in moulding all his work. Hitherto he had not prayed for the supply of money or of helpers, but he was now led to apply this scripture confidently to this new plan, and at once boldly to ask *for premises, and for one thousand pounds in money, and for suitable helpers to take charge of the children.* Two days after, he received, in furtherance of his work, the *first*

*gift of money—one shilling—*and within two days more
the *first donation in furniture*—a large wardrobe.

The day came for the memorable public meeting—
December 9th. During the interval Satan had been busy
hurling at Mr. Müller his fiery darts, and he was very low
in spirit. He was taking a step not to be retraced without both much humiliation to himself and reproach to his
Master : and what if it were a *misstep* and he were moving
without real guidance from above ! But as soon as he began
to speak, help was given him. He was borne up on the
Everlasting Arms, and had the assurance that the work was
of the Lord. He cautiously avoided all appeals to the
transient feelings of his hearers, and took no collection,
desiring all these first steps to be calmly taken, and every
matter carefully and prayerfully weighed before a decision.
Excitement of emotion or kindlings of enthusiasm might
obscure the vision and hinder clear apprehension of the
mind of God. After the meeting there was a voluntary
gift of ten shillings, and one sister offered herself for the
work. The next morning a statement concerning the new
orphan work was put in print, and on January 16, 1836,
a supplementary statement appeared.*

At every critical point Mr. Müller is entitled to explain his own views and actions; and the work he was now
undertaking is so vitally linked with his whole after-life
that it should here have full mention As to his proposed
orphan house he gives three chief reasons for its establishment :

1. That God may be glorified in so furnishing the
means as to show that it is not a vain thing to trust in
Him ;

2. That the spiritual welfare of fatherless and motherless children may be promoted ;

3. That their temporal good may be secured.

He had frequent reminders in his pastoral labours that the *faith of God's children greatly needed strengthening;* and he longed to have some visible proof to point to, that the heavenly Father is the same faithful Promiser and Provider as ever, and as willing to PROVE Himself the LIVING GOD to *all who put their trust in Him,* and that even in their old age He does not forsake those who rely only upon Him. Remembering the great blessing that had come to himself through the work of faith of Francké, he judged that he was bound to serve the Church of Christ *in being able to take God at His word and rely upon it.*

If he, a poor man, *without asking any one but God,* could get means to carry on an orphan house, it would be seen that God is FAITHFUL STILL and STILL HEARS PRAYER. While the orphan work was to be a branch of the Scriptural Knowledge Institution, only those funds were to be applied thereto which should be expressly given for that purpose ; and it would be carried on only so far and so fast as the Lord should provide both money and helpers.

It was proposed to receive only such children as had been bereft of both parents, and to take in such from their seventh to their twelfth year, though later on younger orphans were admitted ; and to bring up the boys for a trade, and the girls for service, and to give them all a plain education likely to fit them for their life-work.

So soon as the enterprise was fairly launched, the Lord's power and will to provide began at once and increasingly to appear ; and, from this point on, the journal is one long record of man's faith and supplication and of God's faithfulness and interposition. It only remains to note the new steps in advance which mark the growth of the work, and the new straits which arise and how they are met, together with such questions and perplexing crises as from time to time demand and receive a new divine solution.

A foremost need was that of able and suitable *helpers*, which only God could supply. In order fully to carry out his plans, Mr. Müller felt that he must have men and women like-minded, who would naturally care for the state of the orphans and of the work. If one Achan could disturb the whole camp of Israel, and one Ananias or Sapphira, the whole church of Christ, one faithless, prayerless, self-seeking assistant would prove not a helper but a hinderer both to the work itself and to all fellow-workers. No step was therefore hastily taken. He had patiently waited on God hitherto, and he now waited to receive at His hands His own chosen servants to join in this service and give to it unity of plan and spirit.

Before he called, the Lord answered. As early as December 10th a brother and sister had willingly offered themselves, and the spirit that moved them will appear in the language of their letter :

" We propose ourselves for the service of the intended orphan house, if you think us qualified for it ; also to give up all the furniture, etc., which the Lord has given us, for its use ; and to do this without receiving any salary whatever ; believing that, if it be the will of the Lord to employ us, He will supply all our need."

Other similar self-giving followed, proving that God's people are willing in the day of His power. He who wrought in His servant to will and to work, sent helpers to share his burdens, and to this day has met all similar needs out of His riches in glory. There has never yet been any lack of competent, cheerful, and devoted helpers, although the work so rapidly expanded and extended.

The gifts whereby the work was supported need a separate review that many lessons of interest may find a

record. But it should here be noted that, among the first
givers, was a poor needlewoman who brought the sur-
prising sum of *one hundred pounds*, the singular self-denial
and whole hearted giving exhibited making this a peculiarly sacred offering and a token of God's favour. There was a
felt significance in His choice of a poor sickly seamstress
as His instrument for laying the foundations for this great
work. He who worketh all things after the counsel of His
own will, passing by the rich, mighty, and noble some-
things of this world, chose again the poor, weak, base, despised nothings, that no flesh should glory in His presence.

For work among orphans a *house* was needful, and for
this definite prayer was offered ; and April 1, 1836, was
fixed as the date for opening such house for *female* orphans, as the most helplessly destitute. The building,
No. 6 Wilson Street, where Mr. Müller had himself lived
up to March 25th, having been rented for one year, was
formally opened April 21st, the day being set apart for
prayer and praise. The public generally were informed
that the way was open to receive needy applicants, and
the intimation was further made on May 18th that it was
intended shortly to open a second house for infant children—both boys and girls.

We now retrace our steps a little to take special notice
of a fact in Mr. Müller's experience which, in point of
time, belongs earlier.

Though he had brought before the Lord even the most
minute details about his plans for the proposed orphan
work and house and helpers, asking in faith for building
and furnishing, money for rent and other expenses, etc.,
he confesses that *he had never once asked the Lord to send
the orphans!* This seems an unaccountable omission ; but
the fact is he had assumed that there would be applications
in abundance. His surprise and chagrin cannot easily be

imagined, when the appointed time came for receiving applications, February 3rd, and *not one application was made!* Everything was ready *except the orphans.* This led to the deepest humiliation before God. All the evening of that day he literally lay on his face, probing his own heart to read his own motives, and praying God to search him and show him His mind. He was thus brought so low that from his heart he could say that, if God would thereby be more glorified, he would rejoice in the fact that his whole scheme should come to nothing. The very *next day* the first application was made for admission ; on April 11th orphans began to be admitted ; and by May 18th there were in the house twenty-six, and more daily expected. Several applications being made for children *under seven,* the conclusion was reached that, while vacancies were left, the limit of years at first fixed should not be adhered to ; but every new step was taken with care and prayer, that it should not be in the energy of the flesh, or in the wisdom of man, but in the power and wisdom of the Spirit. How often we forget that solemn warning of the Holy Ghost, that even when our whole work is not imperilled by a false beginning, but is well laid upon a true foundation, we may carelessly build into it wood, hay, and stubble, which will be burned up in the fiery ordeal that is to try every man's work of what sort it is !

The first house had scarcely been opened for girls when the way for the second was made plain, suitable premises being obtained at No. 1 in the same street, and a well-fitted matron being given in answer to prayer. On November 28th, some seven months after the opening of the first, this second house was opened. Some of the older and abler girls from the first house were used for the domestic work of the second, partly to save hired help, and partly to accustom them to working for others and thus give a proper dignity to what is sometimes despised as a degrading and menial form of service. By April 8, 1837, there were in each house thirty orphan children.

The founder of this orphan work, who had at the first asked for one thousand pounds of God, tells us that, in his own mind, the thing was *as good as done*, so that he often gave thanks for this large sum as though already in hand. (Mark xi. 24 ; 1 John v. 13, 14.) This habit of counting a promise as fulfilled had much to do with the triumphs of his faith and the success of his labour. Now that the first part of his Narrative of the Lord's Dealings was about to issue from the press, he felt that it would much honour the Master whom he served *if the entire amount should be actually in hand before the Narrative should appear, and without any one having been asked to contribute.* He therefore gave himself anew to prayer ; and on June 15th the whole sum was complete, no appeal having been made but to the Living God, before whom, as he records with his usual mathematical precision, he had daily brought his petition for *eighteen months and ten days.*

In closing this portion of his narrative he hints at a proposed further enlargement of the work in a *third* house for orphan boys above seven years, with accommodations for about forty. Difficulties interposed, but as usual disappeared before the power of prayer. Meanwhile the whole work of the Scriptural Knowledge Institution prospered, four day-schools having been established, with over one thousand pupils, and more than four thousand copies of the word of God having been distributed.

George Müller was careful always to consult and then to obey conviction. Hence his moral sense, by healthy exercise, more and more clearly discerned good and evil. This conscientiousness was seen in the issue of the first edition of his Narrative. When the first five hundred copies came from the publishers, he was so weighed down by misgivings that he hesitated to distribute them. Notwithstanding the spirit of prayer with which he had begun, continued, and ended the writing of it and had made every correction in the proof ; notwithstanding the motive, consciously cherished throughout, that God's glory might be promoted in this record of His faithfulness, he reopened with himself the whole question whether this published Narrative might not turn the eyes of men from the great Master Workman to His human instrument. As he opened the box containing the reports, he felt strongly tempted to withhold from circulation the pamphlets it held ; but from the moment when he gave out the first copy, and the step could not be retraced, his scruples were silenced.

He afterward saw his doubts and misgivings to have been a temptation of Satan, and never thenceforth questioned that in writing, printing, and distributing this and the subsequent parts of the Narrative he had done the will of God. So broad and clear was the divine seal set upon it in the large blessing it brought to many and widely scattered persons that no room was left for doubt. It may be questioned whether any like journal has been as widely read and as remarkably used, both in converting sinners and in quickening saints. Proofs of this will hereafter abundantly appear.

It was in the year 1837 that Mr. Müller, then in his thirty-second year, felt with increasingly deep conviction that to his own growth in grace, godliness, and power for service *two things* were quite indispensable : first, more *retirement for secret communion with God,* even at the apparent expense of his public work ; and second, ampler provision for the *spiritual oversight of the flock of God,* the total number of communicants now being near to four hundred.

The former of these convictions has an emphasis which touches every believer's life at its vital centre. George Müller was conscious of being *too busy to pray as he ought.* His outward action was too constant for inward reflection, and he saw that there was risk of losing peace and power, and that activity even in the most sacred sphere must not be so absorbing as to prevent holy meditation on the Word and fervent supplication. The Lord said first to Elijah, " GO, HIDE THYSELF " ; then, ' GO, SHOW THYSELF." He who does not first hide 'himself in the secret place to be alone with God, is unfit to show himself in the public place to move among men. Mr. Müller afterward used to say to brethren who had " too much to do " to spend proper time with God, that four hours of work for which one hour of prayer prepares, is better than five hours of work with the praying left out ; that our service to our Master is more acceptable and our mission to man more profitable, when saturated with the moisture of God's blessing—the dew of the Spirit. Whatever is gained in quantity is lost in quality whenever one engagement follows another without leaving proper intervals for refreshment and renewal of strength by waiting on God. No man, perhaps, since John Wesley has accomplished so much even in a long life as George Müller ; yet few have ever withdrawn so often or so long into the pavilion of prayer. In fact, from one point of view his life seems more given to supplication and intercession than to mere action or occupation among men.

At the same time he felt that the curacy of souls must not be neglected by reason of his absorption in either work or prayer. Both believers and inquirers needed pastoral oversight ; neither himself nor his brother Craik had time enough for visiting so large a flock, many of whom were scattered over the city ; and about fifty new members were added every year who had special need of teaching and care. Again, as there were two separate congregations, the number of meetings was almost doubled ; and the interruptions of visitors from near and far, the burdens of correspondence, and the oversight of the Lord's work generally, consumed so much time that even with two pastors the needs of the church could not be met. At a meeting of both congregations in October, these matters were frankly brought before the believers, and it was made plain that other helpers should be provided, and the two churches so united as to lessen the number of separate meetings.

In October, 1837, a building was secured for a third orphan house, for boys ; but as the neighbours strongly opposed its use as a charitable institution, Mr .Müller, with meekness of spirit, at once relinquished all claim upon the premises, being mindful of the maxim of Scripture : " As much as lieth in you, live peaceably with all men." (Rom. xiii. 18.)   He felt sure that the Lord would provide, and his faith was rewarded in the speedy supply of a building in the same street where the other two houses were.

Infirmity of the flesh again tried the faith and patience of Mr. Müller. For eight weeks he was kept out of the pulpit. The strange weakness in the head, from which he had suffered before and which at times seemed to threaten his reason, forced him to rest ; and in November he went to Bath and Weston-super-Mare, leaving to higher Hands the work to which he was unequal.

One thing he noticed and recorded : that, even during this head trouble, prayer and Bible-reading could be borne better than anything else.   He concluded that whenever

undue carefulness is expended on the body, it is very hard
to avoid undue carelessness as to the soul ; and that it is
therefore much safer comparatively to disregard the body,
that one may give himself wholly to the culture of his
spiritual health and the care of the Lord's work. Though
some may think that in this he ran to a fanatical extreme,
there is no doubt that such became more and more a law of
his life. He sought to dismiss all anxiety, as a duty ;
and, among other anxious cares, that most subtle and seductive form of solicitude which watches every change of
symptoms and rushes after some new medical man or medical remedy for all ailments real or fancied.

Mr. Müller was never actually reckless of his bodily
health. His habits were temperate and wholesome, but
no man could be so completely wrapped up in his Master's
will and work without being correspondingly forgetful of
his physical frame. There are not a few, even among
God's saints, whose bodily weaknesses and distresses so
engross them that their sole business seems to be to nurse
the body, keep it alive and promote its comfort. As Dr.
Watts would have said, this is living " at a poor dying
rate."

When the year 1838 opened, the weakness and distress
in the head still afflicted Mr. Müller. The symptoms were
as bad as ever, and it particularly tried him that they
were attended by a tendency to irritability of temper, and
even by a sort of satanic feeling wholly foreign to him at
other times. He was often reminded that he was by nature a child of wrath even as others, and that, as a child of
God, he could stand against the wiles of the devil only by
putting on the whole armour of God. The pavilion of
God is the saint's place of rest ; the panoply of God is
his coat of mail. Grace does not at once remove or overcome all tendencies to evil, but, if not *eradicated*, they are

counteracted by the Spirit's wondrous working. Peter
found that so long as his eye was on His Master he could
walk on the water. There is always a tendency to *sink,*
and a holy walk with God, that defies the tendency down-
ward, is a divine art that can neither be learned nor practised except so long as we keep 'looking unto Jesus':
that look of faith counteracts the natural tendency to sink,
so long as it holds the soul closely to Him. This man of
God felt his risk, and, sore as this trial was to him, he
prayed not so much for its removal as that he might be
kept from any open dishonour to the name of the Lord,
beseeching God that he might rather die than ever bring
on Him reproach.

Mr. Müller's journal is not only a record of his outer
life of consecrated labour and its expansion, but it is a
mirror of his inner life and its growth. It is an encouragement to all other saints to find that this growth was,
like their own, in spite of many and formidable hindrances,
over which only grace could triumph. Side by side with
glimpses of habitual conscientiousness and joy in God,
we have revelations of times of coldness and despondency.
It is a wholesome lesson in holy living that we find this
man setting himself to the deliberate task of *cultivating
obedience and gratitude;* by the culture of obedience
growing in knowledge and strength, and by the culture of
gratitude growing in thankfulness and love. Weakness and
coldness are not hopeless states : they have their divine
remedies which strengthen and warm the whole being.

Three entries, found side by side in his journal, furnish
pertinent illustration and most wholesome instruction on
this point. One entry records his deep thankfulness to
God for the privilege of being permitted to be His instrument in providing for homeless orphans, as he watches
the little girls, clad in clean warm garments, pass his win-

dow on their way to the chapel on the Lord's day morning.
A second entry records his determination, with God's help,
to send no more letters in parcels because he sees it to be
a violation of the postal laws of the land, and because he
desires, as a disciple of the Lord Jesus, to submit himself
to all human laws so far as such submission does not conflict with loyalty to God.   A third entry immediately follows which reveals this same man struggling against those
innate tendencies to evil which compel a continual resort
to the throne of grace with its sympathizing High Priest.
" This morning," he writes, " I greatly dishonoured the
Lord by irritability manifested towards my dear wife ;
and that, almost immediately after I had been on my knees
before God, praising Him for having given me such a
wife."

These three entries, put together, convey a lesson which
is not learned from either of them alone.   Here is gratitude for divine mercy, conscientious resolve at once to stop
a doubtful practice, and a confession of inconsistency in
his home life.   All of these are typical experiences and
suggest to us means of gracious growth.   He who lets no
mercy of God escape thankful recognition, who never hesi-
tates at once to abandon an evil or questionable practice,
and who, instead of extenuating a sin because it is comparatively small, promptly confesses and forsakes it,—such
a man will surely grow in Christlikeness.

We must exercise our spiritual senses if we are to discern things spiritual.   There is a clear vision for God's
goodness, and there is a dull eye that sees little to be
thankful for; there is a tender conscience, and there is a
moral sense that grows less and less sensitive to evil; there
is an obedience to the Spirit's rebuke which leads to immediate confession and increases strength for every new
conflict.   Mr. Müller cultivated habits of life which made

his whole nature more and more open to divine impression, and so his sense of God became more and more keen and constant.

One great result of this spiritual culture was a growing absorption in God and jealousy for His glory. As he saw divine things more clearly and felt their supreme im. portance, he became engrossed in the magnifying of them before men ; and this is glorifying God. We cannot make God essentially any more glorious, for He is infinitely perfect ; but we can help men to see what a glorious God He is, and thus come into that holy partnership with the Spirit of God whose office it is to take of the things of Christ and show them unto men, and so glorify Christ. Such fellowship in glorifying God Mr. Müller set before him: and in the light of such sanctified aspiration we may read that humble entry in which, reviewing the year 1837 with all its weight of increasing responsibility, he lifts his heart to his divine Lord and Master in these simple words:

" Lord, Thy servant is a poor man ; but he has trusted in Thee and made his boast in Thee before the sons of men; therefore let him not be confounded ! Let it not be said, ' All this is enthusiasm, and therefore it is come to naught.' "

One is reminded of Moses in his intercession for Israel, of Elijah in his exceeding jealousy for the Lord of hosts, and of that prayer of Jeremiah that so amazes us by its boldness:

" Do not abhor us for Thy name's sake !
Do not disgrace the throne of Thy glory ! " *

Looking back over the growth of the work at the end

* Comp. Numbers xiv. 13–19.   1 Kings xix. 10 ; Jer. xiv. 21.

of the year 1837, he puts on record the following facts and figures:

Three orphan houses were now open with eighty-one children, and nine helpers in charge of them. In the Sunday-schools there were three hundred and twenty, and in the day-schools three hundred and fifty ; and the Lord had furnished over three hundred and seven pounds for temporal supplies.

From this same point of view it may be well to glance back over the five years of labour in Bristol up to July, 1837. Between himself and his brother Craik uninterrupted harmony had existed from the beginning. They had been perfectly at one in their views of the truth, in their witness to the truth, and in their judgment as to all matters affecting the believers over whom the Holy Ghost had made them overseers. The children of God had been kept from heresy and schism under their joint pastoral care ; and all these blessings Mr. Müller and his true yoke-fellow humbly traced to the mercy and grace of the great Shepherd and Bishop of souls. Thus far over one hundred and seventy had been converted and admitted to fellowship, making the total number of communicants three hundred and seventy, nearly equally divided between Bethesda and Gideon. The whole history of these years is lit up with the sunlight of God's smile and blessing.

CHAPTER X

THE WORD OF GOD AND PRAYER

HABIT both *shows* and *makes* the man, for it is at once historic and prophetic, the mirror of the man as he is and the mould of the man as he is to be. At this point, therefore, special attention may properly be given to the two marked habits which had principally to do with the man we are studying.

Early in the year 1838, he began reading that third biography which, with those of Francké and John Newton, had such a singular influence on his own life—Philip's Life of George Whitefield. The life-story of the orphan's friend had given the primary impulse to his work; the life-story of the converted blasphemer had suggested his narrative of the Lord's dealings; and now the life-story of the great evangelist was blessed of God to shape his general character and give new power to his preaching and his wider ministry to souls. These three biographies together probably affected the whole inward and outward life of George Müller more than any other volumes but the Book of God, and they were wisely fitted of God to co-work toward such a blessed result. The example of Francké incited to faith in prayer and to a work whose sole dependence was on God. Newton's witness to grace led to a testimony to the same sovereign love and mercy as seen in his own case. Whitefield's experience inspired to greater fidelity and earnestness in preaching the Word, and to greater confidence in the power of the anointing Spirit.

Particularly was this impression deeply made on Mr. Müller's mind and heart: that Whitefield's unparalleled success in evangelistic labours was plainly traceable to two causes and could not be separated from them as direct effects; namely, his *unusual prayerfulness, and his habit of reading the Bible on his knees.*

The great evangelist of the last century had learned that first lesson in service, his own utter nothingness and help-lessness: that he was nothing, and could do nothing, with-out God. He could neither understand the Word for him-self, nor translate it into his own life, nor apply it to others with power, unless the Holy Spirit became to him both *insight* and *unction.* Hence his success; he was filled with the Spirit: and this alone accounts both for the quality and the quantity of his labours. He died in 1770, in the fifty-sixth year of his age, having preached his first sermon in Gloucester in 1736. During this thirty-four years his labours had been both unceasing and untiring. While on his journeyings in America, he preached one hundred and seventy-five times in seventy-five days, besides travelling, in the slow vehicles of those days, upwards of eight hun-dred miles. When health declined, and he was put on ' short allowance,' even that was *one sermon each week-day and three on Sunday.* There was about his preaching, more-over, a nameless charm which held thirty thousand hearers half-breathless on Boston Common and made tears pour down the sooty faces of the colliers at Kingswood.

The passion of George Müller's soul was to know fully the secrets of prevailing with God and with man. George Whitefield's life drove home the truth that God alone could create in him a holy earnestness to win souls and qualify him for such divine work by imparting a compassion for the lost that should become an absorbing passion for their salvation. And—let this be carefully marked as another secret of this life of service—*he now began himself to read the word of God upon his knees,* and often found for hours great blessing in such meditation and prayer over a single psalm or chapter.

Here we stop and ask what profit there can be in thus prayerfully reading and searching the Scriptures in the very attitude of prayer. Having tried it for ourselves, we may add our humble witness to its value.

First of all, this habit is a constant reminder and recognition of the need of spiritual teaching in order to the understanding of the holy Oracles. No reader of God's word can thus bow before God and His open book, without a feeling of new reverence for the Scriptures, and dependence on their Author for insight into their mysteries. The attitude of worship naturally suggests sobermindedness and deep seriousness, and banishes frivolity. To treat that Book with lightness or irreverence would be doubly profane when one is in the posture of prayer.

Again, such a habit naturally leads to self-searching and comparison of the actual life with the example and pattern shown in the Word. The precept compels the practice to be seen in the light of its teaching; the command challenges the conduct to appear for examination. The prayer, whether spoken or unspoken, will inevitably be:

> " Search me, O God, and know my heart,
>   Try me, and know my thoughts;
>   And see if there be any wicked way in me,
>   And lead me in the way everlasting ! "
>   (Psalm cxxxix. 23, 24.)

The words thus reverently read will be translated into the life and mould the character into the image of God.

"Beholding as in a glass the glory of the Lord, we are changed into the same image from glory to glory, even as by the Lord the Spirit." *

But perhaps the greatest advantage will be that the Holy Scriptures will thus suggest the *very words* which become the dialect of prayer. "We know not what we should pray for as we ought"—neither *what* nor *how* to pray. But here is the Spirit's own inspired utterance, and, if the praying be moulded on the model of His teaching, how can we go astray? Here is our God-given liturgy and litany—a divine prayer-book. We have here God's promises, precepts, warnings, and counsels, not to speak of all the Spirit-inspired literal prayers therein contained; and, as we reflect upon these, our prayers take their cast in this matrix. We turn precept and promise, warning and counsel into supplication, with the assurance that we *cannot be asking anything that is not according to His will,*† for are we not turning His own word into prayer?

So Mr. Müller found it to be. In meditating over Hebrews xiii. 8: "Jesus Christ the same yesterday and to-day and for ever," translating it into prayer, he besought God, with the confidence that the prayer was already granted, that, as Jesus had already in His love and power supplied all that was needful, in the same unchangeable love and power He would so continue to provide. And so a promise was not only turned into a prayer, but into a prophecy—an assurance of blessing—and a river of joy at once poured into and flowed through his soul.

The prayer habit, on the knees, with the Word open before the disciple, has thus an advantage which it is difficult to put into words: *It provides a sacred channel of approach to God.* The inspired Scriptures form the vehicle of the Spirit in communicating to us the knowledge of the will of God. If we think of God on the one side and man on the other, the word of God is the mode of conveyance from God to man, of His own mind and heart. It therefore becomes a channel of God's approach to us, a channel prepared by the Spirit for the purpose, and unspeakably sacred as such. When therefore the believer uses the word of God as the guide to determine both the spirit and the dialect of his prayer, he is inverting the process of divine revelation and using the channel of God's approach to him as the channel of his approach to God. How can such use of God's word fail to help and strengthen spiritual life ? What medium or channel of approach could so insure in the praying soul both an acceptable frame and language taught of the Holy Spirit ? If the first thing is not to pray but to hearken, this surely is hearkening for God to speak to us that we may know how to speak to Him.

It was habits of life such as these, and not impulsive feelings and transient frames, that made this man of God what he was and strengthened him to lift up his hands in God's name, and follow hard after Him and in Him rejoice.* Even his sore affliction, seen in the light of such prayer—prayer itself illuminated by the word of God— became radiant; and his soul was brought into that state where he so delighted in the will of God as to be able from his heart to say that he would not have his disease removed until through it God had wrought the blessing it was meant to convey. And when his acquiescence in the will of God had become thus complete he instinctively felt that he would speedily be restored to health.

Subsequently, in reading Proverbs iii. 5–12, he was

* Psalm lxiii. 4, 8, 11.

struck with the words, " Neither be *weary* of His correction." He felt that, though he had not been permitted to
" despise the chastening of the Lord," he had at times
been somewhat " weary of His correction," and he lifted
up the prayer that he might so patiently bear it as neither
to faint nor be weary under it, till its full purpose was
wrought.

Frequent were the instances of the habit of translating
promises into prayers, immediately applying the truth
thus unveiled to him. For example, after prolonged meditation over the first verse of Psalm lxv, " *O Thou that
hearest prayer,*" he at once asked and recorded certain
definite petitions. This writing down specific requests for
permanent reference has a blessed influence upon the
prayer habit. It assures practical and exact form for our
supplications, impresses the mind and memory with what
is thus asked of God, and leads naturally to the record of
the answers when given, so that we accumulate evidences
in our own experience that God is to us personally a
prayer-hearing God, whereby unbelief is rebuked and importunity encouraged.

On this occasion eight specific requests are put on
record, together with the solemn conviction that, having
asked in conformity with the word and will of God, and
in the name of Jesus, he has confidence in Him that He
heareth and that he has the petitions thus asked of Him.*
He writes:

" I believe *He has heard me.* I believe He will make
it *manifest* in His own good time *that He has heard me;*
and I have recorded these my petitions this fourteenth day
of January, 1838, that when God has answered them He
may get, through this, glory to His name."

* 1 John v. 13.

The thoughtful reader must see in all this a man of weak faith, feeding and nourishing his trust in God that his faith may grow strong. He uses the promise of a prayer-hearing God as a staff to stay his conscious feebleness, that he may lean hard upon the strong Word which cannot fail. He records the day when he thus takes this staff in hand, and the very petitions which are the burdens which he seeks to lay on God, so that his act of committal may be the more complete and final. Could God ever dishonour such trust ?

It was in this devout reading on his knees that his whole soul was first deeply moved by that phrase,

"A FATHER OF THE FATHERLESS." (Psalm lxviii. 5.)

He saw this to be one of those "names" of Jehovah which He reveals to His people to lead them to trust in Him, as it is written in Psalm ix. 10:

"They that know Thy name
Will put their trust in Thee."

These five words from the sixty-eighth psalm became another of his life-texts, one of the foundation stones of all his work for the fatherless. These are his own words:

"By the help of God, this shall be my argument before Him, respecting the orphans, in the hour of need. He is their Father, and therefore has pledged Himself, as it were, to provide for them; and I have only to remind Him of the need of these poor children in order to have it supplied."

This is translating the promises of God's word, not only into praying, but into living, doing, serving. Blessed was the hour when Mr. Müller learned that one of God's chosen names is " the Father of the fatherless " !

To sustain such burdens would have been quite impossible but for faith in such a God. In reply to oft-repeated remarks of visitors and observers who could not understand the secret of his peace, or how any man who had so many children to clothe and feed could carry such prostrating loads of care, he had one uniform reply: " By the grace of God, this is no cause of anxiety to me. These children I have years ago cast upon the Lord. The whole work is His, and it becomes me to be without carefulness. In whatever points I am lacking, in this point I am able by the grace of God to roll the burden upon my heavenly Father." *

In tens of thousands of cases this peculiar title of God, chosen by Himself and by Himself declared, became to Mr. Müller a peculiar revelation of God, suited to his special need. The natural inferences drawn from such a title became powerful arguments in prayer, and rebukes to all unbelief. Thus, at the outset of his work for the orphans, the word of God put beneath his feet a rock basis of confidence that he could trust the almighty Father to support the work. And, as the solicitudes of the work came more and more heavily upon him, he cast the loads he could not carry upon Him who, before George Müller was born, was the Father of the fatherless.

About this time we meet other signs of the conflict going on in Mr. Müller's own soul. He could not shut his eyes to the lack of earnestness in prayer and fervency of spirit which at times seemed to rob him of both peace and power. And we notice his experience, in common with so many saints, of the *paradox* of spiritual life. He saw that "such fervency of spirit is altogether the gift of God," and yet he adds, " I have to ascribe to myself the loss of it." He did not run divine sovereignty into blank fatalism as so many do. He saw that God must be sovereign in His gifts, and yet man must be free in his reception and rejection of them. He admitted the mystery without attempting to reconcile the apparent contradiction. He confesses also that the same book, Philip's Life of Whitefield, which had been used of God to kindle such new fires on the altar of his heart, had been also used of Satan to tempt him to neglect for its sake the systematic study of the greatest of books.

Thus, at every step, George Müller's life is full of both encouragement and admonition to fellow disciples. While away from Bristol he wrote in February, 1838, a tender letter to the saints there, which is another revelation of the man's heart. He makes grateful mention of the mercies of God, to him, particularly His gentleness, long-suffering, and faithfulness and the lessons taught him through affliction. The letter makes plain that much sweetness is mixed in the cup of suffering, and that our privileges are not properly prized until for a time we are deprived of them. He particularly mentions how *secret prayer*, even when reading, conversation, or prayer with others was a burden, *always brought relief to his head*. Converse with the Father was an indispensable source of refreshment and blessing at all times. As J. Hudson Taylor says ," Satan, the Hinderer, may build a barrier about us, but he can never *roof us in*, so that we cannot *look up*." Mr. Müller also gives a valuable hint that has already been of value to many afflicted saints, that he found he could help by prayer to fight the battles of the Lord even when he could not by preaching.

After a short visit to Germany, partly in quest of health and partly for missionary objects, and after more than twenty-two weeks of retirement from ordinary public duties, his head was much better, but his mental health allowed only about three hours of daily work. While in

Germany he had again seen his father and elder brother, and spoken with them about their salvation. To his father his words brought apparent blessing, for he seemed at least to feel his lack of the one thing needful. The separation from him was the more painful as there was so little hope that they should meet again on earth.

In May he once more took part in public services in Bristol, a period of six months having elapsed since he had previously done so. His head was still weak, but there seemed no loss of mental power.

About three months after he had been in Germany part of the fruits of his visit were gathered, for twelve brothers and three sisters sailed for the East Indies.

On June 13, 1838, Mrs. Müller gave birth to a stillborn babe,—another parental disappointment,—and for more than a fortnight her life hung in the balance. But once more prayer prevailed for her and her days were prolonged.

One month later another trial of faith confronted them in the orphan work. A twelvemonth previous there were in hand seven hundred and eighty pounds; now that sum was reduced to one thirty-ninth of the amount—twenty pounds. Mr. and Mrs. Müller, with Mr. Craik and one other brother, connected with the Boys' Orphan House, were the only four persons who were permitted to know of the low state of funds; and they gave themselves to united prayer. And let it be carefully observed that Mr. Müller testifies that his own faith was kept even stronger than when the larger sum was on hand a year before; and this faith was no mere fancy, for, although the supply was so low and shortly thirty pounds would be needed, notice was given for seven more children to enter, and it was further proposed to announce readiness to receive five others !

The trial-hour had come, but was not past. Less than two months later the money-supply ran so low that it was needful that the Lord should give *by the day and almost by the hour* if the needs were to be met. In answer to prayer for help God seemed to say, " Mine hour is not yet come." Many pounds would shortly be required, toward which there was not one penny in hand. When, one day, over four pounds came in, the thought occurred to Mr. Müller, " Why not lay aside three pounds against the coming need ? " But immediately he remembered that it is written : " SUFFICIENT UNTO THE DAY IS THE EVIL THEREOF." * He unhesitatingly cast himself upon God, and paid out the whole amount for salaries then due, leaving himself again penniless.

At this time Mr. Craik was led to preach a sermon on Abraham, from Genesis xii, making prominent two facts: first, that so long as he acted in faith and walked in the will of God, all went on well; but that, secondly, so far as he distrusted the Lord and disobeyed Him, all ended in failure. Mr. Müller heard this sermon and conscientiously applied it to himself. He drew two most practical conclusions which he had abundant opportunity to put into practice:

First, that he must go into no byways or paths of his own for deliverance out of a crisis;

And, secondly, that in proportion as he had been permitted to honour God and bring some glory to His name by trusting Him, he was in danger of dishonouring Him.

Having taught him these blessed truths, the Lord tested him as to how far he would venture upon them. While in such sore need of money for the orphan work, he had in the bank some two hundred and twenty pounds,

* Matt. vi. 34.

intrusted to him for other purposes. He might *use this money for the time at least,* and so relieve the present distress. The temptation was the stronger so to do, because he knew the donors and knew them to be liberal supporters of the orphans; and he had only to explain to them the straits he was in and they would gladly consent to any appropriation of their gift that he might see best ! Most men would have cut that Gordian knot of perplexity without hesitation.

Not so George Müller. He saw at once that this would be *finding a way of his own out of difficulty, instead of waiting on the Lord for deliverance.* Moreover, he also saw that it would be *forming a habit of trusting to such expedients of his own, which in other trials would lead to a similar course and so hinder the growth of faith.* We use italics here because here is revealed one of the *tests* by which this man of faith was proven; and we see how he kept consistently and persistently to the one great purpose of his life—to demonstrate to all men that to *rest solely on the promise of a faithful God* is the only way to know for one's self and prove to others, His faithfulness.

At this time of need—the type of many others—this man who had determined to risk everything upon God's word of promise, turned from doubtful devices and questionable methods of relief to *pleading with God.* And it may be well to mark his *manner* of pleading. He used *argument* in prayer, and at this time he piles up *eleven reasons* why God should and would send help.

This method of *holy argument*—ordering our cause before God, as an advocate would plead before a judge— is not only almost a lost art, but to many it actually seems almost puerile. And yet it is abundantly taught and exemplified in Scripture. Abraham in his plea for Sodom is the first great example of it. Moses excelled in this art, in many crises interceding in behalf of the people with consummate skill, marshalling arguments as a general-in-chief marshals batallions. Elijah on Carmel is a striking example of power in this special pleading. What holy zeal and jealousy for God! It is probable that if we had fuller records we should find that all pleaders with God, like Noah, Job, Samuel, David, Daniel, Jeremiah, Paul, and James, have used the same method.

Of course God does not *need to be convinced:* no arguments can make any plainer to Him the claims of trusting souls to His intervention, claims based upon His own word, confirmed by His oath. And yet He will be inquired of and argued with. That is His way of blessing. He loves to have us set before Him our cause and His own promises: He delights in the well-ordered plea, where argument is piled upon argument. See how the Lord Jesus Christ commended the persistent argument of the woman of Canaan, who with the *wit of importunity* actually turned his own *objection* into a *reason.* He said, " It is not meet to take the children's bread and cast it to the little dogs." * " Truth, Lord," she answered, " yet the little dogs under the master's tables eat of the crumbs which fall from the children's mouths!" What a triumph of argument! Catching the Master Himself in His words, as He meant she should, and turning His apparent reason for not granting into a reason for granting her request! " O woman," said He, " great is thy faith! Be it unto thee even as thou wilt "—thus, as Luther said, " flinging the reins on her neck."

This case stands unique in the word of God, and it is this use of argument in prayer that makes it thus solitary in grandeur. But one other case is at all parallel,—that of

* Cf. Matt. vii. 6, xv. 26, 27. Not κυνὶς, but κυναρίοις, the diminutive for little pet dogs.

the centurion of Capernaum,* who, when our Lord promised to go and heal his servant, argued that such coming was
not needful, since He had only to speak the healing word.
And notice the basis of his argument: if he, a commander
exercising authority and yielding himself to higher
authority, both obeyed the word of his superior and ex-
acted obedience of his subordinate, how much more could
the Great Healer, in his absence, by a word of command,
wield the healing Power that in His presence was obedient
to His will! Of him likewise our Lord said: "I have not
found so great faith, no, not in Israel!"

We are to argue our case with God, not indeed to convince *Him*, but to convince *ourselves*. In proving to Him
that, by His own word and oath and character, He has
bound Himself to interpose, we demonstrate *to our own
faith* that He has given us the right to ask and claim, and
that He will answer our plea because He cannot deny Himself.

There are two singularly beautiful touches of the Holy
Spirit in which the right thus to order argument before
God is set forth to the reflective reader. In Micah. vii. 20
we read:

> "Thou wilt perform the *truth* to Jacob,
>   The *mercy* to Abraham,
>   Which thou hast sworn unto our fathers,
>   From the days of old."

Mark the progress of the thought. What was mercy to
Abraham was truth to Jacob. God was under no obligation to extend covenant blessings; hence it was to Abraham a simple act of pure *mercy;* but, having so put Him-

* Matt. viii. 8.

self under voluntary bonds, Jacob could claim as *truth* what to Abraham had been mercy. So in 1 John i. 9:

> " If we confess our sins
> He is *faithful and just* to forgive us our sins,
> And to cleanse us from all unrighteousness."

Plainly, forgiveness and cleansing are not originally matters of faithfulness and justice, but of mercy and grace. But, after God had pledged Himself thus to forgive and cleanse the penitent sinner who confesses and forsakes his sins,* what was originally grace and mercy becomes faithfulness and justice; for God owes it to Himself and to His creature to stand by His own pledge, and fulfil the lawful expectation which His own gracious assurance has created.

Thus we have not only examples of argument in prayer, but concessions of the living God Himself, that when we have His word to plead we may claim the fulfilment of His promise, on the ground not of His mercy only, but of His truth, faithfulness, and justice. Hence the holy boldness with which we are bidden to present our plea at the throne of grace. God owes to His faithfulness to do what He has promised, and to His justice not to exact from the sinner a penalty already borne in his behalf by His own Son.

No man of his generation, perhaps, has been more wont to plead thus with God, after the manner of holy argument, than he whose memoir we are now writing. He was one of the elect few to whom it has been given to revive and restore this lost art of pleading with God. And if all disciples could learn the blessed lesson, what a period of *renaissance* of faith would come to the church of God!

George Müller stored up reasons for God's intervention.

* Proverbs xxviii. 13.

As he came upon promises, authorized declarations of God concerning Himself, names and titles He had chosen to express and reveal His true nature and will, injunctions and invitations which gave to the believer a right to pray and boldness in supplication—as he saw all these, fortified and exemplified by the instances of prevailing prayer, he laid these arguments up in memory, and then on occasions of great need brought them out and spread them before a prayer-hearing God. It is pathetically beautiful to follow this humble man of God into the secret place, and there *hear* him pouring out his soul in these argumentative pleadings, as though he would so order his cause before God as to convince Him that He must interpose to save His own name and word from dishonour !

These were *His* orphans, for had He not declared Himself the Father of the fatherless ? This was *His* work, for had He not called His servant to do His bidding, and what was that servant but an instrument that could neither fit itself nor use itself ? Can the rod lift itself, or the saw move itself, or the hammer deal its own blow, or the sword make its own thrust ? And if this were God's work, was He not bound to care for His own work ? And was not all this deliberately planned and carried on for His own glory ? And would He suffer His own glory to be dimmed ? Had not His own word been given and confirmed by His oath, and could God allow His promise, thus sworn to, to be dishonoured even in the least particular ? Were not the half-believing church and the unbelieving world looking on, to see how the Living God would stand by His own unchanging assurance, and would He supply an argument for the skeptic and the scoffer ? Would He not, must He not, rather put new proofs of His faithfulness in the mouth of His saints, and furnish increasing arguments wherewith to silence the cavilling tongue and put to shame the hesitating disciple ?*

In some such fashion as this did this lowly-minded saint in Bristol plead with God for more than threescore years, *and prevail*—as every true believer may who with a like boldness comes to the throne of grace to obtain mercy and find grace to help in every time of need. How few of us can sincerely sing:

> I believe God answers prayer,
> Answers always, everywhere ;
> I may cast my anxious care,
> Burdens I could never bear,
> On the God who heareth prayer.
> Never need my soul despair
> Since He bids me boldly dare
> To the secret place repair,
> There to prove He answers prayer.

* Mr. Müller himself tells how he argued his case before the Lord at this time. (Appendix F. Narrative, vol. 1, 243, 244.

CHAPTER XI

TRIALS OF FAITH, AND HELPERS TO FAITH

GOD has His own mathematics : witness that miracle of the loaves and fishes. Our Lord said to His disciples: " Give ye them to eat," and as they divided, He multiplied, the scanty provision ; as they subtracted from it He added to it; as they decreased it by distributing, He increased it for distributing. And it has been beautifully said of all holy partnerships, that griefs shared are divided, and joys shared are multiplied.

We have already seen how the prayer circle had been enlarged. The founder of the orphan work, at the first, had only God for his partner, telling Him alone his own wants or the needs of his work. Later on, a very few, including his own wife, Mr. Craik, and one or two helpers, were permitted to know the condition of the funds and supplies. Later still, in the autumn of 1838, he began to feel that he ought more fully to open the doors of his confidence to his associates in the Lord's business. Those who shared in the toils should also share in the prayers, and therefore in the knowledge of the needs which prayer was to supply; else how could they fully be partakers of the faith, the work, and the reward ? Or, again, how could they feel the full proof of the presence and power of God in the answers to prayer, know the joy of the Lord which such answers inspire, or praise Him for the deliverance which such answers exhibit ? It seemed plain that, to the highest glory of God, they must know the depths of need, the extremities of want out of which God had lifted them, and then ascribe all honour and praise to His name.

Accordingly Mr. Müller called together all the beloved brothers and sisters linked with him in the conduct of the work, and fully stated the case, keeping nothing back. He showed them the distress they were in, while he bade them be of good courage, assuring them of his own confidence that help was nigh at hand, and then united them with himself and the smaller praying circle which had previously existed, in supplication to Jehovah Jireh.

The step thus taken was of no small importance to all concerned. A considerable number of praying believers were henceforth added to the band of intercessors that gave God no rest day nor night. While Mr. Müller withheld no facts as to the straits to which the work was reduced, he laid down certain principles which from time to time were reiterated as unchanging laws for the conduct of the Lord's business. For example, nothing must be bought, whatever the extremity, for which there was not money in hand to pay : and yet it must be equally a settled principle that the children must not be left to lack anything needful ; for better that the work cease, and the orphans be sent away, than that they be kept in a nominal home where they were really left to suffer from hunger or nakedness.

Again, nothing was ever to be revealed to outsiders of existing need, lest it should be construed into an appeal for help ; but the only resort must be to the living God. The helpers were often reminded that the supreme object of the institutions, founded in Bristol, was to prove God's faithfulness and the perfect safety of trusting solely to His promises ; jealousy for Him must therefore restrain all tendency to look to man for help. Moreover, they were earnestly besought to live in such daily and hourly fellowship with God as that their own unbelief and disobedience might not risk either their own power in prayer, or the agreement, needful among them, in order to common supplication. One discordant note may prevent the harmonious symphony of united prayer, and so far hinder the acceptableness of such prayer with God.

Thus informed and instructed, these devoted coworkers, with the beloved founder of the orphan work, met the crisis intelligently. If, when there were *no funds,* there must be *no leaning upon man, no debt* incurred, and yet *no lack* allowed, clearly the only resort or resource must be waiting upon the unseen God ; and so, in these straits and in every succeeding crisis, they went to Him alone. The orphans themselves were never told of any existing need; in every case their wants were met, though they knew not how. The barrel of meal might be empty, yet there was always a handful when needed, and the cruse of oil was never so exhausted that a few drops were not left to moisten the handful of meal. Famine and drought never reached the Bristol orphanage : the supplies might come slowly and only for one day at a time, but somehow, when the need was urgent and could no longer wait, there was enough—though it might be barely enough to meet the want.

It should be added here, as completing this part of the Narrative, that, in August, 1840, this circle of prayer was still further enlarged by admitting to its intimacies of fellowship and supplication the brethren and sisters who laboured in the day-schools, the same solemn injunctions being repeated in their case against any betrayal to outsiders of the crises that might arise.

To impart the knowledge of affairs to so much larger a

band of helpers brought in every way a greater blessing, and especially so to the helpers themselves. Their earnest, believing, importunate prayers were thus called forth, and God only knows how much the consequent progress of the work was due to their faith, supplication, and self-denial. The practical knowledge of the exigencies of their common experience begat an unselfishness of spirit which prompted countless acts of heroic sacrifice that have no human record or written history, and can be known only when the pages of the Lord's own journal are read by an assembled universe in the day when the secret things are brought to light. It has, since Mr. Müller's departure, transpired how large a share of the donations received are to be traced to him ; but there is no means of ascertaining as to the aggregate amount of the secret gifts of his coworkers in this sacred circle of prayer.

We do know, however, that Mr. Müller was not the only self-denying giver, though he may lead the host. His true yoke-fellows often *turned the crisis* by their own offerings, which though small were costly ! Instrumentally they were used of God to relieve existing want by their gifts, for out of the abundance of their deep poverty abounded the riches of their liberality. The money they gave was sometimes like the widow's two mites—all their living ; and not only the last penny, but ornaments, jewels, heirlooms, long kept and cherished treasures, like the alabaster flask of ointment which was broken upon the feet of Jesus, were laid down on God's altar as a willing sacrifice. They gave all they could spare and often what they could ill spare, so that there might be meat in God's house and no lack of bread or other needed supplies for His little ones. In a sublime sense this work was not Mr. Müller's only, but *theirs* also, who with him took part in prayers and tears, in cares and toils, in self-denials and self-offerings, whereby God chose to carry forward His plans for these homeless waifs ! It was in thus *giving* that all these helpers found also new power, assurance, and blessing in *praying;* for, as one of them said, he felt that it would scarcely be " *upright to pray, except he were to give what he had.*" *

The helpers, thus admitted into Mr. Müller's confidence, came into more active sympathy with him and the work, and partook increasingly of the same spirit. Of this some few instances and examples have found their way into his journal.

A gentleman and some ladies visiting the orphan houses saw the large number of little ones to be cared for. One of the ladies said to the matron of the Boys' House : " Of course you cannot carry on these institutions without a good stock of funds " ; and the gentleman added, " Have you a good stock ? " The quiet answer was, " Our funds are deposited in a bank which cannot break." The reply drew tears from the eyes of the lady, and a gift of five pounds from the pocket of the gentleman—a donation most opportune, as there was *not one penny then in hand.*

Fellow labourers such as these, who asked nothing for themselves, but cheerfully looked to the Lord for their own supplies, and willingly parted with their own money or goods in the hour of need, filled Mr. Müller's heart with praise to God, and held up his hands, as Aaron and Hur sustained those of Moses, till the sun of his life went down. During all the years of his superintendence these were the main human support of his faith and courage. They met with him in daily prayer, faithfully kept among themselves the secrets of the Lord's work in the great trials of

* Narrative, 1 : 246.

faith ; and, when the hour of triumph came, they felt it
to be both duty and privilege in the annual report to publish their deliverance, to make their boast in God, that
all men might know His love and faithfulness and ascribe
unto Him glory.

From time to time, in connection with the administration of the work, various questions arose which have a
wider bearing on all departments of Christian service, for
their solution enters into what may be called the ethics
and economics of the Lord's work.   At a few of these we
may glance.

As the Lord was dealing with them by the day, it
seemed clear that they were to *live by the day.*   No dues
should be allowed to accumulate, even such as would
naturally accrue from ordinary weekly supplies of bread,
milk, etc.   From the middle of September, 1838, it was
therefore determined that every article bought was to be
paid for at the time.

Again, rent became due in stated amounts and at stated
times.   This want was therefore not unforeseen, and, looked
at in one aspect, rent was due daily or weekly, though col-
lected at longer intervals.   The principle having been laid
down that no debt should be incurred, it was considered as
implying that the amount due for rent should be *put aside*
daily, or at least weekly, even though not then payable.   This
rule was henceforth adopted, with this understanding, that
money thus laid aside was sacred to that end, and not to
be drawn upon, even temporarily, for any other.

Notwithstanding such conscientiousness and consistency
the trial of faith and patience continued.   Money came in
only in small sums, and barely enough with rigid economy
to meet each day's wants.   The outlook was often most
dark and the prospect most threatening ; but *no real need
ever failed to be supplied:* and so praise was continually

mingled with prayer, the incense of thanksgiving making fragrant the flame of supplication. God's interposing power and love could not be doubted, and in fact made the more impression as unquestionable facts, because help came so frequently at the hour of extremity, and in the exact form or amount needed. Before the provision was entirely exhausted, there came new supplies or the money wherewith to buy, so that these many mouths were always fed and these many bodies always clad.

To live up to such principles as had been laid down was not possible without faith, kept in constant and lively exercise. For example, in the closing months of 1838 God seemed purposely putting them to a severe test, whether or not they *did trust Him alone.* The orphan work was in continual straits : at times not one half-penny was in the hands of the matrons in the three houses. But not only was no knowledge of such facts ever allowed to leak out, or any hint of the extreme need ever given to outsiders, *but even those who inquired, with intent to aid, were not informed.*

One evening a brother ventured to ask how the balance would stand when the next accounts were made up, and whether it would be as great in favour of the orphans as when the previous balance-sheet had been prepared. Mr. Müller's calm but evasive answer was : " *It will be as great as the Lord pleases.*" This was no intentional rudeness. To have said more would have been turning from the one Helper to make at least an indirect appeal to man for help; and every such snare was carefully avoided lest the one great aim should be lost sight of : to prove to all men that it is safe to trust only in the Living God.

While admitting the severity of the straits to which the whole work of the Scriptural Knowledge Institution was often brought, Mr. Müller takes pains to assure his readers

that these straits were never a surprise to him, and that
his expectations in the matter of funds were not disappointed, but rather the reverse. He had looked for
great emergencies as essential to his full witness to a
prayer-hearing God. The almighty Hand can never be
clearly seen while any human help is sought for or is in
sight. We must turn absolutely away from all else if we
are to turn fully unto the living God. The deliverance
is signal, only in proportion as the danger is serious, and is
most significant when, without God, we face absolute
despair. Hence the exact end for which the whole work
was mainly begun could be attained only through such
conditions of extremity and such experiences of interposition in extremity.

Some who have known but little of the interior history
of the orphan work have very naturally accounted for the
regularity of supplies by supposing that the public statements, made about it by word of mouth, and especially by
the pen in the printed annual reports, have constituted
appeals for aid. Unbelief would interpret all God's working
however wonderful, by 'natural laws,' and the carnal
mind, refusing to see in any of the manifestations of God's
power any supernatural force at work, persists in thus ex-
plaining away all the 'miracles of prayer.'

No doubt humane and sympathetic hearts have been
strongly moved by the remarkable ways in which God has
day by day provided for all these orphans, as well as the
other branches of work of the Scriptural Knowledge
Institution ; and believing souls have been drawn into
loving and hearty sympathy with work so conducted, and
have been led to become its helpers. It is a well-known
fact that God has used these annual reports to accomplish
just such results. Yet it remains true that these reports
were never intended or issued as appeals for aid, and no de-

pendence has been placed upon them for securing timely
help. It is also undeniable that, however frequent their
issue, wide their circulation, or great their influence, the
regularity and abundance of the supplies of all needs must
in some other way be accounted for.

Only a few days after public meetings were held or
printed reports issued, funds often fell to their lowest ebb.
Mr. Müller and his helpers were singularly kept from all
undue leaning upon any such indirect appeals, and frequently and definitely asked God that they might never
be left to look for any inflow of means through such
channels. For many reasons the Lord's dealings with
them were made known, the main object of such publicity
always being a *testimony to the faithfulness of God*. This
great object Mr. Müller always kept foremost, hoping and
praying that, by such records and revelations of God's
fidelity to His promises, and of the manner in which He
met each new need, his servant might awaken, quicken, and
stimulate faith in Him as the Living God. One has only
to read these reports to see the conspicuous absence of
any appeal for human aid, or of any attempt to excite pity,
sympathy and compassion toward the orphans. The burden of every report is to induce the reader to venture
wholly upon God, to taste and see that the Lord is good,
and find for himself how blessed are all they that put their
trust in Him. Only in the light of this supreme purpose
can these records of a life of faith be read intelligently
and intelligibly.

Weakness of body again, in the autumn of 1839, compelled, for a time, rest from active labour, and Mr. Müller
went to Trowbridge and Exeter, Teignmouth and Plymouth. God had precious lessons for him which He could
best teach in the school of affliction.

While at Plymouth Mr. Müller felt anew the impulse to

early rising for purposes of devotional communion. At Halle he had been an early riser, influenced by zeal for excellence in study. Afterwards, when his weak head and feeble nerves made more sleep seem needful, he judged that, even when he rose late, the day would be long enough to exhaust his little fund of strength ; and so often he lay in bed till six or even seven o'clock, instead of rising at four ; and after dinner took a nap for a quarter-hour. It now grew upon him, however, that he was losing in spiritual vigour, and that his soul's health was declining under this new regimen. The work now so pressed upon him as to prevent proper reading of the Word and rob him of leisure for secret prayer.

A ' chance remark '—there is no *chance* in a believer's life !—made by the brother at whose house he was abiding at Plymouth, much impressed him. Referring to the sacrifices in Leviticus, he said that, as the refuse of the animals was never offered up on the altar, but only the best parts and the fat, so the choicest of our time and strength, the best parts of our day, should be especially given to the Lord in worship and communion. George Müller meditated much on this ; and determined, even at the risk of damage to bodily health, that he would no longer spend his best hours in bed. Henceforth he allowed himself but *seven hours' sleep* and gave up his after-dinner rest. This resumption of early rising secured long seasons of uninterrupted interviews with God, in prayer and meditation on the Scriptures, before breakfast and the various inevitable interruptions that followed. He found himself not worse but better, physically, and became convinced that to have lain longer in bed as before would have kept his nerves weak ; and, as to spiritual life, such new vitality and vigour accrued from thus waiting upon God while others slept, that it continued to be the habit of his after-life.

In November, 1839, when the needs were again great and the supplies very small, he was kept in peace : " I was not," he says, " looking at the *little in hand, but at the fulness of God.*"

It was his rule to empty himself of all that he had, in order to greater boldness in appealing for help from above. All needless articles were sold if a market could be found. But what was useful in the Lord's work he did not reckon as needless, nor regard it right to sell, since the Father knew the need.   One of his fellow labourers had put forward his valuable watch as a security for the return of money laid by for rent, but drawn upon for the time ; yet even this plan was not felt to be scriptural, as the watch might be reckoned among articles needful and useful in the Lord's service, and, if such expedients were quite abandoned, the deliverance would be more manifest as of the Lord.   And so, one by one, all resorts were laid aside that might imperil full trust and sole dependence upon the one and only Helper.

When the poverty of their resources seemed most pinching, Mr. Müller still comforted himself with the daily proof that God had not forgotten, and would day by day feed them with ' the bread of their convenience.'   Often he said to himself, If it is even a proverb of the world that " Man's necessity is God's opportunity," how much more may God's own dear children in their great need look to Him to make their extremity the fit moment to display His love and power !

In February, 1840, another attack of ill health combined with a mission to Germany to lead Mr. Müller for five weeks to the Continent.   At Heimersleben, where he found his father weakened by a serious cough, the two rooms in which he spent most time in prayer and reading of the Word, and confession of the Lord, were the same in which, nearly twenty years before, he had passed most time as an unreconciled sinner against God and man. Later on, at Wolfenbüttel, he saw the inn whence in 1821 he ran away in debt. In taking leave once more of his father he was pierced by a keen anguish, fearing it was his last farewell, and an unusual tenderness and affection were now exhibited by his father, whom he yearned more and more to know as safe in the Lord Jesus, and depending no longer on outward and formal religiousness, or substituting the reading of prayers and of Scripture for an inward conformity to Christ. This proved the last interview, for the father died on March 30th of the same year.

The main purpose of this journey to Germany was to send forth more missionaries to the East. At Sandersleben Mr. Müller met his friend, Mr. Stahlschmidt, and found a little band of disciples meeting in secret to evade the police. Those who have always breathed the atmosphere of religious liberty know little of such intolerance as, in that nominally Christian land, stifled all freedom of worship. Eleven years before, when Mr. Stahlschmidt's servant had come to this place, he had found scarce one true disciple beside his master. The first meetings had been literally of but two or three, and, when they had grown a little larger, Mr. Kroll was summoned before the magistrates and, like the apostles in the first days of the church, forbidden to speak in His name. But again, like those same primitive disciples, believing that they were to obey God rather than men, the believing band had continued to meet, notwithstanding police raids which were so disturbing, and government fines which were so exacting. So secret, however, were their assemblies, as to have neither stated place nor regular time.

George Müller found these persecuted believers, meeting
in the room of a humble weaver where there was but one
chair.   The twenty-five or thirty who were present found
such places to sit or stand as they might, in and about the
loom, which itself filled half the space.

In Halberstadt Mr. Müller found seven large Protestant
churches without one clergyman who gave evidence of
true conversion, and the few genuine disciples there were
likewise forbidden to meet together.

A few days after returning to Bristol from his few
weeks in Germany, and at a time of great financial distress
in the work, a letter reached him from a brother who had
often before given money, as follows :

" Have you any *present* need for the Institution under
your care ?   I know you do not *ask*, except indeed of Him
whose work you are doing ; but to *answer when asked*
seems another thing, and a right thing.   I have a reason
for desiring to know the present state of your means towards the objects you are labouring to serve : viz., should
you *not have* need, other departments of the Lord's work,
or other people of the Lord, *may have* need.   Kindly then
inform me, and to what amount, i.e. what amount you at
this present time need or can profitably lay out."

To most men, even those who carry on a work of faith
and prayer, such a letter would have been at least a temptation.   But Mr. Müller did not waver.   To announce even
to an inquirer the exact needs of the work would, in his
opinion, involve two serious risks :

1. It would turn his own eyes away from God to man ;

2. It would turn the minds of saints away from dependence solely upon Him.

This man of God had staked everything upon one great
experiment—he had set himself to prove that the prayer
which *resorts to God only* will bring help in every crisis,

even when the crisis is unknown to His people whom He
uses as the means of relief and help.

At this time there remained in hand but twenty-seven
pence ha'penny, in all, to meet the needs of hundreds
of orphans. Nevertheless this was the reply to the
letter :

"Whilst I thank you for your love, and whilst I agree
with you that, in general, there is a difference between *ask-*
ing for money and *answering when asked,* nevertheless, in our
case, I feel not at liberty to speak about the state of our
funds, as the primary object of the work in my hands is
to lead those who are weak in faith to see that there is
reality in dealing with God *alone.*"

Consistently with his position, however, no sooner was
the answer posted than the appeal went up to the Living
God : "Lord, thou knowest that, for Thy sake, I did not
tell this brother about our need.   Now, Lord, show afresh
that there is *reality* in speaking to Thee only, about our
need, and speak therefore to this brother so that he may
help us."   In answer, God moved this inquiring brother to
send one hundred pounds, which came when *not one penny*
was in hand.

The confidence of faith, long tried, had its increasing
reward and was strengthened by experience.   In July,
1845, Mr. Müller gave this testimony reviewing these very
years of trial :

"Though for about seven years, our funds have been so
exhausted that it has been comparatively a rare case that
there have been means in hand to meet the necessities of the
orphans *for three days* together, yet I have been only once
tried in spirit, and that was on September 18, 1838, when
for the first time the Lord seemed not to regard our prayer.
But when He did send help at that time, and I saw that it
was only for the trial of our faith, and not because He had

forsaken the work, that we were brought so low, my soul was so strengthened and encouraged that I have not only not been allowed to distrust the Lord since that time, but I have not even been cast down when in the deepest poverty."

CHAPTER XII

THE teacher must also be a learner, and therefore only he who continues to learn is competent to continue to teach. Nothing but new lessons, daily mastered, can keep our testimony fresh and vitalizing and enable us to give advance lessons. Instead of being always engaged in a sort of review, our teaching and testimony will thus be drawn each day from a new and higher level.

George Müller's experiences of prevailing prayer went on constantly accumulating, and so qualified him to speak to others, not 'as on a matter of speculation, theory, or doctrinal belief, but of long, varied, and successful personal experiment. Patiently, carefully and frequently, he seeks to impress on others the conditions of effective supplication. From time to time he met those to whom his courageous, childlike trust in God was a mystery; and occasionally unbelief's secret misgivings found a voice in the question, *what he would do if God did not send help!* what, if a meal-time actually came with no food, and no money to procure it; or if clothing were worn out, and nothing to replace it?

To all such questions there was always ready this one answer: that *such a failure on God's part is inconceivable,* and must therefore be put among the impossibilities. There are, however, conditions necessary on *man's* part: *the suppliant soul must come to God in the right spirit and attitude.* For the sake of such readers as might need further guidance as to the proper and acceptable manner of approach to God, he was wont to make very plain the scripture teaching upon this point.

Five grand conditions of prevailing prayer were ever before his mind :

1. Entire dependence upon the merits and mediation of the Lord Jesus Christ, as the only ground of any claim for blessing. (See John xiv. 13, 14 ; xv. 16, etc.)

2. Separation from all known sin. If we regard iniquity in our hearts, the Lord will not hear us, for it would be sanctioning sin. (Psalm lxvi. 18.)

3. Faith in God's word of promise as confirmed by His oath. Not to believe Him is to make Him both a liar and a perjurer. (Hebrews xi. 6; vi. 13–20.)

4. Asking in accordance with His will. Our motives must be godly : we must not seek any gift of God to consume it upon our own lusts. (1 John v. 13 ; James iv. 3.)

5. Importunity in supplication. There must be *waiting* on God and waiting for God, as the husbandman has long patience to wait for the harvest. (James v. 7 ; Luke xviii. 1-10.)

The importance of firmly fixing in mind principles such as these cannot be overstated. The first lays the basis of all prayer, in our oneness with the great High Priest. The second states a condition of prayer, found in abandonment of sin. The third reminds us of the need of honouring God by faith that He is, and is the Rewarder of the diligent seeker. The fourth reveals the sympathy with God that helps us to ask what is for our good and His glory. The last teaches us that, having laid hold of God in prayer, we are to keep hold until His arm is outstretched in blessing.

Where these conditions do not exist, for God to answer prayer would be both a dishonour to Himself and a damage to the suppliant. To encourage those who come to Him in their own name, or in a self-righteous, self-seeking, and disobedient spirit, would be to set a premium upon continuance in sin. To answer the requests of the unbelieving would be to disregard the double insult put upon His word of promise and His oath of confirmation, by persistent doubt of His truthfulness and distrust of His faithfulness. Indeed not one condition of prevailing prayer exists which is not such in the very nature of things. These are not arbitrary limitations affixed to prayer by a despotic will; they are necessary alike to God's character and man's good.

All the lessons learned in God's school of prayer made Mr. Müller's feelings and convictions about this matter more profound and subduing. He saw the vital relation of prayer to holiness, and perpetually sought to impress it upon both his hearers and readers; and, remembering that for the purpose of persuasion the most effective figure of speech is *repetition,* he hesitated at no frequency of restatement by which such truths might find root in the minds and hearts of others.

There has never been a saint, from Abel's day to our own, who has not been taught the same essential lessons. All prayer which has ever brought down blessing has prevailed by the same law of success—*the inward impulse of God's Holy Spirit.* If, therefore, that Spirit's teachings be disregarded or disobeyed, or His inward movings be hindered, in just such measure will prayer become formal or be altogether abandoned. Sin, consciously indulged, or duty, knowingly neglected, makes supplication an offence to God.

Again, all prayer prevails only in the measure of our

real, even if not conscious, unity with the Lord Jesus Christ as the ground of our approach, and in the degree of our dependence on Him as the medium of our access to God.

Yet again, all prayer prevails only as it is offered in faith ; and the *answer* to such prayer can be recognized and received only *on the plane of faith;* that is, we must maintain the believing frame, expecting the blessing, and being ready to receive it in God's way and time and form, and not our own.

The faith that thus *expects* cannot be surprised at answers to prayer. When, in November, 1840, a sister gave ten pounds for the orphans, and at a time specially opportune, Mr. Müller records his triumphant joy in God as exceeding and defying all expression. Yet he was *free from excitement and not in the least surprised,* because by grace he had been trustfully waiting on God for deliverance. Help had been so long delayed that in one of the houses there was no bread, and in none of them any milk or any money to buy either. It was only a few minutes before the milkman's cart was due, that this money came.

However faithful and trustful in prayer, it behooves us to be none the less careful and diligent in the use of all proper means. Here again Mr. Müller's whole life is a lesson to other believers. For example, when travelling in other lands, or helping other brethren on their way, he besought the Lord's constant guardianship over the conveyances used, and even over the luggage so liable to go astray. But he himself looked carefully to the seaworthiness of the vessel he was to sail in, and to every other condition of safe and speedy transportation for himself and others. In one case where certain German brethren and sisters were departing for foreign shores, he noticed the manner in which the cabman stored away the small luggage in the fly;

and observed that several carpetbags were hastily thrust into a hind boot. He also carefully counted the pieces of luggage and took note of the fact that there were seventeen in all. On arriving at the wharf, where there is generally much hurry and flurry, the dishonest cabman would have driven off with a large part of the property belonging to the party, but for this man of God who not only *prayed* but *watched.* He who trusted God implicitly, no less faithfully looked to the cabman's fidelity, who, after he pretended to have delivered all the luggage to the porters, was compelled to open that hind boot and, greatly to his own confusion, deliver up the five or six bags hidden away there. Mr. Müller adds in his Narrative that " such a circumstance should teach one to make the very smallest affairs a subject of prayer, as, for instance, that all the luggage might be safely taken out of a fly." May we not add that such a circumstance teaches us that companion lesson, quite as important in its way, that we are to be watchful as well as prayerful, and see that a dishonest cab-driver does not run off with another's goods !

This praying saint, who watched man, most of all watched God. Even in the lesser details of his work, his eye was ever looking for God's unfailing supplies, and taking notice of the divine leadings and dealings; and, afterward, there always followed the fruit of the lips, giving thanks to His name. Here is another secret revealed : prayerfulness and thankfulness—those two handmaidens of God—always go together, each helping the other. " Pray without ceasing: in everything give thanks." (1 Thess. v. 17, 18.) These two precepts stand side by side where they belong, and he who neglects one will find himself disobeying the other. This man who prayed so much and so well, offered the sacrifice of praise to God continually.

For example, on September 21, 1840, a specific entry was made in the Narrative, so simple, childlike, and in every way characteristic, that every word of it is precious.

"The Lord, to show His continued care over us, raises up new helpers. They that trust in the Lord shall never be confounded. Some who helped for a while may fall asleep in Jesus ; others grow cold in the service of the Lord; others be as desirous as ever to help, but no longer able ; or, having means, feel it to be His will to lay them out in another way. But in leaning upon God, the Living God alone, we are BEYOND DISAPPOINTMENT and BEYOND *being forsaken because of death, or want of means, or want of love, or because of the claims of other work.* How precious to have learned, in any measure, to be content to stand with God alone in the world, and to know that surely no good thing shall be withheld from us, whilst we walk uprightly !"

Among the gifts received during this long life of stewardship for God some deserve individual mention.

To an offering received in March, 1839, a peculiar history attaches. The circumstances attending its reception made upon him a deep impression. He had given a copy of the Annual Report to a believing brother who had been greatly stirred up to prayer by reading it ; and knowing his own sister, who was also a disciple, to possess sundry costly ornaments and jewels, such as a heavy gold chain, a pair of gold bracelets, and a superb ring set with fine brilliants, this brother besought the Lord so to show her the uselessness of such trinkets that she should be led to lay them all upon His altar as an offering for the orphan work. This prayer was literally answered. Her sacrifice of jewels proved of service to the work at a time of such pressing need that Mr. Müller's heart specially rejoiced in God. By the proceeds of the sale of these ornaments he was helped to meet the expenses of a *whole week*, and besides to *pay the salaries* due to the helpers. But, before disposing of the diamond ring, he wrote with it upon the window-pane of his own room that precious name and title of the Lord—" JEHOVAH JIREH "—and henceforth whenever, in deep poverty, he cast his eyes upon those two words, imperishably written with the point of a diamond upon that pane, he thankfully remembered that " THE LORD WILL PROVIDE."

How many of his fellow believers might find unfailing refreshment and inspiration in dwelling upon the divine promises ! Ancient believers were bidden to write God's words on the palms of their hands, the doorposts of their houses, and on their gates, so that the employments of their hands, their goings out and comings in, their personal and home life, might be constant reminders of Jehovah's everlasting faithfulness. He who inscribed this chosen name of God upon the window-pane of his dwelling, found that every ray of sunlight that shone into his room lit up his Lord's promise.

He thus sums up the experiences of the year 1840 :

1. Notwithstanding multiplied trials of faith, the orphans have lacked nothing.

2. Instead of being disappointed in his expectations or work, the reverse had been true, such trials being seen to be needful to demonstrate that the Lord was their Helper in times of need.

3. Such a way of living brings the Lord very near, as one who daily inspects the need that He may send the more timely aid.

4. Such constant, instant reliance upon divine help does not so absorb the mind in temporal things as to unfit for spiritual employments and enjoyments ; but rather

prompts to habitual communion with the Lord and His Word.

5. Other children of God may not be called to a similar work, but are called to a like faith, and may experience similar interposition if they live according to His will and seek His help.

6. The incurring of debt, being unscriptural, is a sin needing confession and abandonment if we desire unhindered fellowship with God, and experience of His interposition.

It was in this year 1840, also, that a further object was embraced in the work of the Scripture Knowledge Institution, namely, the circulation of Christian books and tracts. But, as the continuance and enlargement of these benevolent activities made the needs greater, so, in answer to prayer, the Hand of the great Provider bestowed larger supplies.

Divine interposition will never be doubted by one who, like George Müller, gives himself to prayer, for the coincidences will prove too exact and frequent between demand and supply, times and seasons of asking and answering, to allow of doubt that God has helped.

The 'ethics of language' embody many lessons. For example, the term 'poetic retribution' describes a visitation of judgment where the penalty peculiarly befits the crime. As poetic lines harmonize, rhyme and rhythm showing the work of a designing hand, so there is often harmony between an offense and its retribution, as when Adonibezek, who had afflicted a like injury upon threescore and five captive kings, had his own thumbs and great toes cut off, or as when Haman was himself hung on the gallows that he built for Mordecai. We read in Psalm ix. 16:

" The Lord is known by the judgment which He exe-
    cuteth :
The wicked is snared in the work of his own hands."
The inspired thought is that the punishment of evil-doers
is in such exact correspondence with the character of their
evil doings as to show that it is the Lord executing ven-
geance—the penalty shows a designing hand. He who
watches the peculiar retributive judgments of God, how
He causes those who set snares and pitfalls for others to
fall into them themselves, will not doubt that behind such
' poetic retribution ' there is an intelligent Judge.

Somewhat so the poetic harmony between prayer and its
answer silences all question as to a discriminating Hearer
of the suppliant soul. A single case of such answered
prayer might be accounted accidental ; but, ever since
men began to call upon the name of the Lord, there have
been such repeated, striking, and marvellous correspond-
ences between the requests of man and the replies of God,
that the inference is perfectly safe, the induction has too
broad a basis and too large a body of particulars to allow
mistake. The coincidences are both too many and too
exact to admit the doctrine of *chance*. We are compelled,
not to say justified, to conclude that the only sufficient
and reasonable explanation must be found in a God who
hears and answers prayer.

Mr. Müller was not the only party to these transactions,
nor the only person thus convinced that God was in the
whole matter of the work and its support. The *donors* as
well as the *receiver* were conscious of divine leading.

Frequent were the instances also when those who gave
most timely help conveyed to Mr. Müller the knowledge of
the experiences that accompanied or preceded their offerings ; as, for example, when, without any intimation
being given them from man that there was special need,

the heart was impressed in prayer to God that there was an emergency requiring prompt assistance.

For example, in June, 1841, fifty pounds were received with these words : " *I am not concerned at my having been prevented for so many days from sending this money; I am confident it has not been needed.*"

" This last sentence is remarkable," says Mr. Müller. " It is now nearly three years since our funds were for the first time exhausted, and only at this period, since then, could it have been said in truth, so far as I remember, that a donation of fifty pounds was *not* needed. From the beginning in July, 1838, till now, there never had been a period when we so abounded as when this donation came; for there were then, in the orphan fund and the other funds, between two and three hundred pounds ! The words of our brother are so much the more remarkable as, on four former occasions, when he likewise gave considerable donations, we were always in need, yea, great need, which he afterwards knew from the printed accounts."

Prevailing prayer is largely conditioned on constant obedience. " Whatsoever we ask we receive of Him, because we keep His commandments, and do those things which are well pleasing in His sight." (1 John iii. 22.) There is no way of keeping in close touch with God unless a *new step* is taken in advance whenever *new light* is given. Here is another of the life-secrets of George Müller. Without unduly counting the cost, he followed every leading of God.

In July, 1841, both Mr. Craik and Mr. Müller were impressed that the existing mode of receiving free-will offerings from those among whom they laboured was inexpedient. These contributions were deposited in boxes, over which their names were placed with an explanation of the purpose to which such offerings were applied. But it was

'felt that this might have the appearance of unduly ele-
vating them above others, as though they were assuming
official importance, or excluding others from full and
equal recognition as labourers in word and doctrine. They
therefore decided to discontinue this mode of receiving
such offerings.

Such an act of obedience may seem to some, overscrupu-
lous, but it cost some inward struggles, for it threatened a
possible and probable decrease in supplies for their own
needs, and the question naturally arose how such lack
should be supplied. Happily Mr. Müller had long ago
settled the question that *to follow a clear sense of duty is
always safe.* He could say, in every such crisis, " O God
my heart is fixed, my heart is fixed, trusting in Thee."
(Psalm cxii. 7.) Once for all having made such a decision,
such apparent risks did not for a moment disturb his peace.
Somehow or other the Lord would provide, and all he had
to do was to serve and trust Him and leave the rest to
His Fatherhood.

In the autumn of 1841 it pleased God that, beyond any
previous period, there should be a severe test of faith.
For some months the supplies had been comparatively
abundant, but now, from day to day and from meal to
meal, the eye of faith had to be turned to the Lord, and,
notwithstanding continuance in prayer, *help seemed at
times to fail,* so much so that it was a special sign of God's
grace that, during this long trial of delay, the confidence
of Mr. Müller and his helpers did not altogether give way.
But he and they were held up, and he unwaveringly rested
on the fatherly pity of God.

On one occasion a poor woman gave two pence, adding,
" It is but a trifle, but I must give it to you." Yet so opportune was the gift of these ' two mites ' that *one of these
two pence* was just what was at that time needed to make

up the sum required to buy bread for immediate use. At another time eight pence more being necessary to provide for the next meal, but *seven* pence were in hand ; but on opening one of the boxes, *one penny* only was found deposited, and thus a single penny was traced to the Father's care.

It was in December of this same year, 1841, that, in order to show how solely dependence was placed on a heavenly Provider, it was determined to *delay for a while* both the holding of any public meeting and the printing of the Annual Report. Mr. Müller was confident that, though no word should be either spoken or printed about the work and its needs, the means would still be supplied. As a matter of fact the report of 1841-2 was thus postponed for five months; and so, *in the midst of deep poverty* and *partly because of the very pressure of such need*, another bold step was taken, which, like the cutting away of the ropes that held the life-boat, in that Mediterranean shipwreck, threw Mr. Müller, and all that were with him in the work, more completely on the promise and the providence of God.

It might be inferred that, where such a decision was made, the Lord would make haste to reward at once such courageous confidence. And yet, so mysterious are His ways, that never, up to that time, had Mr. Müller's faith been tried so sharply as between December 12, 1841, and April 12, 1842. During these four months, again, it was as though God were saying, " I will now see whether indeed you truly lean on Me and look to Me." At any time during this trial, Mr. Müller might have changed his course, holding the public meeting and publishing the report, for, outside the few who were in his councils, *no one knew of the determination*, and in fact many children of God, looking for the usual year's journal of ' The Lord's Dealings,' were surprised at the delay. But the conclusion conscientiously reached was, for the glory of the Lord, as steadfastly pursued, and again Jehovah Jireh revealed His faithfulness.

During this four months, on March 9, 1842, the need was so extreme that, had no help come, the work could not have gone on. But, *on that day*, from a brother living near Dublin, ten pounds came : and the hand of the Lord clearly appeared in this gift, for when the post had already come and no letter had come with it, there was a strong confidence suggested to Mr. Müller's mind that deliverance was at hand; and so it proved, for presently the letter was brought to him, having been delivered at one of the other houses. During this same month, it was necessary once to *delay dinner for about a half-hour*, because of a lack of supplies. Such a postponement had scarcely ever been known before, and very rarely was it repeated in the entire after-history of the work, though thousands of mouths had to be daily fed.

In the spring of 1843, Mr. Müller felt led to open a *fourth orphan house*, the third having been opened nearly six years before. This step was taken with his uniform conscientiousness, deliberation, and prayerfulness. He had seen many reasons for such enlargement of the work, but he had said nothing about the matter even to his beloved wife. Day by day he waited on God in prayer, preferring to take counsel only of Him, lest he might do something in haste, move in advance of clear leading, or be biassed unduly by human judgment.

Unexpected obstacles interfered with his securing the premises which had already been offered and found suitable; but he was in no way ' discomforted.' The burden of his prayer was, " Lord, if *Thou* hast no need of another orphan house, *I* have none " ; and he rightly judged that the calm deliberation with which he had set about the whole matter, and the unbroken peace with which he met new hindrances, were proofs that he was following the guidance of God and not the motions of self-will.

As the public meeting and the publication of the Annual Report had been purposely postponed to show that no undue dependence was placed even on indirect appeals to man, much special prayer went up to God, that, *before July 15*, 1844, when the public meeting was to be held, He would so richly supply all need that it might clearly appear that, notwithstanding these lawful means of informing His servants concerning the work had for a time not been used, the prayer of faith had drawn down help from above. As the financial year had closed in May, it would be more than *two years* since the previous report had been made to the public.

George Müller was jealous for the Lord God of hosts. He desired that " even the shadow of ground might be cut off for persons to say, ' They cannot get any more money ; and therefore they now publish another report.' " Hence, while, during the whole progress of the work, he desired to stand with his Master, without heeding either the favourable or unfavourable judgments of men, he felt strongly that God would be much honoured and glorified as the prayer-hearing God if, before the public had been at all apprised of the situation, an ample supply might be given. In such case, instead of appearing to ask aid of men, he and his associates would be able to witness to the church and the world, God's faithfulness, and offer Him the praise of joyful and thankful hearts. As he had asked, so was it done unto him. Money and other supplies came in, and, on the day before the accounts were closed, such liberal gifts, that there was a *surplus of over twenty pounds* for the whole work.

CHAPTER XIII

FOLLOWING THE PILLAR OF CLOUD AND FIRE

"THE steps of a good man are ordered by the Lord." (Psalm xxxvii. 23.) Some one quaintly adds; "Yes, and the *stops, too!*" The pillar of cloud and fire is a symbol of that divine leadership which guides both as to forward steps and intervals of rest. Mr Müller found it blessed to follow, one step at a time, as God ordered his way, and to stand still and wait when He seemed to call for a halt.

At the end of May, 1843, a crisis was reached, which was a new example of the experiences to which faith is liable in the walk with God; and a new illustration of the duty and delight of depending upon Him in everything and for everything, habitually waiting upon Him, and trusting in Him to remove all hindrances in the way of service.

Some eighteen months previously, a German lady from Würtemberg had called to consult him as to her own plans, and, finding her a comparative stranger to God, he spoke to her about her spiritual state, and gave her the first two parts of his Narrative. The perusal of these pages was so blest to her that she was converted to God, and felt moved to translate the Narrative into her own tongue as a channel of similar blessing to other hearts.

This work of translation she partially accomplished, though somewhat imperfectly ; and the whole occurrence impressed Mr. Müller as an indication that God was once more leading him in the direction of Germany, for another season of labour in his native land. Much prayer deepened his persuasion that he had not misread God's signal, and that His time had now fully come. He records some of the motives which led to this conclusion.

1. First, he yearned to encourage believing brethren who for conscience' sake had felt constrained to separate themselves from the state churches, and meet for worship in such conditions as would more accord with New Testament principles, and secure greater edification.

2. Being a German himself, and therefore familiar with their language, customs, and habits of thought, he saw that he was fitted to wield a larger influence among his fellow countrymen than otherwise.

3. He was minded to publish his Narrative in his own tongue wherein he was born, not so much in the form of a mere translation, as of an independent record of his life's experiences such as would be specially suited to its new mission.

4. An effectual door was opened before him, and more widely than ever, especially at Stuttgart; and although there were many adversaries, they only made his help the more needful to those whose spiritual welfare was in peril.

5. A distinct burden was laid on his heart, as from the Lord, which prayer, instead of relieving, increased—a burden which he *felt* without being able to explain—so that the determination to visit his native land gave him a certain peace which he did not have when he thought of remaining at home.

To avoid mistake, with equal care he records the counter-arguments.

1. The new orphan house, No. 4, was about to be opened, and his presence was desirable if not needful.

2. A few hundred pounds were needed, to be left with his helpers, for current expenses in his absence.

3. Money was also required for travelling expenses of himself and his wife, whose health called for a change.

4. Funds would be needful to publish four thousand copies of his Narrative and avoid too high a market-price

5. A matron for the new orphan house was not yet found, suitable for the position.

In this careful *weighing of matters* many sincere disciples fail, prone to be impatient of delay in making decisions. Impulse too often sways, and self-willed plans betray into false and even disastrous mistakes. Life is too precious to risk one such failure. There is given us a promise of deep meaning :

" The meek will He guide in judgment ;
And the meek will He teach His way."

(Psalm xxv. 9.)

Here is a double emphasis upon *meekness* as a condition of such guidance and teaching. *Meekness is a real pref-erence for God's will.* Where this holy habit of mind exists, the whole being becomes so open to impression that, without any *outward* sign or token, there is an *inward* recognition and choice of the will of God. God guides, not by a visible sign, but by *swaying the judgment*. To wait before Him, weighing candidly in the scales every consideration for or against a proposed course, and in readiness to see which way the preponderance lies, is a frame of mind and heart in which one is fitted to be guided ; and God touches the scales and makes the bal-ance to sway as He will. *But our hands must be off the scales,* otherwise we need expect no interposition of His,

in our favour. To return to the figure with which this
chapter starts, the meek soul simply and humbly waits,
and *watches the moving of the Pillar.*

One sure sign of this spirit of meekness is the entire *rest-
fulness* with which apparent obstacles to any proposed plan
or course are regarded. When waiting and wishing only
to know and do God's will, hindrances will give no anxiety, but a sort of pleasure, as affording a new opportunity
for divine interposition. If it is the Pillar of God we are
following, the Red Sea will not dismay us, for it will furnish but another scene for the display of the power of Him
who can make the waters to stand up as an heap, and to
become a wall about us as we go through the sea on dry
ground.

Mr. Müller had learned this rare lesson, and in this case
he says : "*I had a secret satisfaction in the greatness of
the difficulties which were in the way.* So far from being
cast down on account of them, they delighted my soul ;
for I only desired to do the will of the Lord in this matter."

Here is revealed another secret of holy serving. To him
who sets the Lord always before him, and to whom the will
of God is his delight, there pertains a habit of soul which,
in advance settles a thousand difficult and perplexing
questions.

The case in hand is an illustration of the blessing found
in such meek preference for God's pleasure. If it were the
will of the Lord that this Continental tour should be
undertaken at that time, difficulties need not cast him
down ; for the *difficulties could not be of God;* and, if not
of God, they should give him no unrest, for, in answer to
prayer, they would all be removed. If, on the other hand,
this proposed visit to the Continent were *not* God's plan
at all, but only the fruit of self-will ; if some secret, selfish, and perhaps subtle motive were controlling, then in-

deed hindrances might well be interferences of God, designed to stay his steps. In the latter case, Mr. Müller rightly judged that difficulties in the way would naturally vex and annoy him ; that he would not like to look at them, and would seek to remove them by his own efforts. Instead of giving him an inward satisfaction as affording God an opportunity to intervene in his behalf, they would arouse impatience and vexation, as preventing self-will from carrying out its own purposes.

Such discriminations have only to be stated to any spiritual mind, to have their wisdom at once apparent. Any believing child of God may safely gauge the measure of his surrender to the will of God, in any matter, by the measure of impatience he feels at the obstacles in the way ; for, in proportion as self-will sways him, whatever seems to oppose or hinder his plans will disturb or annoy ; and, instead of quietly leaving all such hindrances and obstacles to the Lord, to deal with them as He pleases, in His own way and time, the wilful disciple will, impatiently and in the energy of the flesh, set himself to remove them by his own scheming and struggling, and he will brook no delay.

Whenever Satan acts as a hinderer (1 Thess. ii. 18) the obstacles which he puts in our way need not dismay us ; God permits them to delay or deter us for the time, only as a test of our patience and faith, and the satanic hinderer will be met by a divine Helper who will sweep away all his obstacles, as with the breath of His mouth.

Mr. Müller felt this, and he waited on God for light and help. But, after forty days' waiting, the hindrances, instead of decreasing, seemed rather to increase. Much more money was spent than was sent in ; instead of finding another suitable matron, a sister, already at work, was probably about to withdraw, so that two vacancies would need to be filled instead of one. Yet his rest and peace of mind were unbroken. Being persuaded that he was yielded up to the will of God, faith not only held him to his purpose, but saw the obstacles already surmounted, so that he gave thanks in advance. Because Caleb "followed the Lord fully," even the giant sons of Anak with their walled cities and chariots of iron had for him no terrors. Their defence was departed from them, but the Lord was with His believing follower, and made him strong to drive them out and take possession of their very stronghold as his own inheritance.

During this period of patient waiting, Mr. Müller remarked to a believing sister : "Well, my soul is at peace. The Lord's time is not yet come ; but, when it is come, He will blow away all these obstacles, as chaff is blown away before the wind." *A quarter of an hour later,* a gift of seven hundred pounds became available for the ends in view, so that three of the five hindrances to this Continental tour were at once removed. All travelling expenses for himself and wife, all necessary funds for the home work for two months in advance, and all costs of publishing the Narrative in German, were now provided. This was on July 12th ; and so soon afterward were the remaining impediments out of the way that, by August 9th, Mr. and Mrs. Müller were off for Germany.

The trip covered but seven months ; and on March 6, 1844, they were once more in Bristol. During this sojourn abroad no journal was kept, but Mr. Müller's letters serve the purpose of a record. Rotterdam, Weinheim, Cologne, Mayence, Stuttgart, Heidelberg, etc., were visited, and Mr. Müller distributed tracts and conversed with individuals by the way ; but his main work was to expound the Word in little assemblies of believers, who had separated themselves from the state church on account of what they deemed errors in teaching, practice, modes of worship, etc.

The first hour of his stay at Stuttgart brought to him one of the sharpest trials of faith he had ever thus far experienced. The nature of it he does not reveal in his journal, but it now transpires that it was due to the recalling of the seven hundred pounds, the gift of which had led to his going to Germany. This fact could not at the time be recorded because the party would feel it a reproach. Nor was this the only test of faith during his sojourn abroad ; in fact so many, so great, so varied, and so prolonged were some of these trials, as to call into full exercise all the wisdom and grace which he had received from God, and whatever lessons he had previously learned in the school of experience became now of use. Yet not only was his peace undisturbed, but he bears witness that the conviction so rooted itself in his inmost being that in all this God's goodness was being shown, that he would have had nothing different. The greatest trials bore fruit in the fullest blessings and sometimes in clusters of blessings. It particularly moved him to adoring wonder and praise to see God's wisdom in having delayed his visit until the very time when it occurred. Had he gone any earlier he would have gone too soon, lacking the full experience necessary to confront the perplexities of his work. When darkness seemed to obscure his way, faith kept him expectant of light, or at least of guidance in the darkness ; and he found that promise to be literally fulfilled :

" As thou goest, step by step, the way shall open up before thee." (See the Hebrew, of Prov. iv. 12.)

At Stuttgart he found and felt, like Jude, that it was " needful earnestly to contend for the faith once delivered to the saints." Even among believers, errors had found far too deep root. Especially was undue stress laid upon *baptism,* which was made to occupy a prominence and importance out of all due proportion of faith. One brother had been teaching that, without it, there is no new birth, and that, consequently, no one could, before baptism, claim the forgiveness of sins; that the apostles were not born from above until the day of Pentecost, and that our Lord Himself had not been new-born until His own baptism, and had thence, for the rest of His mortal life, ceased to be under the law! Many other fanciful notions were found to prevail, such as that baptism is the actual death of the old man by drowning, and that it is a covenant with the believer into which God enters; that it is a sin to break bread with unbaptized believers or with members of the state church; and that the bread and the cup used in the Lord's Supper not only *mean* but *are* the very body and blood of the Lord, etc.

A more serious and dangerous doctrine which it was needful to confront and confute was what Mr. Müller calls that "awful error," spread almost universally among believers in that land, that at last "all will be saved," not sinful men only, but "even the devil, themselves."

Calmly and courteously, but firmly and courageously, these and kindred errors were met with the plain witness of the Word. Refutation of false teaching aroused a spirit of bitterness in opposers of the truth, and, as is too often the case, faithful testimony was the occasion of acrimony; but the Lord stood by His servant and so strengthened him that he was kept both faithful and peaceful.

One grave practical lack which Mr. Müller sought to remedy was ignorance of those deeper truths of the Word, which relate to the power and presence of the Holy Spirit of God in the church, and to the ministry of saints, one to another, as fellow members in the body of Christ, and as those to whom that same Spirit divides severally, as

He will, spiritual gifts for service. As a natural result of being untaught in these important practical matters, believers' meetings had proved rather opportunities for unprofitable talk than godly edifying which is in faith. The only hope of meeting such errors and supplying such lack lay in faithful scripture teaching, and he undertook for a time to act as the sole teacher in these gatherings, that the word of God might have free course and be glorified. Afterward, when there seemed to be among the brethren some proper apprehension of vital spiritual truths, with his usual consistency and humility he resumed his place as simply a brother among fellow believers, all of whom had liberty to teach as the Spirit might lead and guide. There was, however, no shrinking from any duty or responsibility laid upon him by larger, clearer acquaintance with truth, or more complete experience of its power. When called by the voice of his brethren to expound the Word in public assemblies, he gladly embraced all opportunities for further instruction out of Holy Scripture and of witness to God. With strong emphasis he dwelt upon the presiding presence of the Blessed Spirit in all assemblies of saints, and upon the duty and privilege of leaving the whole conduct of such assemblies to His divine ordering; and in perfect accord with such teaching he showed that the Holy Spirit, if left free to administer all things, would lead such brethren to speak, at such times and on such themes as He might please; and that, whenever their desires and preferences were spiritual and not carnal, such choice of the Spirit would always be in harmony with their own.

These views of the Spirit's administration in the assemblies of believers, and of His manifestation in all believers for common profit, fully accord with scripture teaching. (1 Cor. xii., Romans xii., Ephes. iv., etc.)

Were such views practically held in the church of this day, a radical revolution would be wrought and a revival of apostolic faith and primitive church life would inevitably follow. No one subject is perhaps more misunderstood, or less understood, even among professed believers, than the person, offices, and functions of the Spirit of God. John Owen, long since, suggested that the practical test of soundness in the faith, during the present gospel age, is *the attitude of the church toward the Holy Spirit.* If so, the great apostasy cannot be far off, if indeed it is not already upon us, for there is a shameful ignorance and indifference prevalent, as to the whole matter of His claim to holy reverence and obedience.

In connection with this visit to Germany, a curious misapprehension existed, to which a religious periodical had given currency, that Mr. Müller was deputed by the English Baptists to labour among German Baptists to bring them back to the state church. This rumour was of course utterly unfounded, but he had no chance to correct it until just before his return to Britain, as he had not until then heard of it. The Lord had allowed this false report to spread and had used it to serve His own ends, for it was due in part to this wrong impression of Mr. Müller's mission that he was not molested or interfered with by the officers of the government. Though for months openly and undisguisedly teaching vital gospel truths among believers who had separated from the established church, he had suffered no restraint, for, so long as it was thought that his mission in Germany was to reclaim to the fold of the state church those who had wandered away, he would of course be liable to no interference from state officials.

The Lord went before His servant also in preparing the way for the publishing of his Narrative, guiding him to a bookseller who undertook its sale on commission, enabling the author to retain two thousand copies to give away, while the rest were left to be sold.

Mr. Müller, about this time, makes special mention of his joy and comfort in the spiritual blessing attending his work, and the present and visible good, wrought through the publication of his Narrative. Many believers had been led to put more faith in the promises of the great Provider, and unbelievers had been converted by their perusal of the simple story of the Lord's dealings; and these tidings came from every quarter where the Narrative had as yet found its way.

The name of Henry Craik, hitherto affixed to every report together with George Müller's, appears for the last time in the Report of 1844. This withdrawal of his name resulted, not from any division of feeling or diminution of sympathy, but solely from Mr. Craik's conviction that the honour of being used of God as His instrument in forwarding the great work of the Scriptural Knowledge Institution belonged solely to George Müller.

The trials of faith ceased not although the occasions of praise were so multiplied. On September 4, 1844, at day-dawn, but one farthing was left on hand, and one hundred and forty mouths were to be fed at breakfast!

The lack of money and such supplies was, however, only one form of these tests of faith and incentives to prayer. Indeed he accounted these the lightest of his burdens, for there were other cares and anxieties that called for greater exercise of faith resolutely to cast them on Him who, in exchange for solicitude, gives His own perfect peace. What these trials were, any thoughtful mind must at once see who remembers how these many orphans were needing, not only daily supplies of food and clothing, but education, in mind and in morals; preparation for, and location in, suitable homes; careful guards about their health and every possible precaution and provision to prevent disease; also the character of all helpers must be carefully investigated before they were admitted, and their conduct carefully watched afterward lest any unworthy or unqualified party should find a place, or be retained, in the conduct of the work.

These and other matters, too many to be individually mentioned, had to be borne daily to the great Helper, without whose Everlasting Arms they could not have been carried. And Mr. Müller seeks constantly to impress on all who read his pages or heard his voice, the perfect trustworthiness of God. For any and all needs of the work help was always given, and *it never once came too late.* However poor, and however long the suppliant believer waits on God, he never fails to get help, if he trusts the promises and is in the path of duty. Even the delay in answered prayer serves a purpose. God permits us to call on Him while He answers not a word, both to test our faith and importunity, and to encourage others who hear of His dealings with us.

And so it was that, whether there were on hand much or little, by God's grace the founder of these institutions remained untroubled, confident that deliverance would surely come in the best way and time, not only with reference to temporal wants, but in all things needful.

During the history of the Institution thus far, enlargement had been its law. Mr. Müller's heart grew in capacity for larger service, and his faith in capacity for firmer confidence, so that while he was led to attempt greater things for God, he was led also to expect greater things from God. Those suggestive words of Christ to Nathanael have often prompted like larger expectations: "Believest thou? thou shalt see greater things than these." (John i. 50.)

In the year 1846, *the wants of the mission field* took far deeper hold of him than ever before. He had already been giving aid to brethren abroad, in British Guiana and elsewhere, as well as in fields nearer at home. But he felt a strong yearning to be used of God more largely in sending to their fields and supporting in their labours, the chosen servants of the Lord who were working on a scriptural basis and were in need of help. He had observed that whenever God had put into his heart to devise liberal things, He had put into his hand the means to carry out such liberal purposes; and from this time forth he determined, as far as God should enable him, to aid brethren of good report, labouring in word and doctrine, throughout the United Kingdom, who were faithful witnesses to God and were receiving no regular salary. The special object he had in view was to give a helping hand to such as for the sake of conscience and of Christ had relinquished former stipends or worldly emoluments.

Whatever enlargement took place in the work, however, it was no sign of *surplus funds*. Every department of service or new call of duty had separate and prayerful consideration. Advance steps were taken only when and where and so fast as the Pillar moved, and fresh work was often undertaken at a time when there was a lack rather than an abundance of money.

Some who heard of Mr. Müller's absence in Germany inferred plenty of funds on hand—a conclusion that was neither true nor legitimate. At times when poverty was most pressing, additional expenditure was not avoided nor new responsibility evaded if, after much prayer, the Lord seemed plainly leading in that direction. And it was beautiful to see how He did not permit any existing work to be embarrassed because at His bidding new work was undertaken.

One great law for all who would be truly led by God's Pillar of cloud and fire, is to take no step at the bidding of self-will or without the clear moving of the heavenly Guide. Though the direction be new and the way seem beset with difficulty, there is never any risk, provided we are only led of God. Each new advance needs separate and special authority from Him, and yesterday's guidance is not sufficient for to-day.

It is important also to observe that, if one branch of the work is in straits, it is not necessarily a reason for abandoning another form of service. The work of God depends on Him alone. If the whole tree is His planting, we need not cut off one limb to save another. The whole body is His, and, if one member is weak, it is not necessary to cut off another to make it strong, for the strength of the whole body is the dependence of every part. In our many-branching service each must get vitality and vigour from the same source in God. Nevertheless let us not forget that the *stops*, as well as the *steps*, of a good man are ordered of the Lord. If the work is His work, let Him control it, and, whether we expand or contract, let it be at His bidding, and a matter of equal satisfaction to His servant.

CHAPTER XIV

GOD'S BUILDING: THE NEW ORPHAN HOUSES

How complex are the movements of God's providence ! Some events are themselves eventful. Like the wheels in Ezekiel's vision—a wheel in the middle of a wheel,— they involve other issues within their mysterious mechanism, and constitute epochs of history. Such an epochal event was the building of the first of the New Orphan Houses on Ashley Down.

After October, 1845, it became clear to Mr. Müller that the Lord was leading in this direction. Residents on Wilson Street had raised objections to the noise made by the children, especially in play hours; the playgrounds were no longer large enough for so many orphans; the drainage was not adequate, nor was the situation of the rented houses favourable, for proper sanitary conditions; it was also desirable to secure ground for cultivation, and thus supply outdoor work for the boys, etc. Such were some of the reasons which seemed to demand the building of a new orphan house ; and the conviction steadily gained ground that the highest well-being of all concerned would be largely promoted if a suitable site could be found on which to erect a building adapted to the purpose.

There were objections to building which were carefully weighed: money in large sums would be needed; planning and constructing would severely tax time and strength;

wisdom and oversight would be in demand at every stage
of the work; and the question arose whether such permanent structures befit God's pilgrim people, who have
here no continuing city and believe that the end of all
things is at hand.

Continuance in prayer, however, brought a sense of
quiet and restful conviction that all objections were over-
balanced by other and favourable considerations.   One
argument seemed particularly weighty: Should God provide large amounts of money for this purpose, it would still
further illustrate the power of prayer, offered in faith,
to command help from on high.   A lot of ground, spacious enough, would, at the outset, cost thousands of
pounds; but why should this daunt a true child of God
whose Father was infinitely rich ?   Mr. Müller and his
helpers sought day by day to be guided of God, and, as
faith fed on this daily bread of contact with Him, the
assurance grew strong that help would come.   Shortly
Mr. Müller was as sure of this as though the building
already stood before his eyes, though for five weeks not one
penny had been sent in for this purpose.   Meanwhile
there went on that searching scrutiny of his own heart
by which he sought to know whether any hidden motive
of a selfish sort was swaying his will; but as strict self-
examination brought to light no conscious purpose but to
glorify God, in promoting the good of the orphans, and
provoking to larger trust in God all who witnessed the
work, it was judged to be God's will that he should go
forward.

In November of this year, he was much encouraged
by a visit from a believing brother * who bade him go
on in the work, but wisely impressed on him the need

* Robert C. Chapman, of Barnstaple, yet living—and whom Mr.
Müller cherished as his "oldest friend."

of asking for wisdom from above, at every step, seeking God's help in showing him the *plan* for the building, that all details might accord with the divine mind. On the thirty-sixth day after specific prayer had first been offered about this new house, on December 10, 1845, Mr. Müller received *one thousand pounds* for this purpose, the largest sum yet received *in one donation* since the work had begun, March 5, 1834. Yet he was as calm and composed as though the gift had been only a shilling; having full faith in God, as both guiding and providing, he records that he would not have been surprised had the amount been five or ten times greater.

Three days later, a Christian architect in London voluntarily offered not only to draught the plans, but gratuitously to superintend the building! This offer had been brought about in a manner so strange as to be naturally regarded as a new sign and proof of God's approval and a fresh pledge of His sure help. Mr. Müller's sister-in-law, visiting the metropolis, had met this architect; and, finding him much interested to know more of the work of which he had read in the narrative, she had told him of the purpose to build; whereupon, without either solicitation or expectation on her part, this cheerful offer was made. Not only was this architect not urged by her, but he pressed his proposal, himself, urged on by his deep interest in the orphan work. Thus, within forty days, the first thousand pounds had been given in answer to prayer, and a pious man, as yet unseen and unknown by Mr. Müller, had been led to offer his services in providing plans for the new building and superintending its erection. Surely God was moving before His servant.

For a man, personally penniless, to attempt to erect such a house, on such a scale, without appeal to man and in sole dependence on God was no small venture of faith.

The full risk involved in such an undertaking, and the full force of the testimony which it has since afforded to a prayer-hearing God, can be felt only as the full weight of the responsibility is appreciated and all the circumstances are duly considered.

First of all, ground must be bought, and it must comprise six or seven acres, and the site must be in or near Bristol; for Mr. Müller's general sphere of work was in the city, the orphans and their helpers should be within reasonable reach of their customary meeting-place, and on many other accounts such nearness to the city was desirable. But such a site would cost from two thousand to three thousand pounds.

Next the building must be constructed, fitted up, and furnished, with accommodations for three hundred orphans and their overseers, teachers, and various helpers. However plain the building and its furnishings, the total cost would reach from three to four times the price of the site.

Then, the annual cost of keeping such house open and of maintaining such a large body of inmates would be four or five thousand pounds more.

Here, then, was a prospective outlay of somewhere between ten thousand and fifteen thousand pounds, for site and building, with a further expense of one third as much more every year. No man so poor as George Müller, if at the same time *sane*, would ever have *thought* of such a gigantic scheme, much less have undertaken to work it out, if his faith and hope were not fixed on God. Mr. Müller himself confesses that here lay his whole secret. He was not driven onward by any self-seeking, but drawn onward by a conviction that he was doing the will of God. When Constantine was laying out on a vast scale the new capital on the Bosphorus, he met the misgivings of those about him who wondered at his audacity, by simply saying, " I am following One who is leading me." George Müller's scheme was not self-originated. He followed One who was leading him; and, because confident and conscious of such guidance, he had only to follow, trust, and wait.

In proportion as the undertaking was great, he desired God's hand to be very clearly seen. Hence he forbore even to seem prominent: he issued no circular, announcing his purpose, and spoke of it only to the few who were in his councils, and even then only as conversation led in that direction. He remembered the promise, " I will guide thee with Mine eye," and looking up to God, he took no step unless the divine glance or beck made duty " clear as daylight." As he saw the matter, his whole business was to wait on God in prayer with faith and patience.

The assurance became doubly sure that *God would build for Himself* a large orphan house near Bristol, to show to all, near and far, what a blessed privilege it is to trust in Him. He desired God Himself so manifestly to act as that he should be seen by all men to be nothing but His instrument, passive in His hands. Meanwhile he went on with his daily search into the Word, where he found instruction so rich, and encouragement so timely, that the Scriptures seemed written for his special use—to convey messages to him from above. For example, in the opening of the Book of Ezra, he saw how God, when His time had fully come for the return of His exiled people to their own land and for the rebuilding of His Temple, used Cyrus, an idolatrous king, to issue an edict, and to provide means for carrying out His own unknown purpose. He saw also how God stirred up the people to help the returning exiles in their work; and he said to himself, this same God can and will, in His own way, supply the money and all the needed help of man, stirring up the hearts of His own children to aid as He may please.

The first donations toward the work themselves embody a suggestive lesson. On December 10th, one thousand pounds had been given in one sum; twenty days later, fifty pounds more; and the next day, three and sixpence, followed, the same evening, by a second gift of a thousand pounds. Shortly after, a little bag, made of foreign seeds, and a flower wrought of shells, were sent to be sold for the fund; and, in connection with these last gifts, of very little inherent value, a promise was quoted, which had been prominently before the giver's mind, and which brought more encouragement to Mr. Müller than any mere sum of money:

" Who art thou, O great mountain ?
Before Zerubbabel, thou shalt become a plain ! "
(Zech. iv. 7.)

Gifts, however large, were never estimated by intrinsic worth, but as tokens of God's working in the minds of His people, and of His gracious working with and through His servant; and, for this reason, a thousand pounds caused no more sincere praise to God and no more excitement of mind than the fourpence given subsequently by a poor orphan.

Specially asking the Lord to go before him, Mr. Müller now began to seek a suitable *site*. About four weeks passed in seemingly fruitless search, when he was strongly impressed that very soon the Lord would give the ground, and he so told his helpers on the evening of Saturday, January 31, 1846. Within two days, his mind was drawn to *Ashley Down*, where he found lots singularly suited for his needs. Shortly after, he called twice on the owner, once at his house and again at his office; but on both occasions failing to find him, he only left a message. He judged that God's hand was to be seen *even in his not finding the man he sought,* and that, having twice failed the same day, he was not to push the matter as though self-willed, but patiently wait till the morrow. When he did find the owner, his patience was unexpectedly rewarded. He confessed that he had spent two wakeful hours in bed, thinking about his land, and about what reply he should make to Mr. Müller's inquiry as to its sale for an orphan house; and that he had determined, if it were applied for, to ask but one hundred and twenty pounds an acre, instead of two hundred, his previous price.

The bargain was promptly completed; and thus the Lord's servant, by not being in a hurry, saved, in the purchase of the site of seven acres, five hundred and sixty pounds ! Mr. Müller had asked the Lord to go before him, and He had done so in a sense he had not thought of, first speaking about the matter to the owner, holding his eyes waking till He had made clear to him, as His servant and steward, what He would have him do in the sale of that property.*

Six days after, came the formal offer from the London architect of his services in surveying, in draughting plans, elevations, sections, and specifications, and in overseeing the work of construction; and a week later he came to Bristol, saw the site, and pronounced it in all respects well fitted for its purpose.

Up to June 4, 1846, the total sum in hand for the building was a little more than twenty-seven hundred pounds, a small part only of the sum needful; but Mr. Müller felt no doubt that in God's own time all that was required would be given. Two hundred and twelve days he had been waiting on God for the way to be opened for building, and he resolved to wait still further until the *whole sum* was in hand, using for the purpose only such gifts as were specified or left free for that end. He also wisely decided that others must henceforth share the burden, and that he would look out ten brethren of honest report, full of the Holy Ghost and of wisdom, to act as trustees to hold and administer this property in God's name. He felt that, as this work was now so enlarging, and the foundations of a permanent Institution were to be laid, the Christian public, who would aid in its erection and support, would be entitled to a representation in its conduct. At such a point as this many others have made a serious mistake, forfeiting confidence by administering public benefactions in a private manner and an autocratic spirit—their own head being the office, and their own pocket the treasury, of a public and benevolent institution.

Satan again acted as a hinderer. After the ground for the new orphan house had been found, bought and paid for, unforeseen obstacles prevented prompt possession; but Mr. Müller's peace was not disturbed, knowing even hindrances to be under God's control. If the Lord should allow one piece of land to be taken from him, it would only be because He was about to give him one still better; and so the delay only proved his faith and perfected his patience.

On July 6th, two thousand pounds were given—twice as large a gift as had yet come in one donation; and, on January 25, 1847, another like offering, so that, on July 5th following, the work of building began. Six months later, after four hundred days of waiting upon God for this new orphan house, nine thousand pounds had been given in answer to believing prayer.

As the new building approached completion, with its three hundred large windows, and requiring full preparation for the accommodation of about three hundred and thirty inmates, although above eleven thousand pounds had been provided, several thousand more were necessary. But Mr. Müller was not only helped, but far beyond his largest expectations. Up to May 26, 1848, these latter needs existed, and, had but *one* serious difficulty remained unremoved, the result must have been failure. But all the necessary money was obtained, and even more, and all the helpers were provided for the oversight of the orphans.

On June 18, 1849, more than twelve years after the beginning of the work, the orphans began to be transferred from the four rented houses on Wilson Street to the new orphan house on Ashley Down. Five weeks passed before fresh applicants were received, that everything about the new institution might first be brought into complete order by some experience in its conduct. By May 26, 1850, however, there were in the house two hundred and seventy-five children, and the whole number of inmates was three hundred and eight.

The name—"The New Orphan *House*," rather than "*Asylum*"—was chosen to distinguish it from another institution, near by ; and particularly was it requested that it might never be known as "*Mr. Müller's* Orphan House," lest undue prominence be given to one who had been merely God's instrument in its erection. He esteemed it a sin to appropriate even indirectly, or allow others to attribute to him, any part of the glory which belonged solely to Him who had led in the work, given faith and means for it, and helped in it from first to last.

The property was placed in the hands of eleven trustees, chosen by Mr. Müller, and the deeds were enrolled in chancery. Arrangements were made that the house should be open to visitors only on Wednesday afternoons, as about one hour and a half were necessary to see the whole building.

Scarcely were the orphans thus housed on Ashley Down, before Mr. Müller's heart felt enlarged desire that *one thousand,* instead of three hundred, might enjoy such privileges of temporal provision and spiritual instruction ; and, before the new year, 1851, had dawned, this yearning had matured into a purpose. With his uniform carefulness and prayerfulness, he sought to be assured that he was not following self-will, but the will of God; and again in the scales of a pious judgment the reasons for and against were conscientiously weighed. Would he be going ' beyond his measure,' spiritually, or naturally ? Was not the work, with its vast correspondence and responsibility, already sufficiently great ? Would not a new orphan house for three hundred orphans cost another fifteen thousand pounds, or, if built for seven hundred, with the necessary ground, thirty-five thousand ? And, even when built and fitted and filled, would there not be the providing for daily wants, which is a perpetual care, and cannot be paid for at once like a site and a building ? It would demand eight thousand pounds annual outlay to provide for another seven hundred little ones. To all objections the one all-sufficient answer was the all-sufficient God ; and, because Mr. Müller's eye was on His power, wisdom, and riches, his own weakness, folly, and poverty were forgotten.

Another objection was suggested : What if he should succeed in thus housing and feeding a thousand poor waifs, what would become of the institution *after his death ?* The reply is memorable : " My business is, with all my might, to *serve my own generation by the will of God:* in so doing I shall best serve the next generation, should the Lord Jesus tarry." Were such objection valid, it were as valid against beginning any work likely to outlive the worker. And Mr. Müller remembered how Francké at Halle had to meet the same objection when, now over two hundred years ago, he founded the largest charitable establishment which, up to 1851, existed in the world. But when, after about thirty years of personal superintendence, Francké was taken away, his son-in-law, as we have seen, became the director. That fellow countryman who had spoken to Mr. Müller's soul in 1826, thus twenty-five years later encouraged him to go forward, to do his own duty and leave the future to the Eternal God.

Several reasons are recorded by Mr. Müller as specially influencing still further advance : the many applications that could not, for want of room, be accepted ; the low moral state of the poorhouses to which these children of poverty were liable to be sent ; the large number of distressing cases of orphanhood, known to be deserving of help ; the previous experiences of the Lord's gracious leading and of the work itself ; his calmness in view of the proposed expansion; and the spiritual blessing possible to a larger number of homeless children. But one reason overtopped all others : an enlarged service to man, attempted and achieved solely in dependence upon God, would afford a correspondingly weightier witness to the Hearer of prayer. These reasons, here recorded, will need no repetition in connection with subsequent expansions of the work, for, at every new stage of advance, they were what influenced this servant of God.

On January 4, 1851, another offering was received, of three thousand pounds—the largest single donation up to that date—which, being left entirely to his own disposal, encouraged him to go forward.

Again, he kept his own counsel. Up to January 25th, he had not mentioned, even to his own wife, his thought of a further forward movement, feeling that, to avoid all mistakes, he must first of all get clear light from God, and not darken it by misleading human counsel. Not until the Twelfth Report of the Scriptural Knowledge Institution was issued, was the public apprised of 'his purpose, with God's help to provide for seven hundred more needy orphans.

Up to October 2, 1851, only about eleven hundred pounds had been given directly toward the second proposed orphan house, and, up to May 26th following, a total of some thirty-five hundred pounds. But George Müller remembered one who, " after he had patiently endured, obtained the promise." He had waited over two years before all means needful for the first house had been supplied, and could wait still longer, if so God willed it, for the answers to present prayers for means to build a second.

After waiting upwards of nineteen months for the building fund for the second house, and receiving, almost daily, something in answer to prayer, on January 4, 1853, he had intimation that there were about to be paid him, as *the joint donation of several Christians, eighty-one hundred pounds*, of which he appropriated six thousand for the building fund. Again he was not surprised nor excited, though exceeding joyful and triumphant in God. Just two years previous, when recording the largest donation yet received,—three thousand pounds,—he had recorded also his expectation of still greater things ; and now a donation between two and three times as large was about to come into his hands. It was not the amount of money, however, that gave him his overflowing delight, but the fact that not in vain had he made his boast in God.

As now some four hundred and eighty-three orphans were waiting for admission, he was moved to pray that soon the way might be opened for the new building to be begun. James i. 4 was deeply impressed upon him as the injunction now to be kept before him : " But let patience have her perfect work, that ye may be perfect and entire, wanting nothing."

On May 26, 1853, the total sum available for the new building was about twelve thousand five hundred pounds, and over five hundred orphans had applied. Twice this sum would be needed, however, before the new house could be begun without risk of debt.

On January 8, 1855, several Christian friends united in the promise that fifty-seven hundred pounds should be paid to him for the work of God, and of this, thirty-four hundred was by him set apart for the building fund. As there were now between seven hundred and eight hundred applicants, it seemed of God that, at least, a site should be secured for another new orphan house; and a few weeks later Mr. Müller applied for the purchase of two fields adjoining the site of the first house. As they could not, however, be sold at that time, the only resource was to believe that the Lord had other purposes, or would give better ground than that on which His servant had set his mind.

Further thought and prayer suggested to him that two houses could be built instead of one, and located on each side of the existing building, upon the ground already owned. Accordingly it was determined to begin, on the south side, the erection of a house to accommodate four hundred orphans, there being money in the bank, or soon to be available, sufficient to build, fit up, and furnish it.

On May 26, 1856, nearly thirty thousand pounds were in hand for the new Orphan House No. 2; and on November 12, 1857, this house was opened for four hundred additional orphans, and there was a balance of nearly twenty-three hundred pounds. The God who provided the building furnished the helpers, without either difficulty or advertising.

With the beginning of the new year, Mr. Müller began to lay aside six hundred pounds as the first of the appropriations for the *third* orphan house, and the steps which led to the accomplishment of this work, also, were identical with those taken hitherto. A purchase was made of additional ground, adjoining the two buildings ; and, as there were so many applicants and the cost of providing for a larger number would be but little more, it was determined to build so as to receive four hundred and fifty instead of three hundred, rejoicing that, in every enlargement of the work, it would be more apparent how much one poor man, simply trusting in God, can bring about by prayer ; and that thus other children of God might be led to carry on the work of God in dependence solely on Him, and generally to trust Him more in all circumstances and positions.

Orphan House No. 3 was opened March 12, 1862, and with over ten thousand pounds in hand for current expenses. All the helpers needed had not then been supplied, but this delay was only a new incentive to believing prayer : and, instead of *once, thrice,* a day, God was besought to provide suitable persons. One after another was thus added, and in no case too late, so that the reception of children was not hindered nor was the work embarrassed.

Still further enlargement seemed needful, for the same reasons as previously. There was an increasing demand for accommodation of new applicants, and past experience of God's wondrous dealings urged him both to attempt and to expect greater things. Orphan Houses Nos. 4 and 5 began to loom up above his horizon of faith. By May 26, 1862, he had over sixty-six hundred pounds to

apply on their erection. In November, 1864, a large donation of five thousand pounds was received from a donor
who would let neither his name nor residence be known,
and by this time about twenty-seven thousand pounds
had thus accumulated toward the fifty thousand required.

As more than half the requisite sum was thus in hand,
the purchase of a site might safely be made and the
foundations for the buildings be laid. Mr. Müller's eyes
had, for years, been upon land adjoining the three houses
already built, separated from them only by the turnpike
road. He called to see the agent, and found that the
property was subject to a lease that had yet two years to
run. This obstacle only incited to new prayer, but difficulties seemed to increase : the price asked was too high,
and the Bristol Water-works Company was negotiating for
this same piece of land for reservoir purposes. Nevertheless God successively removed all hindrances, so that the
ground was bought and conveyed to the trustees in March,
1865 ; and, after the purchase-money was paid, about
twenty-five thousand pounds yet remained for the structures. Both the cost and the inconvenience of building
would be greatly lessened by erecting both houses at the
same time ; and God was therefore asked for ample means
speedily to complete the whole work.

In May, 1866, over thirty-four thousand pounds being
at Mr. Müller's disposal, No. 4 was commenced ; and in
January following, No. 5 also. Up to the end of March,
1867, over fifty thousand pounds had been supplied, leaving but six thousand more needful to fit and furnish the
two buildings for occupancy. By the opening of February,
1868, fifty-eight thousand pounds in all had been donated;
so that, on November 5, 1868, new Orphan House No. 4,
and on January 6, 1870, No. 5, were thrown open, a balance of several thousand pounds remaining for general

purposes. Thus, early in 1870, the orphan work had reached its complete outfit, in five large buildings on Ashley Down with accommodations for two thousand orphans and for all needed teachers and assistants.

Thus have been gathered, into one chapter, the facts about the erection of this great monument to a prayer-hearing God on Ashley Down, though the work of building covered so many years. Between the first decision to build, in 1845, and the opening of the third house, in 1862, nearly seventeen years had elapsed, and before No. 5 was opened, in 1870, twenty-five years. The work was one in its plan and purpose. At each new stage it supplies only a wider application and illustration of the same laws of life and principles of conduct, as, from the outset of the work in Bristol, had with growing power controlled George Müller. His one supreme aim was the glory of God ; his one sole resort, believing prayer; his one trusted oracle, the inspired Word ; and his one divine Teacher, the Holy Spirit. One step taken in faith and prayer had prepared for another ; one act of trust had made him bolder to venture upon another, implying a greater apparent risk and therefore demanding more implicit trust. But answered prayer was rewarded faith, and every new risk only showed that there was no risk in confidently leaning upon the truth and faithfulness of God.

One cannot but be impressed, in visiting the orphan houses, with several prominent features, and first of all their magnitude. They are very spacious, with about seventeen hundred large windows, and accommodations for over two thousand inmates. They are also very substantial, being built of stone and made to last. They are scrupulously plain; utility rather than beauty seems conspicuously stamped upon them, within and without. Economy has been manifestly a ruling law in their construction ; the furniture is equally unpretentious and unostentatious ; and, as to garniture, there is absolutely none. To some few, they are almost too destitute of embellishment, and Mr. Müller has been blamed for not introducing some æsthetic features which might relieve this bald utilitarianism and serve to educate the taste of these orphans.

To all such criticisms, there are two or three adequate answers. First, Mr. Müller subordinated everything to his one great purpose, the demonstration of the fact that the Living God is the Hearer of prayer. Second, he felt himself to be the steward of God's property, and he hesitated to spend one penny on what was not necessary to the frugal carrying on of the work of God. He felt that all that could be spared without injury to health, a proper mental training, and a thorough scriptural and spiritual education, should be reserved for the relief of the necessities of the poor and destitute elsewhere. And again, he felt that, as these orphans were likely to be put at service in plain homes, and compelled to live frugally, any surroundings which would accustom them to indulge refined tastes, might by contrast make them discontented with their future lot. And so he studied to promote simply their health and comfort, and to school them to contentment when the necessities of life were supplied.

But, more than this, a moment's serious thought will show that, had he surrounded them with those elegancies which elaborate architecture and the other fine arts furnish, he might have been even more severely criticised. He would have been spending the gifts of the poor who often sorely denied themselves for the sake of these orphans, to purchase embellishments or secure decorations which, if they had adorned the humble homes of thousands of donors, would have made their gifts impossible.

When we remember how many offerings, numbering tens
of thousands, were, like the widow's mites, very small in
themselves, yet, relatively to ability, very large, it will be
seen how incongruous it would have been to use the gifts,
saved only by limiting even the wants of the givers, to buy
for the orphans what the donors could not and would not
afford for themselves.

Cleanness, neatness, method, and order, however, everywhere reign, and honest labour has always had, at the
orphan houses, a certain dignity. The tracts of land, adjoining the buildings, are set apart as vegetable-gardens,
where wholesome exercise is provided for the orphan boys,
and, at the same time, work that helps to provide daily
food, and thus train them in part to self-support.

Throughout these houses studious care is exhibited, as
to methodical arrangement. Each child has a square and
numbered compartment for clothes, six orphans being
told off, at a time, in each section, to take charge. The
boys have each three suits, and the girls, five dresses each,
the girls being taught to make and mend their own garments. In the nursery, the infant children have books and
playthings to occupy and amuse them, and are the objects
of tender maternal care. Several children are often admitted to the orphanage from one family, in order to avoid
needless breaking of household ties by separation. The
average term of residence is about ten years, though some
orphans have been there for seventeen.

The daily life is laid out with regularity and goes on
like clockwork in punctuality. The children rise at six
and are expected to be ready at seven, the girls for knitting
and the boys for reading, until eight o'clock, when breakfast is served. Half an hour later there is a brief morning
service, and the school begins at ten. Half an hour of
recreation on the playground prepares for the one-o'clock

dinner, and school is resumed, until four ; then comes an hour and a half of play or outdoor exercise, a half-hour service preceding the six-o'clock meal. Then the girls ply the needle, and the boys are in school, until bedtime, the younger children going to rest at eight, and the older, at nine. The food is simple, ample, and nutritious, consisting of bread, oatmeal, milk, soups, meat, rice, and vegetables. Everything is adjusted to one ultimate end ; to use Mr. Müller's own words : " We aim at this : that, if any of them do not turn out well, temporally or spiritually, and do not become useful members of society, it shall not at least be *our* fault." The most thorough and careful examination of the whole methods of the institution will only satisfy the visitor that it will not be the fault of those who superintend this work, if the orphans are not well fitted, body and soul, for the work of life, and are not prepared for a blessed immortality.

CHAPTER XV

THE MANIFOLD GRACE OF GOD

Some one has quaintly said, in commenting upon the Twenty-third Psalm, that " the coach in which the Lord's saints ride has not only a driver, but two footmen "— " *goodness and mercy shall follow me.*"

Surely these two footmen of the Lord, in their celestial livery of grace, followed George Müller all the days of his life. Wonderful as is the story of the building of those five orphan houses on Ashley Down, many other events and experiences no less showed the goodness and mercy of God, and must not be unrecorded in these pages, if we are to trace, however imperfectly, His gracious dealings ; and having, by one comprehensive view, taken in the story of the orphan homes, we may retrace our steps to the year when the first of these houses was planned, and, following another path, look at Mr. Müller's personal and domestic life.

He himself loved to trace the Lord's goodness and mercy, and he saw abundant proofs that they had followed him. A few instances may be given, from different departments of experience, as representative examples.

The Lord's tender care was manifest as to his beloved daughter Lydia. It became clear in the year 1843, that, both for the relief of the mother and the profit of the daughter, it would be better that Lydia should be taught elsewhere than at home : and in answer to prayer, her father

was divinely directed to a Christian sister, whose special
gifts in the way of instructing and training children were
manifestly from the Spirit, who divides unto all believers
severally as He will. She seemed to be marked of God, as
the woman to whom was to be intrusted the responsible
task of superintending the education of Lydia. Mr. Müller both expected and desired to pay for such training, and
asked for the account, which in the first instance he paid,
but the exact sum was returned to him anonymously ;
and, for the six remaining years of his daughter's stay, he
could get no further bills for her schooling. Thus God
provided for the board and education of this only child,
not only without cost to her parents, but to their intense
satisfaction as being under the true " nurture and admonition of the Lord;" for while at this school, in April, 1846,
Lydia found peace in believing, and began that beautiful
life in the Lord Jesus Christ, that, for forty-four years
afterward, so singularly exhibited His image.

Many Christian parents have made the fatal mistake
of intrusting their children's education to those whose
gifts were wholly intellectual and not spiritual, and who
have misled the young pupils entrusted to their care, into
an irreligious or infidel life, or, at best, a career of mere
intellectualism and worldly ambition. In not a few instances, all the influences of a pious home have been
counteracted by the atmosphere of a school which, if not
godless, has been without that fragrance of spiritual de-
voutness and consecration which is indispensable to the
true training of impressible children during the plastic
years when character is forming for eternity !

Goodness and mercy followed Mr. and Mrs. Müller conspicuously in their sojourn in Germany in 1845, which
covered about three months, from July 19th to October
11th.

God plainly led to Stuttgart, where brethren had fallen into grievous errors and needed again a helping hand. When the strong impression laid hold of Mr. Müller, more than two months before his departure for the Continent, that he was to return there for a season, he began definitely to pray for means to go with, on May 3rd, and, within a *quarter hour* after, five hundred pounds were received, the donor specifying that the money was given for all expenses needful, " preparatory to, and attendant upon " this proposed journey. The same goodness and mercy followed all his steps while abroad. Provision was made, in God's own strange way, for suitable lodgings in Stuttgart, at a time when the city was exceptionally crowded, a wealthy retired surgeon, who had never before rented apartments, being led to offer them. All Mr. Müller's labours were attended with blessing : during part of the time he held as many as eight meetings a week ; and he was enabled to publish eleven tracts in German, and judiciously to scatter over two hundred and twenty thousand of them, as well as nearly four thousand of his Narrative, and yet evade interference from the police.

One experience of this sojourn abroad should have special mention for the lesson it suggests, both in charity for others' views and loving adaptation to circumstances. A providential opening occurred to address meetings of about one hundred and fifty members of the state church. In his view the character of such assemblies was not wholly conformed to the Scripture pattern, and hence did not altogether meet his approval ; but such opportunity was afforded to bear testimony for the truth's sake, and to exhibit Christian unity upon essentials, for love's sake, that he judged it of the Lord that he should enter this open door. Those who knew Mr. Müller but little, but knew his positive convictions and uncompromising loyalty

to them, might suspect that he would have little forbearance with even minor errors, and would not bend
himself from his stern attitude of inflexibility to accommodate himself to those who were ensnared by them.
But those who knew him better, saw that he held fast the
form of sound words with faith and love which are in
Christ Jesus. Like Paul, ever ready to be made all things
to all men that by all means he might save some, in his
whole character and conduct nothing shone, more radiantly beautiful, than Love. He felt that he who would
lift up others must bow himself to lay hold on them ;
that to help brethren we must bear with them, not in-
sisting upon matters of minor importance as though they
were essential and fundamental. Hence his course, instead of being needlessly repellant, was tenderly concilia-
tory ; and it was a conspicuous sign of grace that, while
holding his own views of truth and duty so positively and
tenaciously, the intolerance of bigotry was so displaced
by the forbearance of charity that, when the Lord so led
and circumstances so required, he could conform for a
time to customs whose propriety he doubted, without
abating either the earnestness of his conviction or the
integrity of his testimony.

God's goodness and mercy were seen in the fact that,
whenever more liberal things were devised for Him, He
responded in providing liberally means to carry out such
desires. This was abundantly illustrated not only in the
orphan work, but in the history of the Scriptural Knowledge Institution; when, for years together, the various
branches of this work grew so rapidly, until the point of
full development was reached. The time indeed came
when, in some departments, it pleased God that contraction should succeed expansion, but even here goodness
ruled, for it was afterward seen that it was because *other*

brethren had been led to take up such branches of the Lord's work, in all of which developments Mr. Müller as truly rejoiced as though it had been his work alone that was honoured of God.

The aiding of brethren in the mission fields grew more and more dear to his heart, and the means to indulge his unselfish desires were so multiplied that, in 1846, he found, on reviewing the history of the Lord's dealings, that he had been enabled to expend about *seven times* as much of late years as previously. It may here be added, again by way of anticipation, that when, nineteen years later, in 1865, he sat down to apportion to such labourers in the Lord as he was wont to assist, the sums he felt it desirable to send to each, he found before him the names of *one hundred and twenty-two* such! Goodness and mercy indeed! Here was but one branch of his work, and yet to what proportions and fruitfulness it had grown! He needed four hundred and sixty-six pounds to send them to fill out his appropriations, and he lacked ninety-two of this amount. He carried the lack to the Lord, and *that evening* received five pounds, and the *next morning* a hundred more, and a further "birthday memorial" of fifty, so that he had in all thirty-seven more than he had asked.

What goodness and mercy followed him in the strength he ever had to bear the heavy loads of care incident to his work! The Lord's coach bore him and his burdens together. Day by day his gracious Master preserved his peace unbroken, though disease found its way into this large family, though fit homes and work must be found for outgoing orphans, and fit care and training for incoming orphans; though crises were constantly arising and new needs constantly recurring, grave matters daily demanded prayer and watching, and perpetual diligence and vigilance were needful; for the Lord was his Helper, and carried all his loads.

During the winter of 1846–7 there was a peculiar season of dearth. Would God's goodness and mercy fail? There were those who looked on, more than half incredulous, saying to themselves if not to others, "I wonder how it is *now* with Mr. Müller and his orphans! If he is able to provide for them now as he has been, we will say nothing." But all through this time of widespread want his witness was, "We lack nothing: God helps us." Faith led when the way was too dark for sight; in fact the darker the road the more was the Hand felt that leads the blind by a way they know not. *They went through that winter as easily as through any other from the beginning of the work!*

Was it no sign that God's 'footmen' followed George Müller that the work never ceased to be both a work of faith and of prayer? that no difficulties or discouragements, no successes or triumphs, ever caused for an hour a departure from the sublime essential principles on which the work was based, or a diversion from the purpose for which it had been built up?

We have heard it said of a brother, much honoured of God in beginning a work of faith, that, when it had grown to greater proportions, he seemed to change its base to that of a business scheme. How it glorifies God that the holy enterprise, planted in Bristol in 1834, has known no such alteration in its essential features during all these years! Though the work grew, and its needs with it, until the expenses were twofold, threefold, fourfold, and, at last, seventyfold what they were when that first Orphan House was opened in Wilson Street, there has been no *change of base*, never any looking to man for patronage or support, never any dependence upon a regular income or fixed endowment. God has been, all through these years, as at first, the sole Patron and Dependence. The Scriptural Knowledge Institution has not been wrecked on the rocks of financial failure, nor has it even drifted away from its original moorings in the safe anchorage-ground of the Promises of Jehovah.

Was it not goodness and mercy that kept George Müller ever grateful as well as faithful! He did not more constantly feel his need of faith and prayer than his duty and privilege of abounding joy and praise. Some might think that, after such experiences of answered prayer, one would be less and less moved by them, as the novelty was lost in the uniformity of such interpositions. But no. When, in June, 1853, at a time of sore need, the Lord sent, in one sum, three hundred pounds, he could scarcely contain his triumphant joy in God. He walked up and down his room for a long time, his heart overflowing and his eyes too, his mouth filled with laughter and his voice with song, while he gave himself afresh to the faithful Master he served. God's blessings were to him always new and fresh. Answered prayers never lost the charm of novelty; like flowers plucked fresh every hour from the gardens of God, they never got stale, losing none of their beauty or celestial fragrance.

And what goodness and mercy was it that never suffered prayerfulness and patience to relax their hold, either when answers seemed to come fast and thick like snowflakes, or when the heavens seemed locked up and faith had to wait patiently and long! Every day brought new demands for continuance in prayer. In fact, as Mr. Müller testifies, the only difference between latter and former days was that the difficulties were greater in proportion as the work was larger. But he adds that this was to be expected, for the Lord gives faith for the very purpose of trying it for the glory of His own name and the good of him who has the faith, and it is by these very trials that trust learns the secret of its triumphs.

Goodness and mercy not only guided but also *guarded* this servant of God. God's footmen bore a protecting shield which was always over him. Amid thousands of unseen perils, occasionally some danger was known, though generally after it was passed. While at Keswick labouring in 1847, for example, a man, taken deranged while lodging in the same house, shot himself. It afterward transpired that he had an impression that Mr. Müller had designs on his life, and had he met Mr. Müller during this insane attack he would probably have shot him with the loaded pistol he carried about on his person.

The pathway of this man of God sometimes led through deep waters of affliction, but goodness and mercy still followed, and held him up. In the autumn of 1852, his beloved brother-in-law, Mr. A. N. Groves, came back from the East Indies, very ill; and in May of the next year, after blessed witness for God, he fell asleep at Mr. Müller's house. To him Mr. Müller owed much through grace at the outset of his labours in 1829. By his example his faith had been stimulated and helped when, with no visible support or connection with any missionary society, Mr. Groves had gone to Bagdad with wife and children, for the sake of mission work in this far-off field, resigning a lucrative practice of about fifteen hundred pounds a year. The tie between these men was very close and tender and the loss of this brother-in-law gave keen sorrow.

In July following, Mr. and Mrs. Müller went through a yet severer trial. Lydia, the beloved daughter and only child,—born in 1832 and new-born in 1846, and at this time twenty years old and a treasure without price,—was taken ill in the latter part of June, and the ailment developed into a malignant typhoid which, two weeks later, brought her to the gates of death. These parents had to face the prospect of being left childless. But faith triumphed and prayer prevailed. Their darling Lydia was spared to be, for many years to come, a blessing beyond words, not only to them and to her future husband, but to many others in a wider circle of influence. Mr. Müller found, in this trial, a special proof of God's goodness and mercy, which he gratefully records, in the growth in grace, evidenced in his entire and joyful acquiescence in the Father's will, when, with such a loss apparently before him, his confidence was undisturbed that all things would work together for good. He could not but contrast with this experience of serenity, that broken peace and complaining spirit with which he had met a like trial in August, 1831, twenty-one years before, How, like a magnet among steel filings, the thankful heart finds the mercies and picks them out of the black dust of sorrow and suffering !

The second volume of Mr. Müller's Narrative closes with a paragraph in which he formally disclaims as impudent presumption and pretension all high rank as a miracle-worker, and records his regret that any work, based on scriptural promises and built on the simple lines of faith and prayer, should be accounted either phenomenal or fanatical.

The common ways of accounting for its success would be absurdly ridiculous and amusing were they not so sadly unbelieving. Those who knew little or nothing, either of the exercise of faith or the experience of God's faithfulness, resorted to the most God-dishonouring explanations of the work. Some said: " Mr. Müller is a foreigner; his methods are so novel as to attract attention." Others thought that the " Annual Reports brought in the money," or suggested that he had "a secret treasure." His quiet reply was, that his being a foreigner would be more likely to repel than to attract confidence; that the novelty would scarcely avail him after more than a score of years; that other institutions which issued reports did not always escape want and debt ; but, as to the *secret treasure* to which he was supposed to have access, he felt constrained to confess that there was *more in that supposition than the objectors were aware of.* He had indeed a Treasury, inexhaustible—in the promises of a God unchangeably faithful—from which he admits that he had already in 1856 drawn for twenty-two years, and in all over one hundred and thirteen thousand pounds. As to the Reports, it may be worth while to notice that he never but once in his life advertised the public of any need, and that was the *need of more orphans*—more to care for in the name of the Lord—a single and singular case of advertising, by which he sought not to increase his *income,* but his *expenditure*—not asking the public to aid him in supporting the needy, but to increase the occasion of his outlay !

So far was he from depending upon any such sources of supply as the unbelieving world might think, that it was in the drying up of all such channels that he found the opportunity of his faith and of God's power. The visible treasure was often so small that it was reduced to nothing, but the invisible Treasure was God's Riches in glory, and could be drawn from without limit. This it was to which he looked alone, and in which he felt that he had a river of supply that can never run dry.*

The orphan work had, to Mr. Müller, many charms which grew on him as he entered more fully into it. While his main hope was to be the means of spiritual health to these children, he had the joy of seeing how God used these homes for the promotion of their physical welfare also, and, in cases not a few, for the entire renovation of their weak and diseased bodies. It must be remembered that most of them owed their orphan condition to that great destroyer, Consumption. Children were often brought to the orphan houses thoroughly permeated by the poison of bad blood, with diseased tendencies, and sometimes emaciated and half-starved, having had neither proper food nor medical care.

For example, in the spring of 1855, four children from five to nine years old, and of one family, were admitted to the orphanage, all in a deplorable state from lack of both nursing and nutrition. It was a serious question whether they should be admitted at all, as such cases tended to turn the institution into a hospital, and absorb undue care and time. But to dismiss them seemed almost inhuman, certainly *inhumane*. So, trusting in God, they were taken in and cared for with parental love. A few weeks later these children were physically unrecognizable, so rapid had been the improvement in health, and probably there were with God's blessing four graves less to be dug.

The trials incident to the moral and spiritual condition of the orphans were even greater, however, than those caused by ill health and weakness. When children proved incorrigibly bad, they were expelled, lest they should corrupt others, for the institution was not a *reformatory*, as it was not a *hospital*. In 1849, a boy, of less than eight years, had to be sent away as a confirmed liar and thief, having twice run off with the belongings of other children and gloried in his juvenile crimes. Yet the forbearance exercised even in his case was marvellously godlike, for, during over five years, he had been the subject of private admonitions and prayers and all other methods of reclamation; and, when expulsion became the last resort, he was solemnly and with prayer, before all the others, sent away from the orphan house, that if possible such a course might prove a double blessing, a remedy to him and a warning to others; and even then this young practised sinner was followed, in his expulsion, by loving supplication.

Towards the end of November, 1857, it was found that a serious leak in the boiler of the heating apparatus of house No. 1 would make repairs at once necessary, and as the boilers were encased in bricks and a new boiler might be required, such repairs must consume time. Meanwhile how could three hundred children, some of them very young and tender, be kept warm? Even if gas-stoves could be temporarily set up, chimneys would be needful to carry off the impure air : and no way of heating was available during repairs, even if a hundred pounds were expended to prevent risk of cold. Again Mr. Müller turned to the Living God, and, trusting in Him, decided to have the repairs begun. A day or so before the fires had to be put out, a bleak north wind set in. The work could no longer be delayed ; yet weather, prematurely cold for the season, threatened these hundreds of children with hurtful exposure. The Lord was boldly appealed to. " Lord, these are *Thy* orphans : be pleased to change this north wind into a south wind, and give the workmen a mind to work that the job may be speedily done."

The evening before the repairs actually began, the cold blast was still blowing ; but *on that day a south wind blew, and the weather was so mild that no fire was needful!* Not only so, but, as Mr. Müller went into the cellar with the overseer of the work, to see whether the repairs could in no way be expedited, he heard him say, in the hearing of the men, "they will work late this evening, and come very early again to-morrow." "*We would rather, sir,*" was the reply, "*work all night.*" And so, within about thirty hours, the fire was again burning to heat the water in the boiler; and, until the apparatus was again in order, that merciful soft south wind had continued to blow. Goodness and mercy were following the Lord's humble servant, made the more conspicuous by the crises of special trial and trouble.

Every new exigency provoked new prayer and evoked new faith. When, in 1862, several boys were ready to be apprenticed, and there were no applications such as were desired, prayer was the one resort, as advertising would tend to bring applications from masters who sought apprentices for the sake of the premium. But every one of the eighteen boys was properly bound over to a Christian master, whose business was suitable and who would receive the lad into his own family.

About the same time one of the drains was obstructed which runs about eleven feet underground. When three holes had been dug and as many places in the drain tapped in vain, prayer was offered that in the fourth case the workmen might be guided to the very spot where the stoppage existed—and the request was literally answered.

Three instances of marked deliverance, in answer to prayer, are specially recorded for the year between May 26, 1864, and the same date in 1865, which should not be passed by without at least a mention.

First, in the great drought of the summer of 1864, when the fifteen large cisterns in the three orphan houses were empty, and the nine deep wells, and even the good spring which had never before failed, were almost all dry. Two or three thousand gallons of water were daily required, and daily prayer was made to the God of the rain. See how God provided, while pleased to withhold the supply from above ! A farmer, near by, supplied, from his larger wells, about half the water needful, the rest being furnished by the half-exhausted wells on Ashley Down; and, when he could no longer spare water, without a day's interval, another farmer offered a supply from a brook which ran through his fields, and thus there was abundance until the rains replenished cisterns and wells.*

Second, when, for three years, scarlet and typhus fevers and smallpox, being prevalent in Bristol and the vicinity, threatened the orphans, prayer was again made to Him who is the God of health as well as of rain. There was no case of scarlet or typhus fever during the whole time, though smallpox was permitted to find an entrance into the smallest of the orphan houses. Prayer was still the one resort. The disease spread to the other houses, until at one time fifteen were ill with it. The cases, however, were mercifully light, and the Lord was besought to allow the epidemic to spread *no further*. Not another child was taken ; and when, after nine months, the disease altogether disappeared, not one child had died of it, and only one teacher or adult had had an attack, and that was very mild. What ravages the disease might have made among the twelve hundred inmates of these orphan houses, had it then prevailed as later, in 1872 !

Third, tremendous gales visited Bristol and neighbourhood in January, 1865. The roofs of the orphan houses were so injured as to be laid open in at least twenty places, and large panes of glass were broken. The day was Saturday, and no glazier and slater could be had before Monday. So the Lord of wind and weather was besought to protect the exposed property during the interval. The wind calmed down, and the rain was restrained until

---

* About twenty years later the Bristol Water Works Co. introduced pipes and thus a permanent and unfailing supply.

midday of Wednesday, when the repairs were about finished, but heavy rainfalls drove the slaters from the roof. One exposed opening remained and much damage threatened ; but, in answer to prayer, the rain was stayed, and the work resumed. No damage had been done while the last opening was unrepaired for it had exposed the building from the *south*, while the rain came from the *north*.

Mr. Müller records these circumstances with his usual particularity, as part of his witness to the Living God, and to the goodness and mercy that closely and continually followed him.

During the next year, 1865-6, scarlet fever broke out in the orphanage. In all thirty-nine children were ill, but all recovered. Whooping-cough also made its appearance; but though, during that season, it was not only very prevalent but very malignant in Bristol, in all the three houses there were but seventeen cases, and the only fatal one was that of a little girl with constitutionally weak lungs.

During this same year, however, the Spirit of God wrought mightily among the girls, as in the previous year among the boys, so that over one hundred became deeply earnest seekers after salvation ; and so, even in tribulation, consolation abounded in Christ. Mr. Müller and his wife and helpers now implored God to deepen and broaden this work of His Spirit. Towards the end of the year closing in May, 1866, Emma Bunn, an orphan girl of seventeen, was struck with consumption. Though, for fourteen years, she had been under Mr. Müller's care, she was, in this dangerous illness, still careless and indifferent ; and, as she drew near to death, her case continued as hopeless as ever. Prayer was unceasing for her ; and it pleased God suddenly to reveal Christ to her as her Saviour. Great self-loathing now at once took the place of former indifference ; confession of sin, of previous callousness of conscience ; and unspeakable joy in the Lord, of former apathy and coldness. It was a spiritual miracle —this girl's sudden transformation into a witness for God, manifesting deepest conviction for past sin and earnest concern for others. Her thoughtless and heedless state had been so well known that her conversion and dying messages were now the Lord's means of the *most extensive and God-glorifying work ever wrought up to that time among the orphans.* In one house alone three hundred and fifty were led to seek peace in believing.

What lessons lie hidden—nay, lie on the very surface— to be read of every willing observer of these events ! Prayer can break even a hard heart ; a memory, stored with biblical truth and pious teaching, will prove, when once God's grace softens the heart and unlooses the tongue, a source of both personal growth in grace and of capacity for wide service to others. We are all practically too careless of the training of children, and too distrustful of young converts. Mr. Müller was more and more impressed by the triumphs of the grace of God as seen in children converted at the tender age of nine or ten and holding the beginning of their confidence steadfast unto the end.

These facts and experiences, gleaned, like handfuls of grain, from a wide field, show the character both of the seed sown and the harvest reaped, from the sowing.

Again, when, in 1866, cholera developed in England, in answer to special prayer *not one* case of this disease was known in the orphan houses ; and when, in the same autumn, whooping-cough and measles broke out, though eight children had the former and two hundred and sixty-two, the latter, not one child died, or was afterward debilitated by the attack. From May, 1866, to May, 1867, out of over thirteen hundred children under care, only eleven died, considerably less than one per cent.

That severe and epidemic disease should find its way into the orphanages at all may seem strange to those who judge God's faithfulness by appearances, but many were the compensations for such trials. By them not only were the hearts of the children often turned to God, but the hearts of helpers in the Institution were made more sympathetic and tender, and the hearts of God's people at large were stirred up to practical and systematic help. God uses such seeming calamities as 'advertisements' of His work; many who would not have heard of the Institution, or on whom what they did hear would have made little impression, were led to take a deep interest in an orphanage where thousands of little ones were exposed to the ravages of some malignant and dangerous epidemic.

Looking back, in 1865, after thirty-one years, upon the work thus far done for the Lord, Mr. Müller gratefully records that, during the entire time, he had been enabled to hold fast the original principles on which the work was based on March 5, 1834. He had never once gone into debt ; he had sought for the Institution no patron but the Living God ; and he had kept to the line of demarkation between believers and unbelievers, in all his seeking for active helpers in the work.

His grand purpose, in all his labours, having been, from the beginning, the glory of God, in showing what could be done through prayer and faith, without any leaning upon man, his unequivocal testimony is: " Hitherto hath the Lord helped us." Though for about five years they had, almost daily, been in the constant trial of faith, they were as constantly proving His faithfulness. The work had rapidly grown, till it assumed gigantic proportions, but so did the help of God keep pace with all the needs and demands of its growth.

In January, 1866, Mr. Henry Craik, who had for thirty-six years been Mr. Müller's valued friend, and, since 1832, his coworker in Bristol, fell asleep after an illness of seven months. In Devonshire these two brethren had first known each other, and the acquaintance had subsequently ripened, through years of common labour and trial, into an affection seldom found among men. They were nearly of an age, both being a little past sixty when Mr. Craik died. The loss was too heavy to have been patiently and serenely borne, had not the survivor known and felt beneath him the Everlasting Arms. And even this bereavement, which in one aspect was an irreparable loss, was seen to be only another proof of God's love. The look ahead might be a dark one, the way desolate and even dangerous, but goodness and mercy were still following very close behind, and would in every new place of danger or difficulty be at hand to help over hard places and give comfort and cheer in the night season.

CHAPTER XVI

THE SHADOW OF A GREAT SORROW

" WITH clouds He covereth the light." No human life is without some experience of clouded skies and stormy days, and sometimes " the clouds return after the rain." It is a blessed experience to recognize the silver lining on the darkest storm-cloud, and, better still, to be sure of the shining of God's light behind a sky that seems wholly and hopelessly overcast.

The year 1870 was made forever pathetically memorable by the decease of Mrs. Müller, who lived just long enough to see the last of the New Orphan Houses opened. From the outset of the work in November, 1835, for more than thirty-four years, this beloved, devoted wife had been also a sympathetic helper.

This wedded life had approached very near to the ideal of connubial bliss, by reason of mutual fitness, common faith in God and love for His work, and long association in prayer and service. In their case, the days of courtship were never passed ; indeed the tender and deli- cate mutual attentions of those early days rather increased than decreased as the years went on; and the great maxim was both proven and illustrated, that the secret of winning love is the secret of keeping it. More than that, such affection grows and becomes more and more a fountain of mutual delight. Never had his beloved " Mary " been so precious to her husband as during the very year of her departure.

This marriage union was so happy that Mr. Müller could not withhold his loving witness that he never saw her at any time after she became his wife, without a new feeling of delight. And day by day they were wont to find at least a few moments of rest together, sitting after dinner, hand in hand, in loving intercourse of mind and heart, made the more complete by this touch of physical contact, and, whether in speech or silence, communing in the Lord. Their happiness in God and in each other was perennial, perpetual, growing as the years fled by.

Mr. Müller's solemn conviction was that all this wedded bliss was due to the fact that she was not only a devoted Christian, but that their one united object was to live only and wholly for God; that they had always abundance of work for God, in which they were heartily united; that this work was never allowed to interfere with the care of their own souls, or their seasons of private prayer and study of the Scriptures; and that they were wont daily, and often thrice a day, to secure a time of united prayer and praise when they brought before the Lord the matters which at the time called for thanksgiving and supplication.

Mrs. Müller had never been a very vigorous woman, and more than once had been brought nigh unto death. In October, 1859, after twenty-nine years of wedded life and love, she had been laid aside by rheumatism and had continued in great suffering for about nine months, quite helpless and unable to work; but it was felt to be a special mark of God's love and faithfulness that this very affliction was used by Him to reëstablish her in health and strength, the compulsory rest made necessary for the greater part of a year being in Mr. Müller's judgment a means of prolonging her life and period of service for the ten years following. Thus a severe trial met by them both in faith had issued in much blessing both to soul and body.

The closing scenes of this beautiful life are almost too sacred to be unveiled to common eyes. For some few years before her departure, it was plain that her health and vitality were declining. With difficulty could she be prevailed on, however, to abate her activity, or, even when a distressing cough attacked her, to allow a physician to be called. Her husband carefully guarded and nursed her, and by careful attention to diet and rest, by avoidance of needless exposure, and by constant resort to prayer, she was kept alive through much weakness and sometimes much pain. But, on Saturday night, February 5th, she found that she had not the use of one of her limbs, and it was obvious that the end was nigh. Her own mind was clear and her own heart at peace. She herself remarked, " He will soon come." And a few minutes after four in the afternoon of the Lord's day, February 6, 1870, she sweetly passed from human toils and trials, to be forever with the Lord.

Under the weight of such a sorrow, most men would have sunk into depths of almost hopeless despair. But this man of God, sustained by a divine love, at once sought for occasions of thanksgiving; and, instead of repining over his loss, gratefully remembered and recorded the goodness of God in *taking* such a wife, releasing her saintly spirit from the bondage of weakness, sickness, and pain, rather than leaving her to a protracted suffering and the mute agony of helplessness; and, above all, introducing her to her heart's desire, the immediate presence of the Lord Jesus, and the higher service of a celestial sphere. Is not that grief akin to selfishness which dwells so much on our own deprivations as to be oblivious of the ecstatic gain of the departed saints who, withdrawn from us and absent from the body, are at home with the Lord?

It is only in those circumstances of extreme trial which prove to ordinary men a crushing weight, that implicit faith in the Father's unfailing wisdom and love proves its full power to sustain. Where self-will is truly lost in the will of God, the life that is hidden in Him is most radiantly exhibited in the darkest hour.

The death of this beloved wife afforded an illustration of this. Within a few hours after this withdrawal of her who had shared with him the planning and working of these long years of service, Mr. Müller went to the Monday-evening prayer meeting, then held in Salem Chapel, to mingle his prayers and praises as usual with those of his brethren. With a literally shining countenance, he rose and said: "Beloved brethren and sisters in Christ, I ask you to join with me in hearty praise and thanksgiving to my precious Lord for His loving kindness in having taken my darling, beloved wife out of the pain and suffering which she has endured, into His own presence; and as I rejoice in everything that is for her happiness, so I now rejoice as I realize how far happier she is, in beholding her Lord whom she loved so well, than in any joy she has known or could know here. I ask you also to pray that the Lord will so enable me to have fellowship in her joy that my bereaved heart may be occupied with her blessedness instead of my unspeakable loss." These remarkable words are supplied by one who was himself present and on whose memory they made an indelible impression.

This occurrence had a marked effect upon all who were at that meeting. Mrs. Müller was known by all as a most valuable, lovely, and holy woman and wife. After nearly

forty years of wedded life and love, she had left the earthly
home for the heavenly. To her husband she had been a
blessing beyond description, and to her daughter Lydia,
at once a wise and tender mother and a sympathetic companion. The loss to them both could never be made up
on earth. Yet in these circumstances this man of God
had grace given to forget his own and his daughter's irreparable loss, and to praise God for the unspeakable gain to
the departed wife and mother.

The body was laid to rest on February 11th, many thousands of sorrowing friends evincing the deepest sympathy.
Twelve hundred orphans mingled in the funeral procession,
and the whole staff of helpers so far as they could be spared
from the houses. The bereaved husband strangely upheld
by the arm of the Almighty Friend in whom he trusted,
took upon himself the funeral service both at chapel and
cemetery. He was taken seriously ill afterward, but, as
soon as his returning strength allowed, he preached his
wife's funeral sermon—another memorable occasion. It
was the supernatural serenity of his peace in the presence
of such a bereavement that led his attending physician to
say to a friend, " I have never before seen so *unhuman* a
man." Yes, *un*human indeed, though far from *in*human,
lifted above the weakness of mere humanity by a power not
of man.

That funeral sermon was a noble tribute to the goodness
of the Lord even in the great affliction of his life. The
text was :

" *Thou art good and doest good.*" (Psalm cxix. 68.)

Its three divisions were : " The Lord was good and did
good: first, in giving her to me ; second, in so long leaving
her to me ; and third, in taking her from me." It is

happily preserved in Mr. Müller's journal, and must be read to be appreciated.*

This union, begun in prayer, was in prayer sanctified to the end. Mrs. Müller's chief excellence lay in her devoted piety. She wore that one ornament which is in the sight of God of great price—the meek and quiet spirit ; the beauty of the Lord her God was upon her. She had sympathetically shared her husband's prayers and tears during all the long trial-time of faith and patience, and partaken of all the joys and rewards of the triumph hours. Mr. Müller's own witness to her leaves nothing more to be added, for it is the tribute of him who knew her longest and best. He writes:

" She was God's own gift, exquisitely suited to me even in natural temperament. Thousands of times I said to her, ' My darling, God Himself singled you out for me, as the most suitable wife I could possibly wish to have had.' "

As to culture, she had a basis of sensible practical education, surmounted and adorned by ladylike accomplishments which she had neither time nor inclination to indulge in her married life. Not only was she skilled in the languages and in such higher studies as astronomy, but in mathematics also ; and this last qualification made her for thirty-four years an invaluable help to her husband, as month by month she examined all the account-books, and the hundreds of bills of the matrons of the orphan houses, and with the eye of an expert detected the least mistake.

All her training and natural fitness indicated a providential adaptation to her work, like " the round peg in the round hole." Her practical education in needlework, and her knowledge of the material most serviceable for various

---

* Narrative, III. 575-594.

household uses, made her competent to direct both in the purchase and manufacture of cloths and other fabrics for garments, bed-linen, etc.   She moved about those orphan houses like an angel of Love, taking unselfish delight in such humble ministries as preparing neat, clean, beds to rest the little ones, and covering them with warm blankets in cold weather.   For the sake of Him who took little children in His arms, she became to these thousands of destitute orphans a nursing mother.

Shortly after her death, a letter was received from a believing orphan some seventeen years before sent out to service, asking, in behalf also of others formerly in the houses, permission to erect a stone over Mrs. Müller's grave as an expression of love and grateful remembrance.   Consent being given, hundreds of little offerings came in from orphans who during the twenty-five years previous had been under her motherly oversight—a beautiful tribute to her worth and a touching offering from those who had been to her as her larger family.

The dear daughter Lydia had, two years before Mrs. Müller's departure, found in one of her mother's pocketbooks a sacred memorandum in her own writing, which she brought to her bereaved father's notice two days after his wife had departed.   It belongs among the precious relics of her history.   It reads as follows:

"Should it please the Lord to remove M. M. [Mary Müller] by a sudden dismissal, let none of the beloved survivors consider that it is in the way of judgment, either to her or to them.   She has so often, when enjoying conscious nearness to the Lord, felt 'How sweet it would be *now* to depart and to be *forever* with Jesus,' that nothing but the shock it would be to her beloved husband and child, etc., has checked in her the longing desire that *thus* her happy spirit might take its flight.   Precious

Jesus ! Thy will in this as in everything else, and not hers, be done ! "

These words were to Mr. Müller her last legacy; and with the comfort they gave him, the loving sympathy of his precious Lydia who did all that a daughter could do to fill a mother's place, and with the remembrance of Him who hath said, ' I will never leave thee nor forsake thee,' he went on his lonely pilgrim way, rejoicing in the Lord, feeling nevertheless a wound in his heart, that seemed rather to deepen than to heal.

Sixteen months passed, when Mr. James Wright, who like Mr. Müller had been bereft of his companion, asked of him the hand of the beloved Lydia in marriage. The request took Mr. Müller wholly by surprise, but he felt that, to no man living, could he with more joyful confidence commit and intrust his choicest remaining earthly treasure ; and, ever solicitous for others' happiness rather than his own, he encouraged his daughter to accept Mr. Wright's proffered love, when she naturally hesitated on her father's account. On November 16, 1871, they were married, and began a life of mutual prayer and sympathy which, like that of her father and mother, proved supremely and almost ideally happy, helpful, and useful.

While as yet this event was only in prospect, Mr. Müller felt his own lonely condition keenly, and much more in view of his daughter's expected departure to her husband's home. He felt the need of some one to share intimately his toils and prayers, and help him in the Lord's work, and the persuasion grew upon him that it was God's will that he should marry again. After much prayer, he determined to ask Miss Susannah Grace Sangar to become his wife, having known her for more than twenty-five years as a consistent disciple, and believing her to be well fitted to be his helper in the Lord. Accordingly, fourteen days

after his daughter's marriage to Mr. Wright, he entered
into similar relations with Miss Sangar, who for years
after joined him in prayer, unselfish giving, and labours
for souls.

The second Mrs. Müller was of one mind with her husband as to the stewardship of the Lord's property. He
found her poor, for what she had once possessed she had
lost ; and had she been rich he would have regarded her
wealth as an obstacle to marriage, unfitting her to be his
companion in a self-denial based on scriptural principle.
Riches or hoarded wealth would have been to both of them
a snare, and so she also felt; so that, having still, before her
marriage, a remnant of two hundred pounds, she at once
put it at the Lord's disposal, thus joining her husband
in a life of voluntary poverty ; and although subsequent
legacies were paid to her, she continued to the day of her
death to be poor for the Lord's sake.

The question had often been asked Mr. Müller what
would become of the *work* when he, the master workman,
should be removed.   Men find it hard to get their eyes off
the instrument, and remember that there is only, strictly
speaking, one AGENT, for an agent is *one who works*, and an
instrument is what *the agent works with*.   Though provision might be made, in a board of trustees, for carrying
on the orphan work, where would be found the man to
take the direction of it, a man whose spirit was so akin
to that of the founder that he would trust in God and
depend on Him just as Mr. Müller had done before him ?
Such were the inquiries of the somewhat doubtful or
fearful observers of the great and many-branched work
carried on under Mr. Müller's supervision.

To all such questions he had always one answer ready—
his one uniform solution of all cares and perplexities :
the Living God. He who had built the orphan houses

could maintain them ; He who had raised up one humble man to oversee the work in His name, could provide for a worthy successor, like Joshua who not only *followed* but *succeeded* Moses. Jehovah of hosts is not limited in resources.

Nevertheless much prayer was offered that the Lord would provide such a successor, and, in Mr. James Wright, the prayer was answered. He was not chosen, as Mr. Müller's son-in-law, for the choice was made before his marriage to Lydia Müller was even thought of by him. For more than thirty years, even from his boyhood, Mr. Wright had been well known to Mr. Müller, and his growth in the things of God had been watched by him. For thirteen years he had already been his " right hand " in all most important matters ; and, for nearly all of that time, had been held up before God as his successor, in the prayers of Mr. and Mrs. Müller, both of whom felt divinely assured that God would fit him more and more to take the entire burden of responsibility.

When, in 1870, the wife fell asleep in Jesus, and Mr. Müller was himself ill, he opened his heart to Mr. Wright as to the succession. Humility led him to shrink from such a post, and his then wife feared it would prove too burdensome for him ; but all objections were overborne when it was seen and felt to be God's call. It was twenty-one months after this, when, in November, 1871, Mr. Wright was married to Mr. Müller's only daughter and child, so that it is quite apparent that he had neither sought the position he now occupies, nor was he appointed to it because he was Mr. Müller's son-in-law, for, at that time, his first wife was living and in health. From May, 1872, therefore, Mr. Wright *shared* with his father-in-law the responsibilities of the Institution, and gave him great joy as a partner and successor in full sympathy with all the great principles on which his work had been based.

A little over three years after Mr. Müller's second marriage, in March, 1874, Mrs. Müller was taken ill, and became, two days later, feverish and restless, and after about two weeks was attacked with hemorrhage which brought her also very near to the gates of death. She rallied ; but fever and delirium followed and obstinate sleeplessness, till, for a second time, she seemed at the point of death. Indeed so low was her vitality that, as late as April 17th, a most experienced London physician said that he had never known any patient to recover from such an illness ; and thus a third time all human hope of restoration seemed gone. And yet, in answer to prayer, Mrs. Müller was raised up, and in the end of May, was taken to the seaside for change of air, and grew rapidly stronger until she was entirely restored. Thus the Lord spared her to be the companion of her husband in those years of missionary touring which enabled him to bear such worldwide witness. Out of the shadow of his griefs this beloved man of God ever came to find that divine refreshment which is as the " shadow of a great rock in a weary land."

CHAPTER XVII

GOD's real answers to prayer are often seeming denials. Beneath the outward request He hears the voice of the inward desire, and He responds to the mind of the Spirit rather than to the imperfect and perhaps mistaken words in which the yearning seeks expression. Moreover, His infinite wisdom sees that a larger blessing may be ours only by the withholding of the lesser good which we seek; and so all true prayer trusts Him to give His own answer, not in our way or time, or even to our own expressed desire, but rather to His own unutterable groaning within us which He can interpret better than we.

Monica, mother of Augustine, pleaded with God that her dissolute son might not go to Rome, that sink of iniquity; but he was permitted to go, and thus came into contact with Ambrose, bishop of Milan, through whom he was converted. God fulfilled the mother's *desire* while denying her *request*.

When George Müller, five times within the first eight years after conversion, had offered himself as a missionary, God had blocked his way; now, at sixty-five, He was about to permit him, in a sense he had never dreamed of, to be a missionary to the world. From the beginning of his ministry he had been more or less an itinerant, spending no little time in wanderings about in Britain and on the Continent; but now he was to go to the regions beyond and spend the major part of seventeen years in witnessing to the prayer-hearing God.

These extensive missionary tours occupied the evening of Mr. Müller's useful life, from 1875 to 1892. They reached, more or less, over Europe, America, Asia, Africa, and Australia ; and would of themselves have sufficed for the work of an ordinary life.

They had a singular suggestion. While, in 1874, compelled by Mrs. Müller's health to seek a change of air, he was preaching in the Isle of Wight, and a beloved Christian brother for whom he had spoken, himself a man of much experience in preaching, told him how ' that day had been the happiest of his whole life ' ; and this remark, with others like it previously made, so impressed him that the Lord was about to use him to help on believers outside of Bristol, that he determined no longer to confine his labours in the Word and doctrine to any one place, but to go wherever a door might open for his testimony.

In weighing this question he was impressed with *seven* reasons or motives, which led to these tours :

1. To *preach the gospel* in its simplicity, and especially to show how salvation is based, not upon feelings or even upon faith, but upon the finished work of Christ ; that justification is ours the moment we believe, and we are to accept and claim our place as accepted in the Beloved without regard to our inward states of feeling or emotion.

2. To *lead believers to know their saved state*, and to realize their standing in Christ, great numbers not only of disciples, but even preachers and pastors, being themselves destitute of any real peace and joy in the Lord, and hence unable to lead others into joy and peace.

3. To *bring believers back to the Scriptures*, to search the Word and find its hidden treasures ; to test everything by this divine touchstone and hold fast only what will stand

this test; to make it the daily subject of meditative and prayerful examination in order to translate it into daily obedience.

4. To *promote among all true believers, brotherly love;* to lead them to make less of those non-essentials in which disciples differ, and to make more of those great essential and foundation truths in which all true believers are united; to help all who love and trust one Lord to rise above narrow sectarian prejudices, and barriers to fellowship.

5. To *strengthen the faith of believers,* encouraging a simpler trust, and a more real and unwavering confidence in God, and particularly in the sure answers to believing prayer, based upon His definite promises.

6. To *promote separation from the world* and deadness to it, and so to increase heavenly-mindedness in children of God; at the same time warning against fanatical extremes and extravagances, such as sinless perfection while in the flesh.

7. And finally to *fix the hope of disciples on the blessed coming of our Lord Jesus;* and, in connection therewith, to instruct them as to the true character and object of the present dispensation, and the relation of the church to the world in this period of the outgathering of the Bride of Christ.

These seven objects may be briefly epitomized thus : Mr. Müller's aim was to lead sinners to believe on the name of the Son of God, and so to *have eternal life;* to help those who have thus believed, to *know* that they have this life ; to teach them so to *build up* themselves on their most holy faith, by diligent searching into the word of God, and praying in the Holy Ghost, as that this life shall be more and more a real possession and a conscious possession ; to promote among all disciples the *unity of the Spirit* and the *charity* which is the bond of perfectness, and to help them to exhibit that life before the world ; to incite them to cultivate an *unworldly and spiritual type of character* such as conforms to the life of God in them ; to lead them to the *prayer of faith* which is both the expression and the expansion of the life of faith ; and to direct their hope to the *final appearing of the Lord,* so that they should purify themselves even as He is pure, and occupy till He comes. Mr. Müller was thus giving himself to the double work of evangelization and edification, on a scale commensurate with his love for a dying world, as opportunity afforded doing good unto all men, and especially to them who are of the household of faith.

Of these long and busy missionary journeys, it is needful to give only the outline, or general survey. March 26, 1875, is an important date, for it marks the starting-point. He himself calls this " the beginning of his missionary tours."

From Bristol he went to Brighton, Lewes, and Sunderland—on the way to Sunderland preaching to a great audience in the Metropolitan Tabernacle, at Mr. Spurgeon's request—then to Newcastle-on-Tyne, and back to London, where he spoke at the Mildmay Park Conference, Talbot Road Tabernacle, and ' Edinburgh Castle.' This tour closed, June 5th, after seventy addresses in public, during about ten weeks.

Less than six weeks passed, when, on August 14th, the second tour began, in which case the special impulse that moved him was a desire to follow up the revival work of Mr. Moody and Mr. Sankey. Their short stay in each place made them unable to lead on new converts to higher attainments in knowledge and grace, and there seemed to be a call for some instruction fitted to confirm these new believers in the life of obedience. Mr. Müller accordingly followed these evangelists in England, Ireland, and Scotland, staying in each place from one week to six, and seeking to educate and edify those who had been led to Christ. Among the places visited on this errand in 1875, were London ; then Kilmarnock, Saltwater, Dundee, Perth, Glasgow, Kirkentilloch in Scotland, and Dublin in Ireland; then, returning to England, he went to Leamington, Warwick, Kenilworth, Coventry, Rugby, etc. In some cases, notably at Mildmay Park, Dundee and Glasgow, Liverpool and Dublin, the audiences numbered from two thousand to six thousand, but everywhere rich blessing came from above. This second tour extended into the new year, 1876, and took in Liverpool, York, Kendal, Carlisle, Annan, Edinburgh, Arbroath, Montrose, Aberdeen, and other places; and when it closed in July, having lasted nearly eleven months, Mr. Müller had preached at least three hundred and six times, an average of about one sermon a day, exclusive of days spent in travel. So acceptable and profitable were these labours that there were over one hundred invitations urged upon him which he was unable to accept.

The third tour was on the Continent. It occupied most of the year closing May 26, 1877, and embraced Paris, various places in Switzerland, Prussia and Holland, Alsace, Wurtemberg, Baden, Hesse Darmstadt, etc. Altogether over three hundred addresses were given in about seventy cities and villages to all of which he had been invited by letter. When this tour closed more than sixty written invitations remained unaccepted, and Mr. Müller found that, through his work and his writings, he was as well known in the continental countries visited, as in England.

Turning now toward America, the fourth tour extended from August, 1877, to June of the next year. For many

years invitations had been coming with growing frequency, from the United States and Canada; and of late
their urgency led him to recognize in them the call of God,
especially as he thought of the many thousands of Germans across the Atlantic, who as they heard him speak in
their own native tongue would keep the more silence.
(Acts xxii. 2.)

Mr. and Mrs. Müller, landing at Quebec, thence went to
the United States, where, during ten months, his labours
stretched over a vast area, including the States of New
York, New Jersey, Massachusetts, Pennsylvania, Mary-
land, District of Columbia, Virginia, South Carolina,
Georgia, Florida, Alabama, Louisiana, and Missouri. Thus
having swept round the Atlantic sea-border, he crossed to
the Pacific coast, and returning visited Salt Lake City in
Utah—the very centre and stronghold of Mormonism—
Illinois, Ohio, etc. He spoke frequently to large congregations of Germans, and, in the Southern States, to the
coloured population; but he regarded no opportunity for
service afforded him on this tour as so inspiring as the repeated meetings with and for ministers, evangelists, pastors, and Christian workers; and, next to them in importance, his interviews with large bodies of students and professors in the universities, colleges, theological seminaries,
and other higher schools of education. To cast the salt
of the gospel into the very springs of social influence, the
sources whence power flows, was to him a most sacred privilege. His singular catholicity, charity, and humility drew
to him even those who differed with him, and all denom-
inations of Christians united in giving him access to the
people. During this tour he spoke three hundred times,
and travelled nearly ten thousand miles; over one hundred
invitations being declined, for simple lack of time and
strength.

After a stay in Bristol of about two months, on September 5, 1878, he and his wife began the fifth of these missionary tours. In this case, it was on the Continent, where he ministered in English, German, and French; and in Spain and Italy, when these tongues were not available, his addresses were through an interpreter. Many open doors the Lord set before him, not only to the poorer and humbler classes, but to those in the middle and higher ranks. In the Riviera, he had access to many of the nobility and aristocracy, who from different countries sought health and rest in the equable climate of the Mediterranean, and at Mentone he and Mr. Spurgeon held sweet converse. In Spain Mr. Müller was greatly gladdened by seeing for himself the schools, entirely supported by the funds of the Scriptural Knowledge Institution, and by finding that, in hundreds of cases, even *popish* parents so greatly valued these schools that they continued to send their children, despite both the threats and persuasions of the Romish priests. He found, moreover, that the pupils frequently at their homes read to their parents the word of God and sang to them the gospel hymns learned at these schools, so that the influence exerted was not bounded by its apparent horizon, as diffused or refracted sunlight reaches with its illumining rays far beyond the visible track of the orb of day.

The work had to contend with governmental opposition. When a place was first opened at Madrid for gospel services, a sign was placed outside, announcing the fact. Official orders were issued that the sign should be painted over, so as to obliterate the inscription. The painter of the sign, unwilling both to undo his own work and to hinder the work of God, painted the sign over with water-colours, which would leave the original announcement half visible, and would soon be washed off by the rains; whereupon the government sent its own workman to daub the sign over with thick oil-colour.

Mr. Müller, ready to preach the gospel to those at Rome also, felt his spirit saddened and stirred within him, as he saw that city wholly given to idolatry—not pagan but papal idolatry—the Rome not of the Cæsars, but of the popes. While at Naples he ascended Vesuvius. Those masses of lava, which seemed greater in bulk than the mountain itself, more impressed him with the power of God than anything else he had ever seen. As he looked upon that smoking cone, and thought of the liquid death it had vomited forth, he said within himself, " What cannot God do ! " He had before felt somewhat of His Almightiness in love and grace, but he now saw its manifestation in judgment and wrath. His visit to the Vaudois valleys, where so many martyrs had suffered banishment and imprisonment, loss of goods and loss of life for Jesus' sake, moved him to the depths of his being and stimulated in him the martyr spirit.

When he arrived again in Bristol, June 18, 1879, he had been absent nine months and twelve days, and preached two hundred and eighty-six times and in forty-six towns and cities. After another ten weeks in Bristol, he and his wife sailed again for America, the last week of August, 1879, landing at New York the first week in September. This visit took in the States lying between the Atlantic Ocean and the valley of the Mississippi—New York and New Jersey, Ohio, Indiana, Michigan and Illinois, Wisconsin, Iowa, Minnesota—and, from London and Hamilton to Quebec, Canada also shared the blessing. This visit covered only two hundred and seventy-two days, but he preached three hundred times, and in over forty cities. Over one hundred and fifty written invitations still remained without response, and the number increased the longer his stay. Mr. Müller therefore assuredly gathered that the Lord called him to return to America, after another brief stay at Bristol, where he felt it needful to spend a season annually, to keep in close touch with the work at home and relieve Mr. and Mrs. Wright of their heavy responsibilities, for a time.

Accordingly on September 15, 1880, again turning from Bristol, these travellers embarked the next day on their seventh mission tour, landing, ten days later, at Quebec. Mr. Müller had a natural antipathy to the sea, in his earlier crossing to the Continent having suffered much from sea-sickness; but he had undertaken these long voyages, not for his own pleasure or profit, but wholly on God's errand; and he felt it to be a peculiar mark of the loving-kindness of the Lord that, while he was ready to endure any discomfort, or risk his life for His sake, he had not in his six crossings of the Atlantic suffered in the least, and on this particular voyage was wholly free from any indisposition.

From Quebec he went to Massachusetts, Connecticut, New York, New Jersey, and Pennsylvania. Among other places of special interest were Boston, Plymouth—the landing-place of the Pilgrims,—Wellesley and South Hadley colleges—the great schools for woman's higher education,—and the centres farther westward, where he had such wide access to Germans. This tour extended over a smaller area than before, and lasted but eight months; but the impression on the people was deep and permanent. He had spoken about two hundred and fifty times in all; and Mrs. Müller had availed herself of many opportunities of personal dealing with inquirers, and of distributing books and tracts among both believers and unbelievers. She had also written for her husband more than seven hundred letters,—this of itself being no light task, inasmuch as it reaches an average of about three a day. On May 30, 1881, they were again on British shores.

The eighth long preaching tour, from August 23, 1881, to May 30, 1882, was given to the Continent of Europe, where again Mr. Müller felt led by the low state of religious life in Switzerland and Germany.

This visit was extended to the Holy Land in a way strikingly providential. After speaking at Alexandria, Cairo, and Port Said, he went to Jaffa, and thence to Jerusalem, on November 28. With reverent feet he touched the soil once trodden by the feet of the Son of God, visiting, with pathetic interest, Gethsemane and Golgotha, and crossing the Mount of Olives to Bethany, thence to Bethlehem and back to Jaffa, and so to Haipha, Mt. Carmel, and Beyrût, Smyrna, Ephesus, Constantinople, Athens, Brindisi, Rome, and Florence. Again were months crowded with services of all sorts whose fruit will appear only in the Day of the Lord Jesus, addresses being made in English, German, and French, or by translation into Arabic, Armenian, Turkish, and modern Greek. Sightseeing was always but incidental to the higher service of the Master. During this eighth tour, covering some eight months, Mr. Müller spoke hundreds of times, with all the former tokens of God's blessing on his seed-sowing.

The *ninth* tour, from August 8, 1882, to June 1, 1883, was occupied with labours in Germany, Austria, and Russia, including Bavaria, Hungary, Bohemia, Saxony, and Poland. His special joy it was to bear witness in Kroppenstädt, his birthplace, after an absence of about sixty-four years. At St. Petersburg, while the guest of Princess Lieven, at her mansion he met and ministered to many of high rank; he also began to hold meetings in the house of Colonel Paschkoff, who had suffered not only persecution but exile for the Lord's sake. While the Scriptures were being read one day in Russ, with seven poor Russians, a policeman summarily broke up the meeting and dispersed the little company. At Lodz in Poland, a letter was received, in behalf of 'almost the whole population,' begging him to remain longer; and so signs seemed to multiply, as he went forward, that he was in the path of duty and that God was with him.

On September 26, 1883, the *tenth* tour began, this time his face being turned toward the Orient. Nearly sixty years before he had desired to go to the East Indies as a missionary; now the Lord permitted him to carry out the desire in a new and strange way, and *India* was the twenty-third country visited in his tours. He travelled over 21,000 miles, and spoke over two hundred times, to missionaries and Christian workers, European residents, Eurasians, Hindus, Moslems, educated natives, native boys and girls in the orphanage at Colar, etc. Thus, in his seventy-ninth year, this servant of God was still in labours abundant, and in all his work conspicuously blessed of God.

After some months of preaching in England, Scotland, and Wales, on November 19, 1885, he and his wife set out on their fourth visit to the United States, and their *eleventh longer mission tour.* Crossing to the Pacific, they went to Sydney, New South Wales, and, after seven months in Australia, sailed for Java, and thence to China, arriving at Hong Kong, September 12th; Japan and the Straits of Malacca were also included in this visit to the Orient. The return to England was by way of Nice; and, after travelling nearly 38,000 miles, in good health Mr. and Mrs. Müller reached home on June 14, 1887, having been absent more than one year and seven months, during which Mr. Müller had preached whenever and wherever opportunity was afforded.

Less than two months later, on August 12, 1887, he sailed for South Australia, Tasmania, New Zealand, Ceylon, and India. This twelfth long tour closed in March, 1890, having covered thousands of miles. The intense heat at one time compelled Mr. Müller to leave Calcutta, and on the railway journey to Darjeeling his wife feared he would die. But he was mercifully spared.

It was on this tour and in the month of January, 1890, while at Jubbulpore, preaching with great help from the Lord, that a letter was put into Mr. Müller's hands, from a missionary at Agra, to whom Mr. Wright had sent a telegram, informing his father-in-law of his dear Lydia's death. For nearly thirty years she had laboured gratuitously at the orphan houses and it would be difficult to fill that vacancy; but for fourteen years she had been her husband's almost ideal companion, and for nearly fifty-eight years her father's unspeakable treasure—and here were two other voids which could never be filled. But Mr. Müller's heart, as also Mr. Wright's, was kept at rest by the strong confidence that, however mysterious God's ways, all His dealings belong to one harmonious spiritual mechanism in which every part is perfect and all things work together for good. (Romans viii. 28.)

This sudden bereavement led Mr. Müller to bring his mission tour in the East to a close and depart for Bristol, that he might both comfort Mr. Wright and relieve him of undue pressure of work.

After a lapse of two months, once more Mr. and Mrs. Müller left home for other extensive missionary journeys. They went to the Continent and were absent from July, 1890, to May, 1892. A twelvemonth was spent in Germany and Holland, Austria and Italy. This absence in fact included two tours, with no interval between them, and concluded the series of extensive journeys reaching through seventeen years.

This man—from his seventieth to his eighty-seventh year—when most men are withdrawing from all activities, had travelled in forty-two countries and over two hundred thousand miles, a distance equivalent to nearly eight journeys round the globe! He estimated that during these seventeen years he had addressed over three million people; and from all that can be gathered from the records of these tours, we estimate that he must have spoken, outside of Bristol, between five thousand and six thousand times. What sort of teaching and testimony occupied these tours, those who have known the preacher and teacher need not be told. While at Berlin in 1891, he gave an address that serves as an example of the vital truths which he was wont to press on the attention of fellow disciples. We give a brief outline:

He first urged that believers should never, even under the greatest difficulties, be discouraged, and gave for his position sound scriptural reasons. Then he pointed out to them that the chief business of every day is first of all to seek to be truly at rest and happy in God. Then he showed how, from the word of God, all saved believers may know their true standing in Christ, and how in circumstances of particular perplexity they might ascertain the will of God. He then urged disciples to seek with intense earnestness to become acquainted with God Himself as revealed in the Holy Scriptures, and carefully to form and maintain godly habits of systematic Bible study and prayer, holy living and consecrated giving. He taught that God alone is the one all-satisfying portion of the soul, and that we must determine to possess and enjoy Him as such. He closed by emphasizing it as the one, single, all-absorbing, daily aim to glorify God in a complete surrender to His will and service.

In all these mission tours, again, the faithfulness of God

was conspicuously seen, in the bounteous supply of every need. Steamer fares and long railway journeys; hotel accommodations, ordinarily preferred to private hospitality, which seriously interfered with private habits of devotion, public work, and proper rest—such expenses demanded a heavy outlay; the new mode of life, now adopted for the Lord's sake, was at least three times as costly as the former frugal housekeeping; and yet, in answer to prayer and without any appeal to human help, the Lord furnished all that was required.

Accustomed to look, step by step, for such tokens of divine approval, as emboldened him to go foward, Mr. Müller records how, when one hundred pounds was sent to him for personal uses, this was recognized as a foretoken from his great Provider, "by which," he writes, " God meant to say to my own heart, ' I am pleased with thy work and service in going about on these long missionary tours. I will pay the expenses thereof, and I give thee here a specimen of what I am yet willing to do for thee.' "

Two other facts Mr. Müller specially records in connection with these tours: first, God's gracious guiding and guarding of the work at Bristol so that it suffered nothing from his absence; and secondly, the fact that these journeys had no connection with collecting of money for the work or even informing the public of it. No reference was made to the Institution at Bristol, except when urgently requested, and not always even then; nor were collections ever made for it. Statements found their way into the press that in America large sums were gathered, but their falsity is sufficiently shown by the fact that in his first tour in America, for example, the sum total of all such gifts was less than sixty pounds, not more than two thirds of the outlay of every day at the orphan houses.

These missionary tours were not always approved even

by the friends and advisers of Mr. Müller. In 1882, while experiencing no little difficulty and trial, especially as to funds, there were not a few who felt a deep interest in the Institution on Ashley Down, who would have had God's servant discontinue his long absences, as to them it appeared that these were the main reason for the falling off in funds. He was always open to counsel, but he always reserved to himself an independent decision; and, on weighing the matter well, these were some of the reasons that led him to think that the work of God at home did not demand his personal presence:

1. He had observed year after year that, under the godly and efficient supervision of Mr. Wright and his large staff of helpers, every branch of the Scriptural Knowledge Institution had been found as healthy and fruitful during these absences as when Mr. Müller was in Bristol.

2. The Lord's approval of this work of wider witness had been in manner conclusive and in measure abundant, as in the ample supply of funds for these tours, in the wide doors of access opened, and in the large fruit already evident in blessing to thousands of souls.

3. The strong impression upon his mind that this was *the* work which was to occupy the 'evening of his life,' grew in depth, and was confirmed by so many signs of God's leading that he could not doubt that he was led both of God's providence and Spirit.

4. Even while absent, he was never out of communication with the heplers at home. Generally he heard at least weekly from Mr. Wright, and any matters needing his counsel were thus submitted to him by letter; prayer to God was as effectual at a distance from Bristol as on the spot; and his periodical returns to that city for some weeks or months between these tours kept him in close touch with every department of the work.

5. The supreme consideration, however, was this: To suppose it necessary for Mr. Müller himself to be at home *in order that sufficient means should be supplied*, was a direct contradiction of the very principles upon which, and to maintain which, the whole work had been begun. *Real trust in God is above circumstances and appearances.* And this had been proven; for, during the third year after these tours began, the income for the various departments of the Scriptural Knowledge Institution was larger than ever during the preceding forty-four years of its existence; and therefore, nothwithstanding the loving counsel of a few donors and friends who advised that Mr. Müller should stay at home, he kept to his purpose and his principles, partly to demonstrate that no man's presence is indispensable to the work of the Lord. "Them that honour Me I will honour." (1 Samuel ii. 39.) He regarded it the greatest honour of his life to bear this wide witness to God, and God correspondingly honoured His servant in bearing this testimony.

It was during the first and second of these American tours that the writer had the privilege of coming into personal contact with Mr. Müller. While I was at San Francisco, in 1878, he was to speak on Sabbath afternoon, May 12th, at Oakland, just across the bay, but conscientious objections to needless Sunday travel caused me voluntarily to lose what then seemed the only chance of seeing and hearing a man whose career had been watched by me for over twenty years, as he was to leave for the East a few days earlier than myself and was likely to be always a little in advance. On reaching Ogden, however, where the branch road from Salt Lake City joins the main line, Mr. and Mrs. Müller boarded my train and we travelled to Chicago together. I introduced myself, and held with him daily converse about divine things, and, while tarry-ing at Chicago, had numerous opportunities for hearing him speak there.

The results of this close and frequent contact were singularly blessed to me, and at my invitation he came to Detroit, Michigan, on his next tour, and spoke in the Fort Street Presbyterian Church, of which I was pastor, on Sundays, January 18 and 25, 1880, and on Monday and Friday evenings, in the interval.

In addition to these numerous and favourable optunities thus providentially afforded for hearing and conversing with Mr. Müller, he kindly met me for several days in my study, for an hour at a time, for conference upon those deeper truths of the word of God and deeper experiences of the Christian life, upon which I was then very desirous of more light.   For example, I desired to understand more clearly the Bible teaching about the Lord's coming.   I had opposed with much persistency what is known as the premillennial view, and brought out my objections, to all of which he made one reply: " My beloved brother, I have heard all your arguments and objections against this view, but they have one fatal defect: *not one of them is based upon the word of God.*   You will never get at the truth upon any matter of divine revelation unless you lay aside your prejudices and like a little child ask simply what is the testimony of Scripture."

With patience and wisdom he unravelled the tangled skein of my perplexity and difficulty, and helped me to settle upon biblical principles all matters of so-called expediency.   As he left me, about to visit other cities, his words fixed themselves in my memory.   I had expressed to him my growing conviction that the worship in the churches had lost its primitive simplicity; that the pew-rent system was pernicious; that fixed salaries for ministers of the gospel were unscriptural; that the church of God should be administered only by men full of the Holy Ghost, and that the duty of Christians to the non-church-going masses was grossly neglected, etc. He solemnly said to me: " My beloved brother, the Lord has given you much light upon these matters, and will hold you correspondingly responsible for its use. If you obey Him and walk in the light, you will have more; if not, the light will be withdrawn."

It is a singular lesson on the importance of an anointed tongue, that forty simple words, spoken over twenty years ago, have had a daily influence on the life of him to whom they were spoken. Amid subtle temptations to compromise the claims of duty and hush the voice of conscience, or of the Spirit of God, and to follow the traditions of men rather than the word of God, those words of that venerated servant of God have recurred to mind with ever fresh force. We risk the forfeiture of privileges which are not employed for God, and of obscuring convictions which are not carried into action. God's word to us is " *use or lose.*" " To him that hath shall be given: from him that hath not shall be taken away even that which he seemeth to have." It is the hope and the prayer of him who writes this memoir that the reading of these pages may prove to be an interview with the man whose memorial they are, and that the witness borne by George Müller may be to many readers a source of untold and lifelong blessing.

It need not be said that to carry out conviction into action is a costly sacrifice. It may make necessary renunciations and separations which leave one to feel a strange sense both of deprivation and loneliness. But he who will fly as an eagle does into the higher levels where cloudless day abides, and live in the sunshine of God, must consent to live a comparatively lonely life. No bird is so solitary as the eagle. Eagles never fly in flocks: one, or at most two, and the two, mates, being ever seen at once. But the life that is lived unto God, however it forfeits human companionship, knows divine fellowship, and the child of God who like his Master undertakes to " do always the things that please Him," can like his Master say, " The Father hath not left me alone." " I am alone; yet not alone, for the Father is with me." Whosoever will promptly follow whatever light God gives, without regard to human opinion, custom, tradition, or approbation, will learn the deep meaning of these words: " Then shall we know, if we follow on to know the Lord."

CHAPTER XVIII

QUANTITY of service is of far less importance than quality. To do well, rather than to do much, will be the motto of him whose main purpose is to please God. Our Lord bade His disciples tarry until endued with power from on high, because it is such enduement that gives to all witness and work the celestial savour and flavour of the Spirit.

Before we come to the closing scenes, we may well look back over the life-work of George Müller, which happily illustrates both quantity and quality of service. It may be doubted whether any other one man of this century accomplished as much for God and man, and yet all the abundant offerings which he brought to his Master were characterized by a heavenly fragrance.

The orphan work was but one branch of that tree— the Scriptural Knowledge Institution—which owed its existence to the fact that its founder devised large and liberal things for the Lord's cause. He sought to establish or at least to aid Christian schools wherever needful, to scatter Bibles and Testaments, Christian books and tracts; to aid missionaries who were witnessing to the truth and working on a scriptural basis in destitute parts; and though each of these objects might well have engrossed his mind, they were all combined in the many-sided work which his love for souls suggested.

An aggressive spirit is never content with what has been done, but is prompt to enter any new door that is providentially opened. When the Paris Exposition of 1867 offered such rare opportunities, both for preaching to the crowds passing through the French capital, and for circulating among them the Holy Scriptures, he gladly availed himself of the services of two brethren whom God had sent to labour there, one of whom spoke three, and the other, eight, modern languages ; and through them were circulated, chiefly at the Exposition, and in thirteen different languages, nearly twelve thousand copies of the word of God, or portions of the same. It has been estimated that at this International Exhibition there were distributed in all over one and a quarter million Bibles, in sixteen tongues, which were gratefully accepted, even by Romish priests. Within six months those who thus entered God's open door scattered more copies of the Book of God than in ordinary circumstances would have been done by ten thousand colporteurs in twenty times that number of months, and thousands of souls are known to have found salvation by the simple reading of the New Testament. Of this glorious work, George Müller was permitted to be so largely a promoter.

At the Havre Exhibition of the following year, 1868, a similar work was done ; and in like manner, when a providential door was unexpectedly opened into the Land of the Inquisition, Mr. Müller promptly took measures to promote the circulation of the Word in Spain. In the streets of Madrid the open Bible was seen for the first time, and copies were sold at the rate of two hundred and fifty in an hour, so that the supply was not equal to the demand. The same facts were substantially repeated when free Italy furnished a field for sowing the seed of the Kingdom. This wide-awake servant of God watched the signs of the times and, while others slept, followed the Lord's signals of advance.

One of the most fascinating features of the Narrative is found in the letters from his Bible distributors. It is interesting also to trace the story of the growth of the tract enterprise, until, in 1874, the circulation exceeded three and three-quarter millions, God in His faithfulness supplying abundant means.*

The good thus effected by the distributors of evangelical literature must not be overlooked in this survey of the many useful agencies employed or assisted by Mr. Müller. To him the world was a field to be sown with the seed of the Kingdom, and opportunities were eagerly embraced for widely disseminating the truth. Tracts were liberally used, given away in large quantities at open-air services, fairs, races and steeplechases, and among spectators at public executions, or among passengers on board ships and railway trains, and by the way. Sometimes, at a single gathering of the multitudes, fifteen thousand were distributed judiciously and prayerfully, and this branch of the work has, during all these years, continued with undiminished fruitfulness to yield its harvest of good.

All this was, from first to last, and of necessity, a work of faith. How far faith must have been kept in constant and vigorous exercise can be appreciated only by putting one's self in Mr. Müller's place. In the year 1874, for instance, about forty-four thousand pounds were needed, and he was compelled to count the cost and face the situation. Two thousand and one hundred hungry mouths were daily to be fed, and as many bodies to be clad and cared for. One hundred and eighty-nine missionaries were needing assistance; one hundred schools, with about nine thousand pupils, to be supported; four million pages of

* Narrative, IV. 244.

tracts and tens of thousands of copies of the Scriptures to be yearly provided for distribution ; and, beside all these ordinary expenses, inevitable crises or emergencies, always liable to arise in connection with the conduct of such extensive enterprises, would from time to time call for extraordinary outlay. The man who was at the head of the Scriptural Knowledge Institution had to look at this array of unavoidable expenses, and at the same time face the human possibility and probability of an empty treasury whence the last shilling had been drawn.

Let him tell us how he met such a prospect:

" God, our infinitely rich Treasurer, remains to us. It is this which gives me peace. . . . Invariably, with this probability before me, I have said to myself: ' God who has raised up this work through me ; God who has led me generally year after year to enlarge it ; God, who has supported this work now for more than forty years, will still help and will not suffer me to be confounded, because I rely upon Him. I commit the whole work to Him, and He will provide me with what I need, in future also, though I know not whence the means are to come.' " *

Thus he wrote in his journal, on July 28, 1874. Since then twenty-four years have passed, and to this day the work goes on, though he who then had the guidance of it sleeps in Jesus. Whoever has had any such dealings with God, on however small a scale, cannot even *think* of the Lord as failing to honour a faith so simple, genuine, and childlike, a faith which leads a helpless believer thus to cast himself and all his cares upon God with utter abandonment of all anxiety. This man put God to proof, and proved to himself and to all who receive his testimony that it is blessed to wait only upon Him. The particular point which he had in view, in making these entries in his jour-

* Narrative, IV. 386, 387.

nal, is the object also of embodying them in these pages, namely, to show that, while the annual expenses of this Institution were so exceedingly large and the income so apparently uncertain, the soul of this believer was, to use his own words, "THROUGHOUT, without the least wavering, stayed upon God, believing that He who had through him begun the Institution, enlarged it almost year after year, and upheld it for forty years in answer to prayer by faith, would do this still and not suffer this servant of His to be confounded." * Believing that God would still help, and supply the means, George Müller was willing, and THOROUGHLY in heart prepared, if necessary, to pass again through similar severe and prolonged seasons of trial as he had already endured.

The Living God had kept him calm and restful, amid all the ups and downs of his long experience as the superintendent and director of this many-sided work, though the tests of faith had not been light or short of duration. For more than ten years at a time—as from August, 1838, to April, 1849, day by day, and for months together from meal to meal—it was necessary to look to God, almost without cessation, for daily supplies. When, later on, the Institution was twentyfold larger and the needs proportionately greater, for months at a time the Lord likewise constrained His servant to lean from hour to hour, in the same dependence, upon Him. All along through these periods of unceasing want, the Eternal God was his refuge and underneath were the Everlasting Arms. He reflected that God was aware of all this enlargement of the work and its needs; he comforted himself with the consoling thought that he was seeking his Master's glory; and that if in this way the greater glory would accrue to Him for the good of His people and of those who were still unbelievers,

* Narrative, IV. 389.

it was no concern of the servant; nay, more than this, it behooved the servant to be willing to go on in this path of trial, even unto the end of his course, if so it should please his Master, who guides His affairs with divine discretion.

The trials of faith did not cease even until the end. July 28, 1881, finds the following entry in Mr. Müller's journal:

" The income has been for some time past only about a third part of the expenses. Consequently all we have for the support of the orphans is nearly gone ; and for the first four objects of the Institution we have nothing at all in hand. The natural appearance now is that the work cannot be carried on. But I BELIEVE that the Lord will help, both with means for the orphans and also for other objects of the Institution, and that we shall not be confounded; also that the work shall not need to be given up. I am fully expecting help, and have written this to the glory of God, that it may be recorded hereafter for the encouragement of His children. The result will be seen. I expect that we shall not be confounded, though for some years we have not been so poor."

While faith thus leaned on God, prayer took more vigorous hold. Six, seven, eight times a day, he and his dear wife were praying for means, looking for answers, and firmly persuaded that their expectations would not be disappointed. Since that entry was made, seventeen more years have borne their witness that this trust was not put to shame. Not a branch of this tree of holy enterprise has been cut off by the sharp blade of a stern necessity.

Though faith had thus tenaciously held fast to the promises, the pressure was not at once relieved. When, a fortnight after these confident records of trust in God had been spread on the pages of the journal, the balance for the orphans was less than it had been for twenty-five years, it would have seemed to human sight as though God had forgotten to be gracious. But, on August 22d, over one thousand pounds came in for the support of the orphans and thus relief was afforded for a time.

Again, let us bear in mind how in the most unprecedented straits God alone was made the confidant, even the best friends of the Institution, alike the poor and the rich, being left in ignorance of the pressure of want. It would have been no sin to have made known the circumstances, or even to have made an appeal for aid to the many believers who would gladly have come to the relief of the work. But the *testimony to the Lord* was to be jealously guarded, and the main object of this work of faith would have been imperilled just so far as by any appeal to men this witness to God was weakened.

In this crisis, and in every other, faith triumphed, and so the testimony to a prayer-hearing God grew in volume and power as the years went on. It was while as yet this period of testing was not ended, and no permanent relief was yet supplied, that Mr. Müller, with his wife, left Bristol on August 23d, for the Continent, on his eighth long preaching tour. Thus, at a time when, to the natural eye, his own presence would have seemed well-nigh indispensable, he calmly departed for other spheres of duty, leaving the work at home in the hands of Mr. Wright and his helpers. The tour had been already arranged for, under God's leading, and it was undertaken, with the supporting power of a deep conviction that God is as near to those who in prayer wait on Him in distant lands, as on Ashley Down, and needs not the personal presence of any man in any one place, or at any time, in order to carry on His work.

In an American city, a half-idiotic boy who was bearing a heavy burden asked a drayman, who was driving an empty cart, for a ride. Being permitted, he mounted the cart with his basket, but thinking he might so relieve the horse a little, while still himself riding, lifted his load and carried it. We laugh at the simplicity of the idiotic lad, and yet how often we are guilty of similar folly! We profess to cast ourselves and our cares upon the Lord, and then persist in bearing our own burdens, as if we felt that He would be unequal to the task of sustaining us and our loads. It is a most wholesome lesson for Christian workers to learn that all true work is primarily the Lord's, and only secondarily ours, and that therefore all 'carefulness' on our part is distrust of Him, implying a sinful self-conceit which overlooks the fact that He is the one Worker and all others are only His instruments.

As to our trials, difficulties, losses, and disappointments, we are prone to hesitate about committing them to the Lord, trustfully and calmly. We think we have done well if we take refuge in the Lord's promise to his reluctant disciple Peter, "What I do thou knowest not now, but thou shalt know hereafter," referring this 'hereafter' to the future state where we look for the solution of all problems. In Peter's case the hereafter appears to have come when the feet-washing was done and Christ explained its meaning; and it is very helpful to our faith to observe Mr. Müller's witness concerning all these trying and disappointing experiences of his life, that, without one exception, he had found already in this life that they worked together for his good; so that he had reason to praise God for them all. In the ninetieth psalm we read:

" Make us glad according to the days wherein Thou hast afflicted us
And the years wherein we have seen evil."

(Psalm xc. 15.)

This is an inspired prayer, and such prayer is a prophecy. Not a few saints have found, this side of heaven, a divine gladness for every year and day of sadness, when their afflictions and adversities have been patiently borne.

Faith is the secret of both peace and steadfastness, amid all tendencies to discouragement and discontinuance in well-doing. James was led by the Spirit of God to write that the unstable and unbelieving man is like the " wave of the sea driven with the wind and tossed." There are two motions of the waves—one up and down, which we call undulation, the other to and fro, which we call fluctuation. How appropriately both are referred to— " tossed " up and down, " driven " to and fro ! The double-minded man lacks steadiness in both respects: his faith has no uniformity of experience, for he is now at the crest of the wave and now in the trough of the sea; it has no uniformity of progress, for whatever he gains to-day he loses to-morrow.

Fluctuations in income and apparent prosperity did not take George Müller by surprise. He expected them, for if there were no crises and critical emergencies how could there be critical deliverances ? His trust was in God, not in donors or human friends or worldly circumstances: and because he trusted in the Living God who says of Himself, " I am the Lord, I change not," amid all other changes, his feet were upon the one Rock of Ages that no earthquake shock can move from its eternal foundations.

Two facts Mr. Müller gratefully records at this period of his life: (Narrative, IV. 411, 418.)

First. " For above fifty years I have now walked, by His grace, in a path of complete reliance upon Him who is the faithful one, for everything I have needed; and yet I am increasingly convinced that it is by His help *alone* I am enabled to continue in this course; for, if left to myself, even after the precious enjoyment so long experienced of walking thus in fellowship with God, I should yet be tempted to abandon this path of entire dependence upon Him. To His praise, however, I am able to state that for more than half .a century I have never had the least desire to do so."

Second. From May, 1880, to May 1881, a gracious work of the Spirit had visited the orphans on Ashley Down and in many of the schools. During the three months spent by Mr. Müller at home before sailing for America in September, 1880, he had been singularly drawn out in prayer for such a visitation of grace, and had often urged it on the prayers of his helpers. The Lord is faithful, and He cheered the heart of His servant in his absence by abundant answers to his intercessions. Before he had fairly entered on his work in America, news came from home of a blessed work of conversion already in progress, and which went on for nearly a year, until there was good ground for believing that in the five houses five hundred and twelve orphans had found God their Father in Christ, and nearly half as many more were in a hopeful state.

The Lord did not forget His promise, and He did keep the plant He had permitted His servant to set in His name in the soil on Ashley Down. Faith that was tried, triumphed. On June 7, 1884, a legacy of over eleven thousand pounds reached him, the *largest single gift* ever yet received, the largest donations which had preceded being respectively one thousand, two thousand, three thousand, five thousand, eight thousand one hundred, and nine thousand and ninety-one pounds.

This last amount, eleven thousand, had been due for over six years from an estate, but had been kept back by the delays of the Chancery Court. Prayer had been made day by day that the bequest might be set free for its uses, and now the full answer had come; and God had singularly timed the supply to the need, for there was at that time only forty-one pounds ten shillings in hand, not one half of the average daily expenses, and certain sanitary improvements were just about to be carried out which would require an outlay of over two thousand pounds.

As Mr. Müller closed the solemn and blessed records of 1884, he wrote:

"Thus ended the year 1884, during which we had been tried, greatly tried, in various ways, no doubt for the exercise of our faith, and to make us know God more fully; but during which we had also been helped and blessed, and *greatly* helped and blessed. Peacefully, then, we were able to enter upon the year 1885, fully assured that, as we had God FOR US and WITH US, ALL, ALL would be well." John Wesley had in the same spirit said a century before, "Best of all, God is with us."

Of late years the orphanage at Ashley Down has not had as many inmates as formerly, and some four or five hundred more might now be received. Mr. Müller felt constrained, for some years previous to his death, to make these vacancies known to the public, in hopes that some destitute orphans might find there a home. But it must be remembered that the provision for such children has been greatly enlarged since this orphan work was begun. In 1834 the total accommodation for all orphans, in England, reached thirty-six hundred, while the prisons contained nearly twice as many children under eight years of age. This state of things led to the rapid enlargement of the work until over two thousand were housed on Ashley Down alone; and this colossal enterprise stimulated others to open similar institutions until, fifty years after Mr. Müller began his work, at least one hundred thousand orphans were cared for in England alone. Thus God used Mr. Müller to give such an impetus to this form of philanthropy, that destitute children became the object of a widely organized charity both on the part of individuals and of societies, and orphanages now exist for various classes.

In all this manifold work which Mr. Müller did he was, to the last, self-oblivious. From the time when, in October, 1830, he had given up all stated salary, as pastor and minister of the gospel, he had never received any salary, stipend nor fixed income, of any sort, whether as a pastor or as a director of the Scriptural Knowledge Institution. Both principle and preference led him to wait only upon God for all personal needs, as also for all the wants of his work. Nevertheless God put into the hearts of His believing children in all parts of the world, not only to send gifts in aid of the various branches of the work which Mr. Müller superintended, but to forward to him money for his own uses, as well as clothes, food, and other temporal supplies. He never appropriated one penny which was not in some way indicated or designated as for his own personal needs, and subject to his personal judgment. No straits of individual or family want ever led him to use, even for a time, what was sent to him for other ends. Generally gifts intended for himself were wrapped up in paper with his name written thereon, or in other equally distinct ways designated as meant for him. Thus as early as 1874 his year's income reached upwards of twenty-one hundred pounds. Few nonconformist ministers, and not one in twenty of the clergy of the establishment, have any such income, which averages about six pounds for every day in the year—and all this came from the Lord, simply in answer to prayer, and without appeal of any sort to man or even the revelation of personal needs. If we add legacies paid at the end of the year 1873, Mr. Müller's entire income in about thirteen months exceeded thirty-one hundred pounds. Of this he gave, out and out to the needy, and to the work of God, the whole amount save about two hundred and fifty, expended on personal and family wants; and thus started the year 1875 as poor as he had begun forty-five years before; and if his personal expenses were scrutinized it would be found that even what he ate and drank and wore was with equal conscientiousness expended for the glory of God, so that in a true sense we may say he spent nothing on himself.

In another connection it has already been recorded that, when at Jubbulpore in 1890, Mr. Müller received tidings of his daughter's death. To any man of less faith that shock might have proved, at his advanced age, not only a stunning but a fatal blow. His only daughter and only child, Lydia, the devoted wife of James Wright, had been called home, in her fifty-eighth year, and after nearly thirty years of labour at the orphan houses. What this death meant to Mr. Müller, at the age of eighty-four, no one can know who has not witnessed the mutual devotion of that daughter and that father: and what that loss was to Mr. Wright, the pen alike fails to portray. If the daughter seemed to her father humanly indispensable, she was to her husband a sort of inseparable part of his being; and over such experiences as these it is the part of delicacy to draw the curtain of silence. But it should be recorded that no trait in Mrs. Wright was more pathetically attractive than her humility. Few disciples ever felt their own nothingness as she did, and it was this ornament of a meek and quiet spirit—the only ornament she wore— that made her seem so beautiful to all who knew her well enough for this 'hidden man of the heart' to be disclosed to their vision. Did not that ornament in the Lord's sight appear as of great price ? Truly " the beauty of the Lord her God was upon her."

James Wright had lived with his beloved Lydia for more than eighteen years, in " unmarred and unbroken felicity." They had together shared in prayers and tears before God, bearing all life's burdens in common. Weak as she was physically, he always leaned upon her and found her a tower of spiritual strength in time of heavy responsibility. While, in her lowly-mindedness, she thought of herself as a ' little useless thing,' he found her both a capable and cheerful supervisor of many most important domestic arrangements where a competent woman's hand was needful: and, with rare tact and fidelity, she kept watch of the wants of the orphans as her dear mother had done before her. After her decease, her husband found among her personal effects a precious treasure—a verse written with her own hand:

> " I have seen the face of Jesus,
>   Tell me not of aught beside ;
>   I have heard the voice of Jesus,
>   All my soul is satisfied."

This invaluable little fragment, like that other writing found by this beloved daughter among her mother's effects, became to Mr. Wright what that had been to Mr. Müller, a sort of last legacy from his departed and beloved wife. Her desires were fulfilled; she had seen the face and heard the voice of Him who alone could satisfy her soul.

In the Fifty-third Report, which extends to May 26, 1892, it is stated that the expenses exceeded the income for the orphans by a total of over thirty-six hundred pounds, so that many dear fellow labourers, without the least complaint, were in arrears as to salaries. This was the second time only, in fifty-eight years, that the income thus fell short of the expenses. Ten years previous, the expenses had been in excess of the income by four hundred and eighty-eight pounds, but, within one month after the new financial year had begun, by the payment of legacies three times as much as the deficiency was paid in; and, adding donations, six times as much. And now the question arose whether God would not have Mr. Müller contract rather than expand the work.

He says: "The Lord's dealings with us during the last year indicate that it is His will we should contract our operations, and we are waiting upon Him for directions as to how and to what extent this should be done; for we have but one single object—the glory of God. When I founded this Institution, one of the principles stated was, 'that there would be no enlargement of the work by going into debt': and in like manner we cannot go on with *that which already exists* if we have not sufficient means coming in to meet the current expenses." Thus the godly man who loved to expand his service for God was humble enough to bow to the will of God if its contraction seemed needful.

Prayer was much increased, and faith did not fail under the trial, which continued for weeks and months, but was abundantly sustained by the promises of an unfailing Helper. This distress was relieved in March by the sale of ten acres of land, at one thousand pounds an acre, and at the close of the year there was in hand a balance of over twenty-three hundred pounds.

The exigency, however, continued more or less severe until again, in 1893–4, after several years of trial, the Lord once more bountifully supplied means. And Mr. Müller is careful to add that though the *appearance* during those years of trial was many times as if God had forgotten or forsaken them and would never care any more about the

Institution, it was only in appearance, for He was as mindful of it as ever, and he records how by this discipline faith was still further strengthened, God was glorified in the patience and meekness whereby He enabled them to endure the testing, and tens of thousands of believers were blessed in afterward reading about these experiences of divine faithfulness.*

Five years after Mrs. Wright's death, Mr. Müller was left again a widower. His last great mission tour had come to an end in 1892, and in 1895, on the 13th of January, the beloved wife who in all these long journeys had been his constant companion and helper, passed to her rest, and once more left him peculiarly alone, since his devoted Lydia had been called up higher. Yet by the same grace of God which had always before sustained him he was now upheld, and not only kept in unbroken peace, but enabled to " kiss the Hand which administered the stroke."

At the funeral of his second wife, as at that of the first, he made the address, and the scene was unique in interest. Seldom does a man of ninety conduct such a service. The faith that sustained him in every other trial held him up in this. He lived in such habitual communion with the unseen world, and walked in such uninterrupted fellowship with the unseen God, that the exchange of worlds became too real for him to mourn for those who had made it, or to murmur at the infinite Love that numbers our days. It moved men more deeply than any spoken word of witness to see him manifestly borne up as on everlasting Arms.

I remember Mr. Müller remarking that he waited eight years before he understood at all the purpose of God in re-

* Fifty-fifth Report, p. 32.

moving his first wife, who seemed so indispensable to him
and his work. His own journal explains more fully this
remark. When it pleased God to take from him his second
wife, after over twenty-three years of married life,
again he rested on the promise that " All things work
together for good to them that love God " and reflected
on his past experiences of its truth. When he lost
his first wife after over thirty-nine years of happy
wedlock, while he bowed to the Father's will, *how*
that sorrow and bereavement could work good had
been wholly a matter of *faith*, for no compensating
good was apparent to sight ; yet he believed God's word
and waited to *see* how it would be fulfilled. That loss
seemed one that could not be made up. Only a little before, two orphan houses had been opened for nine hundred more orphans, so that there were total accommodations for over two thousand; she, who by nature, culture,
gifts, and graces, was so wonderfully fitted to be her husband's helper, and who had with motherly love cared for
these children, was suddenly removed from his side. Four
years after Mr. Müller married his second wife, he saw it
plainly to be God's will that he should spend life's even-
ing-time in giving witness to the nations. These mission
tours could not be otherwise than very trying to the physical powers of endurance, since they covered over two hundred thousand miles and obliged the travellers to spend a
week at a time in a train, and sometimes from four to six
weeks on board a vessel. Mrs. Müller, though never taking
part in public, was severely taxed by all this travel, and always busy, writing letters, circulating books and tracts, and
in various ways helping and relieving her husband. All at
once, while in the midst of these fatiguing journeys and
exposures to varying climates, it flashed upon Mr. Müller
that his first wife, who had died in her seventy-third year,

could never have undertaken these tours, and that the Lord
had thus, in taking her, left him free to make these extensive journeys. She would have been over fourscore years old
when these tours began, and, apart from age, could not
have borne the exhaustion, because of her frail health ;
whereas the second Mrs. Müller, who, at the time, was not
yet fifty-seven, was both by her age and strength fully
equal to the strain thus put upon her.

CHAPTER XIX

AT EVENING-TIME—LIGHT

THE closing scene of this beautiful and eventful life-history has an interest not altogether pathetic. Mr. Müller seems like an elevated mountain, on whose summit the evening sun shines in lingering splendour, and whose golden peak rises far above the ordinary level and belongs to heaven more than earth, in the clear, cloudless calm of God.

From May, 1892, when the last mission tour closed, he devoted himself mainly to the work of the Scriptural Knowledge Institution, and to preaching at Bethesda and elsewhere as God seemed to appoint. His health was marvellous, especially considering how, when yet a young man, frequent and serious illnesses and general debility had apparently disqualified him from all military duty, and to many prophesied early death or hopeless succumbing to disease. He had been in tropic heat and arctic cold, in gales and typhoons at sea, and on journeys by rail, sometimes as continuously long as a sea-voyage. He had borne the pest of fleas, mosquitoes, and even rats. He had endured changes of climate, diet, habits of life, and the strain of almost daily services, and come out of all unscathed. This man, whose health was never robust, had gone through labours that would try the mettle of an iron constitution; this man, who had many times been laid aside by illness and sometimes for months and who in 1837 had feared that a persistent head trouble might unhinge his mind, could say, in his ninety-second year: " I have been able, every day and all the day, to work, and that with ease, as seventy years since." When the writer was holding meetings in Bristol in 1896, on an anniversary very sacred to himself, he asked his beloved father Müller to speak at the closing meeting of the series, in the Y. M. C. A. Hall; and he did so, delivering a powerful address of forty-five minutes, on Prayer in connection with Missions, and giving his own life-story in part, with a vigour of voice and manner that seemed a denial of his advanced age.*

The marvellous preservation of such a man at such an age reminds one of Caleb, who at eighty-five could boast in God that he was as strong even for war as in the day that he was sent into the land as one of the spies; and Mr. Müller himself attributed this preservation to three causes: first, the exercising of himself to have always a conscience void of offence both toward God and toward men; secondly to the love he felt for the Scriptures, and the constant recuperative power they exercised upon his whole being; and third, to that happiness he felt in God and His work, which relieved him of all anxiety and needless wear and tear in his labours.

The great fundamental truth that this heroic man stamped on his generation was that the Living God is the same to day and forever as yesterday and in all ages past, and that, with equal confidence with the most trustful souls of any age, we may believe His word, and to every promise add, like Abraham, our ' Amen '—IT SHALL BE SO! † When, a few days after his death, Mr. E. H. Glenny, who is known to many as the beloved and self-sacrificing friend

* Appendix K.   † Gen. xv. 6. (Hebrew.)

of the North African Mission, passed through Barcelona, he found written in an album over his signature the words: "Jesus Christ, the same yesterday and to-day and for ever." And, like the writer of the Epistle to the Hebrews, quoting from the 102d Psalm, we may say of Jehovah, while all else changes and perishes :

" THOU REMAINEST " ;
" THOU ART THE SAME."

Toward the close of life Mr. Müller, acting under medical advice, abated somewhat of his active labours, preaching commonly but once a Sunday. It was my privilege to hear him on the morning of the Lord's day, March 22, 1896. He spoke on the 77th Psalm ; of course he found here his favourite theme—prayer : and, taking that as a fair specimen of his average preaching, he was certainly a remarkable expositor of Scripture even at ninety-one years of age. Later on the outline of this discourse will be found.

On Sunday morning, March 6, 1898, he spoke at Alma Road Chapel, and on the Monday evening following was at the prayer service at Bethesda, on both occasions in his usual health. On Wednesday evening following, he took his wonted place at the Orphan House prayer meeting and gave out the hymns :

" The countless multitude on high."

and

" We'll sing of the Shepherd that died."

When he bade his beloved son-in-law "good-night," there was no outward sign of declining strength. He seemed to the last the vigorous old man, and retired to rest as usual. It had been felt that one so advanced in years should have some night-attendant, especially as indications of heart-weakness had been noticed of late, and he had yielded to the pressure of love and consented to such an arrangement *after that night*. But the consent came too late. He was never more to need human attendance or attention. On Thursday morning, March 10th, at about seven o'clock, the usual cup cf tea was taken to his room. To the knock at the door there was no response save an ominous silence. The attendant opened the door, only to find that the venerable patriarch lay dead, on the floor beside the bed. He had probably risen to take some nourishment—a glass of milk and a biscuit being always put within reach—and, while eating the biscuit, he had felt faint, and fallen, clutching at the table-cloth as he fell, for it was dragged off, with certain things that had lain on the table. His medical adviser, who was promptly summoned, gave as his opinion that he had died of heart-failure some hour or two before he had been found by his attendant.

Such a departure, even at such an age, produced a world-wide sensation. That man's moral and spiritual forces reached and touched the earth's ends. Not in Bristol, or in Britain alone, but across the mighty waters toward the sunrise and sunset was felt the responsive pulse-beat of a deep sympathy. Hearts bled all over the globe when it was announced, by telegraph wire and ocean cable, that George Müller was dead. It was said of a great Englishman that his influence could be measured only by " parallels of latitude " ; of George Müller we may add, and by meridians of longitude. He belonged to the whole church and the whole world, in a unique sense; and the whole race of man sustained a loss when he died.

The funeral, which took place on the Monday following, was a popular tribute of affection, such as is seldom seen. Tens of thousands of people reverently stood along the route of the simple procession ; men left their workshops and offices, women left their elegant homes or humble kitchens, all seeking to pay a last token of respect. Bristol had never before witnessed any such scene.

A brief service was held at Orphan House No. 3, where over a thousand children met, who had for a second time lost a 'father'; in front of the reading-desk in the great dining-room, a coffin of elm, studiously plain, and by request without floral offerings, contained all that was mortal of George Müller, and on a brass plate was a simple inscription, giving the date of his death, and his age.

Mr. James Wright gave the address, reminding those who were gathered that, to all of us, even those who have lived nearest God, death comes while the Lord tarries; that it is blessed to die in the Lord; and that for believers in Christ there is a glorious resurrection waiting. The tears that ran down those young cheeks were more eloquent than any words, as a token of affection for the dead.

The procession silently formed. Among those who followed the bier were four who had been occupants of that first orphan home in Wilson Street. The children's grief melted the hearts of spectators, and eyes unused to weeping were moistened that day. The various carriages bore the medical attendants, the relatives and connections of Mr. Müller, the elders and deacons of the churches with which he was associated, and his staff of helpers in the work on Ashley Down. Then followed forty or fifty other vehicles with deputations from various religious bodies, etc.

At Bethesda, every foot of space was crowded, and hundreds sought in vain for admission. The hymn was sung which Mr. Müller had given out at that last prayer meeting the night before his departure. Dr. Maclean of Bath offered prayer, mingled with praise for such a long life of service and witness, of prayer and faith, and Mr. Wright spoke from Hebrews xiii. 7, 8 :

" Remember them which have the rule over you,
Who have spoken unto you the word of God :
Whose faith follow,
Considering the end of their conversation :
Jesus Christ, the same yesterday and to-day and for-
ever."

He spoke of those spiritual rulers and guides whom
God sets over his people; and of the privilege of imitating
their faith, calling attention to the two characteristics of
his beloved father-in-law's faith: first, that it was based
on that immovable Rock of Ages, God's written word; and
secondly, that it translated the precepts and promises of
that word into daily life.

Mr. Wright made very emphatic Mr. Müller's acceptance
of the whole Scriptures, as divinely inspired. He had been
wont to say to young believers, " Put your finger on the
passage on which your faith rests," and had himself read
the Bible from end to end nearly two hundred times. He
fed on the Word and therefore was strong. He found the
centre of that Word in the living Person it enshrines, and
his one ground of confidence was His atoning work. Always
in his own eyes weak, wretched, and vile, unworthy of the
smallest blessing, he rested solely on the merit and mediation of His great High Priest.

George Müller *cultivated* faith. He used to say to his
helpers in prayer and service, " Never let enter your minds
a shadow of doubt as to the love of the Father's heart
or the power of the Father's arm." And he projected his
whole life forward, and looked at it in the light of the
Judgment Day.

Mr. Wright's address made prominent one or two other
most important lessons, as, for example, that the Spirit
bids us imitate, not the idiosyncrasies or philanthropy of

others, but *their faith*. And he took occasion to remind his hearers that philanthropy was not the foremost aim or leading feature of Mr. Müller's life, but above all else to magnify and glorify God, as *still the living God who, now as well as thousands of years ago, hears the prayers of His children and helps those who trust Him.*" He touchingly referred to the humility that led Mr. Müller to do the mightiest thing for God without self-consciousness, and showed that God can take up and use those who are willing to be only instruments.

Mr. Wright further remarked: "I have been asked again and again lately as to whether the orphan work would go on. It is going on. Since the commencement of the year we have received between forty and fifty fresh orphans, and this week expect to receive more. The other four objects of the Institution, according to the ability God gives us, are still being carried on. We believe that whatever God would do with regard to the future will be worthy of Him. We do not know much more, and do not want to. He knows what He will do. I cannot think, however, that the God who has so blessed the work for so long will leave our prayers as to the future unanswered."

Mr. Benjamin Perry then spoke briefly, characterizing Mr. Müller as the greatest personality Bristol had known as a citizen. He referred to his power as an expounder of Scripture, and to the fact that he brought to others for their comfort and support what had first been food to his own soul. He gave some personal reminiscences, referring, for instance, to his ability at an extreme old age still to work without hindrance either mental or physical, free from rheumatism, ache, or pain, and seldom suffering from exhaustion. He briefly described him as one who, in response to the infinite love of God, which called him from a life of sin to a life of salvation and service, wholly loved God above everybody and everything, so that his highest pleasure was to please and serve Him. As an illustration of his humility, he gave an incident. When of late a friend had said, " When God calls you home, it will be like a ship going into harbour, full sail "—" Oh no ! " said Mr. Müller, " it is poor George Müller who needs daily to pray, " Hold Thou me up in my goings, that my footsteps slip not.' " The close of such lives as those of Asa and Solomon were to Mr. Müller a perpetual warning, leading him to pray that he might never thus depart from the Lord in his old age.

After prayer by Mr. J. L. Stanley, Col. Molesworth gave out the hymn,

" 'Tis sweet to think of those at rest."

And after another prayer by Mr. Stanley Arnot, the body was borne to its resting-place in Arno's Vale Cemetery, and buried beside the bodies of Mr. Müller's first and second wives, some eighty carriages joining in the procession to the grave. Everything from first to last was as simple and unostentatious as he himself would have wished. At the graveside Col. Molesworth prayed, and Mr. George F. Bergin read from 1 Cor. xv. and spoke a few words upon the tenth verse, which so magnifies the grace of God both in what we *are* and what we *do*.

Mr. E. K. Groves, nephew of Mr. Müller, announced as the closing hymn the second given out by him at that last prayer meeting at the orphanage.

" We'll sing of the Shepherd that died."

Mr. E. T. Davies then offered prayer, and the body was left to its undisturbed repose, until the Lord shall come.

Other memorial services were held at the Y. M. C. A. Hall, and very naturally at Bethesda Chapel, which brought to a fitting close this series of loving tributes to the departed. On the Lord's day preceding the burial, in nearly all the city pulpits, more or less extended reference had been made to the life, the character, and the career of the beloved saint who had for so many years lived his irreproachable life in Bristol. Also the daily and weekly press teemed with obituary notices, and tributes to his piety, worth, and work.

It was touchingly remarked at his funeral that he first confessed to feeling weak and weary in his work that last night of his earthly sojourn; and it seemed specially tender of the Lord not to allow that sense of exhaustion to come upon him until just as He was about to send His chariot to bear him to His presence. Mr. Müller's last sermon at Bethesda Chapel, after a ministry of sixty-six years, had been from 2 Cor. v. 1:

" For we know that, if our earthly house of this tabernacle were dissolved, we have a building of God, a house not made with hands, eternal in the heavens."

It was as though he had some foretokens of his being about shortly to put off this his tabernacle. Evidently he was not taken by surprise. He had foreseen that his days were fast completing their number. Seven months before his departure, he had remarked to his medical attendant, in connection with the irregularity of his pulse: " It means *death*."

Many of the dear orphans—as when the first Mrs. Müller died—wrote, asking that they might contribute toward the erection of a monument to the memory of their beloved benefactor. Already one dear young servant had gathered, for the purpose, over twenty pounds. In conformity with the known wishes of his father-in-law that only the simplest headstone be placed over his remains, Mr. Wright thought necessary to check the inflow of such gifts, the sum in hand being quite sufficient.

Further urgent appeals were made both from British

and American friends, for the erection of some statue or other large visible monument or memorial, and in these appeals the local newspapers united. At length private letters led Mr. Wright to communicate with the public press, as the best way at once to silence these appeals and express the ground of rejecting such proposals. He wrote as follows:

"You ask me, as one long and closely associated with the late Mr. George Müller, to say what I think would be most in accordance with his own wishes as a fitting memorial of himself.

"Will not the best way of replying to this question be to let him speak for himself?

"1st. When he erected Orphan House No. 1, and the question came what is the building to be called, he deliberately avoided associating his own name with it, and named it 'The New Orphan House, Ashley Down.' N.B.—To the end of his life he *disliked* hearing or reading the words 'Müller's Orphanage.' In keeping with this, for years, in *every Annual Report*, when referring to the Orphanage he reiterated the statement, 'The New Orphan Houses on Ashley Down, Bristol, are not *my* Orphan Houses, . . . they are God's Orphan Houses.' (See, for example, the Report for 1897, p. 69.)

"2d. For years, in fact until he was nearly eighty years old, he steadily refused to allow any *portrait* of himself to be published; and only most reluctantly (for reasons which he gives with characteristic minuteness in the preface to 'Preaching Tours') did he at length give way on this point.

"3d. In the last published Report, at page 66, he states: 'The primary object I had in view in carrying on this work,' viz., 'that it might be seen that now, in the nineteenth century, *God is still the Living God, and that now, as well as thousands of years ago, He listens to the prayers of His children and helps those who trust in Him.'* From these words and ways of acting, is it not evident, that the only 'memorial' that George Müller cared about was that which consists in the effect of his example, Godward, upon his fellow men ? Every soul converted to God (instrumentally) through his words or example constitutes a permanent memorial to him as the father in Christ of such an one. Every believer strengthened in faith (instrumentally) through his words or example constitutes a similar memorial to his spiritual teacher.

" He knew that God had, already, in the riches of His grace, given him many such memorials; and he departed this life, as I well know, cherishing the most lively hope that he should greet *above* thousands more to whom it had pleased God to make him a channel of rich spiritual blessing.

" He used often to say to me, when he opened a letter in which the writer poured out a tale of sore pecuniary need, and besought his help to an extent twice or three or ten times exceeding the sum total of his (Mr. Müller's) earthly possessions at the moment, ' Ah ! these dear people entirely miss the lesson I am *trying* to teach them, for they come to *me,* instead of going to *God.'* And if he could come back to us for an hour, and listen to an account of what his sincerely admiring, but mistaken, friends are proposing to do to *perpetuate* his memory, I can hear him, with a sigh, exclaiming, ' Ah ! these *dear* friends are entirely missing the lesson that I tried for seventy years to teach them,' viz., ' That a *man* can receive nothing except it be *given* him *from above,'* and that, therefore, it is the Blessed *Giver,* and not the poor receiver, that is to be glorified.

" Yours faithfully,

" JAMES WRIGHT."

CHAPTER XX

DEATH shuts the door upon earthly service, whatever door it may open to other forms and spheres of activity. There are many intimations that service beyond the grave is both unceasing and untiring : the blessed dead "rest indeed from their *labours* "—toilsome and painful tasks—" but their *works* "—activities for God—" do follow them," where exertion is without exhaustion.

This is therefore a fit point for summing up the results of the work over which, from its beginning, one man had specially had charge. One sentence from Mr. Müller's pen marks the purpose which was the very pivot of his whole being : " I have joyfully dedicated my whole life to the object of exemplifying how much may be accomplished by prayer and faith." This prepared both for the development of the character of him who had such singleness of aim, and for the development of the work in which that aim found action. Mr. Müller's oldest friend, Robert C. Chapman of Barnstaple, beautifully says that " when a man's chief business is to serve and please the Lord, all his circumstances become his servants "; and we shall find this maxim true in Mr. Müller's life-work.

The Fifty-ninth Report, issued May 26, 1898, was the last up to the date of the publication of this volume, and the first after Mr. Müller's death. In this, Mr. Wright gives the brief but valuable summary not only of the whole work of the year preceding, but of the whole work from its beginning, and thus helps us to a comprehensive survey.

This report is doubly precious as it contains also the last contribution of Mr. Müller's own pen to the record of the Lord's dealings. It is probable that on the afternoon of March 9th he laid down his pen, for the last time, all unconscious that he was never again to take it up. He had made, in a twofold sense, his closing entry in life's solemn journal! In the evening of that day he took his customary part in the prayer service in the orphan house— then went to sleep for the last time on earth ; there came a waking hour, when he was alone with God, and suddenly departed, leaving his body to its long sleep that knows no waking until the day of the Lord's coming, while his spirit returned unto God who gave it.

The afternoon of that day of death, and of ' birth ' into the heavenly life—as the catacomb saints called it—found the helpers again assembled in the same prayer room to commit the work to him " who only hath immortality," and who, amid all changes of human administration, ever remains the divine Master Workman, never at a loss for His own chosen instruments.

Mr. Wright, in this report, shows himself God's chosen successor in the work, evidently like-minded with the departed director. The first paragraph, after the brief and touching reference to his father-in-law, serves to convey to all friends of this work the assurance that he to whom Mr. Müller left its conduct has also learned the one secret of all success in coworking with God. It sounds, as the significant *keynote* for the future, the same old keynote of the past, carrying on the melody and harmony, without change, into the new measures. It is the same oratorio, without alteration of theme, time, or even key : the leading performer is indeed no more, but another hand takes up his instrument and, trembling with emotion, continues the unfinished strain so that there is no interruption. Mr. Wright says :

"It is written (Job xxvi. 7): 'He hangeth the earth upon *nothing*'—that is, no *visible* support. And so we exult in the fact that 'the Scriptural Knowledge Institution for Home and Abroad' hangs, as it has ever hung, since its commencement, now more than sixty-four years ago, 'upon nothing,' that is, upon no VISIBLE support. It hangs upon no human patron, upon no endowment or funded property, but solely upon the good pleasure of the blessed God."

Blessed lesson to learn ! that to hang upon the invisible God is not to hang "upon nothing," though it be upon nothing *visible*. The power and permanence of the invisible forces that hold up the earth after sixty centuries of human history are sufficiently shown by the fact that this great globe still swings securely in space and is whirled through its vast orbit, and that, without variation of a second, it still moves with divine exactness in its appointed path. We can therefore trust the same invisible God to sustain with His unseen power all the work which faith suspends upon His truth and love and unfailing word of promise, though to the natural eye all these may seem as nothing.

Mr. Wright records also a very striking answer to long-continued prayer, and a most impressive instance of the tender care of the Lord, in the *providing of an associate,* every way like-minded, and well fitted to share the responsibility falling upon his shoulders at the decease of his father-in-law.

Feeling the burden too great for him, his one resource

was to cast his burden on the Lord. He and Mr. Müller
had asked of God such a companion in labour for three
years before his departure, and Mr. Wright and his dear
wife had, for twenty-five years before that—from the time
when Mr. Müller's long missionary tours began to withdraw
him from Bristol—besought of the Lord the same favour.
But to none of them had any *name* been suggested, or, if so,
it had never been mentioned.

After that day of death, Mr. Wright felt that a gracious
Father would not long leave him to sustain this great burden alone, and about a fortnight later he felt assured that
it was the will of God that he should ask Mr. George
Frederic Bergin to join him in the work, who seemed to
him a *" true yoke-fellow."* He had known him well for a
quarter-century ; he had worked by his side in the church;
and though they were diverse in temperament, there had
never been a break in unity or sympathy. Mr. Bergin was
seventeen years his junior, and so likely to survive and succeed him ; he was very fond of children, and had been
much blessed in training his own in the nurture and admonition of the Lord, and hence was fitted to take charge
of this larger family of orphans. Confident of being led
of God, he put the matter before Mr. Bergin, delighted but
not surprised to find that the same God had moved on his
mind also, and in the same direction ; for not only was
he ready to respond to Mr. Wright's appeal, but he had
been led of God to feel that he should, after a certain time,
go to Mr. Wright and offer himself. The Spirit who guided
Philip to the Eunuch and at the same time had made the
Eunuch to inquire after guidance ; who sent men from
Cornelius and, while they were knocking at Simon's house,
was bidding Peter go with them, still moves in a mysterious way, and simultaneously, on those whom He would
bring together for cooperation in loving service. And

thus Mr. Wright found the Living God the same Helper and Supplier of every need, after his beloved father-in-law had gone up higher ; and felt constrained to feel that the God of Elijah was still at the crossing of the Jordan and could work the same wonders as before, supplying the need of the hour when the need came.

Mr. Müller's own gifts to the service of the Lord find in this posthumous report their first full record and recognition.   Readers of the Annual Reports must have noticed an entry, recurring with strange frequency during all these thirty or forty years, and therefore suggesting a giver that must have reached a very ripe age : " from a servant of the Lord Jesus, who, constrained by the love of Christ, seeks to lay up treasure in heaven." If that entry be carefully followed throughout and there be added the personal gifts made by Mr. Müller to various benevolent objects, it will be found that the aggregate sum from this " servant " reaches, up to March 1, 1898, a total of *eighty-one thousand four hundred and ninety pounds eighteen shillings and eightpence.*   Mr. Wright, now that this " servant of the Lord Jesus " is with his Master, who promised, " Where I am there shall also My servant be," feels free to make known that this donor was no other than *George Müller himself* who thus gave out of his own money —money given to him for his own use or left to him by legacies—the total sum of about sixty-four thousand five hundred pounds to the Scriptural Knowledge Institution, and, in other directions, seventeen thousand more.

This is a record of personal gifts to which we know no parallel.   It reminds us of the career of John Wesley, whose simplicity and frugality of habits enabled him not only to limit his own expenditure to a very small sum, but whose Christian liberality and unselfishness prompted him to give all that he could thus save to purely benevolent objects. While he had but thirty pounds a year, he lived on twenty-eight and gave away forty shillings. Receiving twice as much the next year, he still kept his living expenses down to the twenty-eight pounds and had thirty-two to bestow on the needy ; and when the third year his income rose to ninety pounds, he spent no more than before and gave away sixty-two. The fourth year brought one hundred and twenty, and he disbursed still but the same sum for his own needs, having ninety-two to spare. It is calculated that in the course of his life he thus gave away at least thirty thousand pounds, and four silver spoons comprised all the silver plate that he possessed when the collectors of taxes called upon him. Such economy on the one hand and such generosity on the other have seldom been known in human history. But George Müller's record will compare favourably with this or any other of modern days. His frugality, simplicity, and economy were equal to Wesley's, and his gifts aggregated eighty-one thousand pounds. Mr. Müller had received increasingly large sums from the Lord which he *invested* well and most profitably, so that for over sixty years he never lost a penny through a bad speculation ! But his investments were not in lands or banks or railways, but in the *work of God*. He made friends out of the mammon of unrighteousness that when he failed received him into everlasting habitations. He continued, year after year, to make provision for himself, his beloved wife and daughter, by laying up treasure—in heaven. Such a man had certainly a right to exhort others to systematic beneficence. He gave—as not one in a million gives—not a tithe, not any fixed proportion of annual income, but *all that was left* after the simplest and most necessary supply of actual wants. While most Christians regard themselves as doing their duty if, after they have given a portion to the Lord, they spend all the rest on themselves, God led George Müller to reverse this rule and reserve only the most frugal sum for personal needs, that the entire remainder might be given to him that needeth. The utter *revolution* implied in our habits of giving which would be necessary were such a rule adopted is but too obvious. Mr. Müller's own words are :

"My aim never was, how much I could *obtain*, but rather how much I could give."

He kept continually before him *his stewardship* of God's property ; and sought to make the most of the one brief life on earth, and to use for the best and largest good the property held by him in trust. The things of God were deep realities, and, projecting every action and decision and motive into the light of the judgment-seat of Christ, he asked himself how it would appear to him in the light of that tribunal. Thus he sought prayerfully and conscientiously so to live and labour, so to deny himself, and, by love, serve God and man, as that he should not be ashamed before Him at His coming. But not in a spirit of *fear* was this done ; for if any man of his generation knew the perfect love that casts out fear, it was George Müller. He felt that God is love, and love is of God. He saw that love manifested in the greatest of gifts—His only-begotten Son at Calvary—he knew and believed the Love that God hath to us ; he received it into his own heart ; it became an abiding presence, manifested in obedience and benevolence, and, subduing him more and more, it became perfected so as to expel tormenting fear and impart a holy confidence and delight in God.

Among the texts which strongly impressed and moulded Mr. Müller's habits of giving was Luke vi. 38 :

"Give and it shall be given unto you. Good measure, pressed down, shaken together and running over shall men give into your bosom."

He believed this promise and he verified it. His testimony is : " I had GIVEN, and God had caused to be GIVEN TO ME AGAIN, and bountifully."

Again he read : " It is more blessed to give than to receive."

He says that he BELIEVED what he found in the word of God, and by His grace sought to ACT ACCORDINGLY, and thus again records that he was blessed abundantly and his peace and joy in the Holy Ghost increased more and more.

It will not be a surprise, therefore, that, as has been already noted, Mr. Müller's *entire personal estate* at his death, as sworn to, when the will was admitted to probate, was only £169 9s. 4d., of which books, household furniture, etc., were reckoned at over one hundred pounds, the only *money* in his possession being a trifle over sixty pounds, and even this only awaiting disbursement as God's steward.

The will of Mr. Müller contains a pregnant clause which should not be forgotten in this memorial. It closes with a paragraph which is deeply significant as meant to be his posthumous word of testimony—" a last testament " :

" I cannot help admiring God's wondrous grace in bringing me to the knowledge of the Lord Jesus when I was an entirely careless and thoughtless young man, and that He has kept me in His fear and truth, allowing me the great honour, for so long a time, of serving Him."

In the comprehensive summary contained in this Fifty-ninth Report, remarkable growth is apparent during the sixty-four years since the outset of the work in 1834. During the year ending May 26, 1898, the number of day-schools was 7, and of pupils, 354; the number of children in attendance from the beginning, 81,501. The number of home Sunday-schools, 12, and of children in them, 1341; but from the beginning, 32,944. The number of Sunday-schools *aided* in England and Wales, 25. The amount expended in connection with home schools, £736 13s. 10d.; from the outset, £109,992 19s. 10d. The Bibles and parts thereof circulated, 15,411; from the beginning, 1,989,266. Money expended for this purpose the past year, £439; from the first, £41,090 13s. 3d. Missionary labourers aided, 115. Money expended, £2082 9s. 6d.; from the outset, £261,859 7s. 4d. Circulation of books and tracts, 3,101,338. Money spent, £1001 3s.; and from the first, £47,188 11s. 10d. The number of orphans on Ashley Down, 1620; and from the first, 10,024. Money spent in orphan houses, last year, £22,523 13s. 1d.; and from the beginning, £988,829.

To carry out conviction into action is sometimes a costly sacrifice; but whatever Mr. Müller's fidelity to conviction cost in one way, he had stupendous results of his life-work to contemplate, even while he lived. Let any one look at the above figures and facts, and remember that here was one poor man who, dependent on the help of God only in answer to prayer, could look back over threescore years and see how he had built five large orphan houses and taken into his family over ten thousand orphans, expending, for their good, within twelve thousand pounds of a round million. He had given aid to day-schools and Sunday-schools, in this and other lands, where nearly one hundred and fifty thousand children have been taught, at a cost of over one hundred and ten thousand pounds more. He had circulated nearly two million Bibles and parts thereof at the cost of over forty thousand pounds; and over three million books and tracts, at a cost of nearly fifty thousand pounds more. And besides all this he had spent over two hundred and sixty thousand pounds to aid missionary labourers in various lands. The sum total of the money thus spent during sixty years has thus reached very nearly the astonishing aggregate of one and a half million of pounds sterling ($7,500,000).

To summarize Mr. Müller's service we must understand his great secret. Such a life and such a work are the result of one habit more than all else,—daily and frequent communion with God. Unwearied in supplications and intercessions, we have seen how, in every new need and crisis, prayer was the one resort, the prayer of faith. He first satisfied himself that he was in the way of duty; then he fixed his mind upon the unchanging word of promise; then, in the boldness of a suppliant who comes to a throne of grace in the name of Jesus Christ and pleads the assurance of the immutable Promiser, he presented every petition. He was an unwearied intercessor. No delay discouraged him. This is seen particularly in the case of individuals for whose conversion or special guidance into the paths of full obedience he prayed. On his prayer list were the names of some for whom he had besought God, daily, by name, for one, two, three, four, six, ten years before the answer was given. The year just before his death, he told the writer of two parties for whose reconciliation to God he had prayed, day by day, *for over sixty years,* and who had not as yet to his knowledge turned unto God: and he significantly added, " I have not a doubt that I shall meet them both in heaven; for my Heavenly Father would not lay upon my heart a burden of prayer for them for over threescore years, if He had not concerning them purposes of mercy."

This is a sufficient example of his almost unparalleled perseverance and importunity in intercession. However long the delay, he held on, as with both hands clasping the very horns of the altar; and his childlike spirit reasoned simply but confidently, that the very fact of his own spirit being so long drawn out in prayer for one object, and of the Lord's enabling him so to continue patiently and believingly to wait on Him for the blessing, was a promise and prophecy of the answer; and so he waited on, so assured of the ultimate result that he praised God in advance, believing that he had practically received that for which he asked.

It is most helpful here to add that one of the parties for whom for so many years he unceasingly prayed has recently died in faith, having received the promises and embraced them and confessed Jesus as his Lord. Just before leaving Bristol with this completed manuscript of Mr. Müller's life, I met a lady, a niece of the man referred to, through whom I received a knowledge of these facts. He had, before his departure, given most unequivocal testimony to his faith and hope in the Saviour of sinners.

If George Müller could still speak to us, he would again repeat the warning so frequently found in his journal and reports, that his fellow disciples must not regard him as a *miracle-worker*, as though his experience were to be accounted so exceptional as to have little application in our ordinary spheres of life and service. With patient repetition he affirms that in all essentials such an experience is the privilege of all believers. God calls disciples to various forms of *work*, but all alike to the same *faith*. To say, therefore, "I am not called to build orphan houses, etc., and have no right to expect answers to my prayers as Mr. Müller did," is wrong and unbelieving. Every child of God, he maintained, is first to get into the sphere appointed of God, and therein to exercise full trust, and live by faith upon God's sure word of promise.

Throughout all these thousands of pages written by his pen, he teaches that every experience of God's faithfulness is both the reward of past faith and prayer, and the preparation of the servant of God for larger work and more efficient service and more convincing witness to his Lord.

No man can understand such a work who does not see in it the *supernatural* power of God. Without that the enigma defies solution; with that all the mystery is at least an open mystery. He himself felt from first to last that this supernatural factor was the key to the whole work, and without that it would have been even to himself a problem inexplicable. How pathetically we find him often comparing himself and his work for God to "the Burning Bush in the Wilderness" which, always aflame and always threatened with apparent destruction, was not consumed, so that not a few turned aside wondering to see this great sight. And why was it not burnt? Because Jehovah of hosts, who was in the Bush, dwelt in the man and in his work: or, as Wesley said with almost his last breath, "Best of all, God is with us."

This simile of the Burning Bush is the more apt when we consider the *rapid growth of the work*. At first so very small as to seem almost insignificant, and conducted in one small rented house, accommodating thirty orphans, then enlarged until other rented premises became necessary; then one, two, three, four, and even five immense structures being built, until three hundred, seven hundred, eleven hundred and fifty, and finally two thousand and fifty inmates could find shelter within them,—how seldom has the world seen such vast and, at the same time, rapid enlargement! Then look at the outlay! At first a trifling expenditure of perhaps five hundred pounds for the first year of the Scriptural Knowledge Institution, and of five hundred pounds for the first twelve month of the orphan work, and in the last year of Mr. Müller's life a grand total of over twenty-seven thousand five hundred, for all the purposes of the Institution.

The cost of the houses built on Ashley Down might

have staggered a man of large capital, but this poor man only cried and the Lord helped him. The first house cost fifteen thousand pounds; the second, over twenty-one thousand; the third, over twenty-three thousand; and the fourth and fifth, from fifty thousand to sixty thousand more—so that the total cost reached about one hundred and fifteen thousand. Besides all this, there was a yearly expenditure which rose as high as twenty-five thousand for the orphans alone, irrespective of those occasional outlays made needful for emergencies, such as improved sanitary precautions, which in one case cost over two thousand pounds.

Here is a burning bush indeed, always in seeming danger of being consumed, yet still standing on Ashley Down, and still preserved because the same presence of Jehovah burns in it. Not a branch of this many-sided work has utterly perished, while the whole bush still challenges unbelievers to turn aside and see the great sight, and take off the shoes from their feet as on holy ground where God manifests Himself.

Any complete survey of this great life-work must include much that was wholly outside of the Scriptural Knowledge Institution; such as that service which Mr. Müller was permitted to render to the church of Christ and the world at large as a preacher, pastor, witness for truth, and author of books and tracts.

His preaching period covered the whole time from 1826 to 1898, the year of his departure, over seventy years; and from 1830, when he went to Teignmouth, his preaching continued, without interruption except from ill health, until his life closed, with an average through the whole period of probably three sermons a week, or over ten thousand for his lifetime. This is probably a low estimate, for during his missionary tours, which covered over two hundred thousand miles and were spread through seventeen years, he spoke on an average about once a day notwithstanding already advanced age.

His church life was much blessed even in visible and tangible results. During the first two and a half years of work in Bristol, two hundred and twenty-seven members were added, about half of whom were new converts, and it is probable that, if the whole number brought to the knowledge of Christ by his preaching could now be ascertained, it would be found to aggregate full as many as the average of those years, and would thus reach into the thousands, exclusive of orphans converted on Ashley Down. Then when we take into account the vast numbers addressed and impressed by his addresses, given in all parts of the United Kingdom, on the Continent of Europe, and in America, Asia, and Australia, and the still vaster numbers who have read his Narrative, his books and tracts, or who have in various other ways felt the quickening power of his example and life, we shall get some conception—still, at best, inadequate—of the range and scope of the influence he wielded by his tongue and pen, his labours. and his life. Much of the best influence defies all tabulated statistics and evades all mathematical estimates ; it is like the fragrance of the alabaster flask which fills all the house but escapes our grosser senses of sight, hearing, and touch. This part of George Müller's work we cannot summarize: it belongs to a realm where we cannot penetrate. But God sees, knows, and rewards it.